The Folklore of (old) Monmouthshire

LOGASTON PRESS
Little Logaston Woonton Almeley
Herefordshire HR3 6QH

First published by Logaston Press 1998
Copyright © Roy Palmer 1998

All rights reserved. No part of this publication
may be reproduced, stored in a retrieval system,
or transmitted, in any form or by any means,
electronic, mechanical, photocopying, recording
or otherwise, without the prior permission,
in writing of the publisher

ISBN 1 873827 40 7

Set in Times by Logaston Press
and printed in Great Britain by
Antony Rowe, Chippenham, Wiltshire

Contents

		page
	Acknowledgements	*vii*
	Introduction	*ix*
Chapter 1	Saints	1
Chapter 2	Soldiers	25
Chapter 3	Spirits	53
Chapter 4	Earth	95
Chapter 5	Water	107
Chapter 6	Sickness and Health	127
Chapter 7	Life and Death	147
Chapter 8	Words	179
Chapter 9	Work	195
Chapter 10	Play	231
Chapter 11	Calendar Customs	253
	Sources	287
	Index	295

The grey old man in the chimney corner
Of his father heard this story,
Which from his father he had heard,
And after them have I remembered,
So now I tell it unto you.

(Traditional Verse)

Acknowledgements

I should like to thank for their assistance these people and institutions: Abergavenny Museum and Castle, Jeremy Barlow, Mr R. Blatchford, Bodleian Library, John Buchanan-Brown, Chepstow Museum, Mary-Ann Constantine, Arfur Daley, Diocese of Monmouthshire, Folklore Society, Gloucester City Library, Gwent Record Office, Gwent Rural Life Museum at Usk, Rev. Glyndwr Hackett, Tegwen Harrison, Herefordshire Library Service, Keith Kissack, Museum of Welsh Life, National Library of Wales, Nelson Museum at Monmouth, Newport Libraries, Newport Museum and Art Gallery, Gerald Porter, W.L. Rothon, Walter Stokes, Henry Toulouse, Vaughan Williams Memorial Library, Welsh Office, E.J.T. Wiles, Working Class Movement Library at Salford.

I am grateful for translations to Mary-Ann Constantine, Emma Lile, Dr Rhian Davies and Frank Olding, though any errors must be mine. I also thank Mr Olding for much helpful guidance.

I dedicate this book to my wife, Pat, who has shared my excursions in Monmouthshire (not to speak of 45 years of married life), as well as my delight in the beauty and fascination of the old county. I also have to thank her for transcribing and inscribing tunes, and for taking the photographs on pages 16, 20, 21, 30, 33, 34, 41, 44, 49, 59, 65, 71, 72, 78, 87, 92, 94, 98, 100, 101, 102 (both), 103, 105, 106, 109, 112, 120, 123 (upper), 125, 129, 135, 139, 140, 143, 144, 145, 146, 150, 154, 162, 163, 165, 167, 173, (lower), 175, 177, 181, 183, 190, 196 and 225.

For other illustrations I am grateful to Abergavenny Museum (pp. 251 and 275), Chris Barber (pp. 159, 198 and 284), Chepstow Museum (pp. 119, 121, 221 and 265), John Crawley (p. 223), Robin Gwyndaf (pp. 11 and 54), the Warden of Llandovery College (p. 278), Dr P.T..J. Morgan (p. 136), Museum of Welsh Life (p. 228), National Coracle Centre, Cenarth (p. 116), National Library of Wales (pp. 137 and 252), National Portrait Gallery (p. 47), Nelson Museum and Local History Centre, Monmouth (p. 247, lower), Newport Museum and Art Gallery (pp. 48, 51 and 193), John Summers (p. 118), and Village Publishing (p. 261).

I am indebted to Tony Conran for the loan of tapes and transcripts of interviews with members of mining communities; John Crawley for 'Poem of Bryngwyn People', by Richard Crawley; Gwyn and Ceinfryn Morris for 'Bells of Rhymney', by Idris Davies, and Pete Seeger for the tune; Bob Patten for 'The Black Decree' (tune and 1 verse); and Michael Raven for 'Sons of Glyndwr'.

Introduction

'I affronted a Welsh waiter in Monmouthshire,' wrote the songwriter, Charles Dibdin, in 1788, 'by asking him if we might not call ourselves in WALES—to which he answered—"Cot pless hur and luff hur, to be sure it is *Waales*, but it is not Welch *Waales* look you."' At least the waiter had no doubt about the main point. Others are uncertain. Maps from Speed (1610) to Piggot (1840) include Monmouthshire with England. *The Concise Oxford Dictionary of English Place-names* has a number of entries from Monmouthshire. Even Welsh sources often make reference to 'Wales and Monmouthshire', as though the two were somehow separate.

However, a Welsh expression for the breadth, if not the length, of the country, *O Fon i Fynwy*, means 'from Anglesey to Monmouthshire'. Another phrase, *dros Glawdd Offa*, 'across Offa's Dyke', is an alternative way of referring to England which by implication firmly places Monmouthshire on the Welsh side.

Poets had no hesitation. William Thomas (1832-78), better known as Islwyn, born near the village of Ynys-ddu in the Sirhowy Valley, where his father was Lord Llanover's mineral agent, wrote:

> Gwylet Walia ydwyt itihau, Mynwy gu
> Dy enw'n unig a newidiaist ti.
> (Wild Wales art thou still, dear Monmouth,
> Thy name only hast thou changed).

Idris Davies (1905-53), born in the next century 'beneath a Celtic star' at Rhymney, felt just as strongly:

> In Parliament they ponder
>   On Monmouth's pedigree;
> Or is she Welsh or English

> In the page of history?
> But those who know her people
> Among the smoking vales
> Proclaim with pride that they were born
> In Monmouthshire, Wales.

The County of Monmouth, together with those of Brecon, Denbigh, Montgomery and Radnor, came into existence as a result of the Act of Union which annexed Wales to England. The statute specified that from the Feast of All Saints (2 November) in 1536 Monmouthshire should consist of 'the following lordships, townships parishes, commotes and cantreds, viz. Monmouth, Chepstow, Mathern, Llanfihangel, Magor, Goldcliff, Newport, Wentllwg, Llanwern, Caerleon, Usk, Trellech, Tintern, Skenfrith, Grosmont, White Castle, Raglan, Caldicot, Bishton, Abergavenny, Penrhos, Greenfield [Maesglas], Machen and Hochwyslade [?]'.

In fact Henry VIII was amalgamating the whole area between the Wye and Rhymney rivers with his own lordships of Monmouth and the Three Castles, but all this belonged to the ancient Welsh district of Gwynllwg and the kingdom of Gwent, of which the latter owed its origin in turn to the administrative system established by the Romans at Caerwent.

So far as the administration of justice was concerned, Monmouthshire became part of the Oxford Circuit, along with Oxfordshire, Gloucestershire, Worcestershire and Herefordshire; and this may have given rise to the notion that it,was somehow not Welsh. The county boundaries, enclosing an area of some 540 square miles, including 125 parishes, remained largely unchanged for over 400 years. However, under Local Government Reorganisation Act of 1972 which took effect two years later, Monmouthshire lost parts of Gwynllwg to the south, gained Bryn-mawr and Gilwern from Breconshire to the north, and acquired the new, old name of Gwent.

Further changes followed less than 25 years later. From 1 April 1997 the county of Monmouth was reborn with a reduced area, while other parts of Gwent became the new unitary authorities of Blaenau Gwent, Torfaen and Newport. They are all, of course, in Wales, but the voters of only one of them, Blaenau Gwent, produced a majority in favour of a Welsh Assembly in the subsequent referendum.

As the title of a book, *The Folklore of Blaenau Gwent, Torfaen, Newport and Monmouthshire*, would hardly have been attractive, and even this would have omitted Islwyn and the Rhymney valley's move into the jurisdiction of Caerphilly. I have therefore chosen to cover the area occupied for so long by the historic county of Monmouthshire.

After writing on the neighbouring counties of Hereford and Gloucester it seemed a good idea to cross the border into Monmouth, 'an enchanted land', as Arthur Machen saw it, with a long history and a rich folklore. John Rhys wrote that 'one of the folklorist's greatest difficulties is that of drawing the line between story and history'; but the distinction seems less important when one considers that folklore, a body of tales, traditions, songs, beliefs, observances, and customs, is itself part of social history.

Some may find it odd—even unwelcome—that an Englishman should write on the folklore of a Welsh county. I hope that my doing so will be taken not as an impertinence but as a tribute.

*Map of old Monmouthshire showing many of the places
mentioned in the text*

CHAPTER 1

Saints

Wales, famed as the land of song, is also celebrated for its saints. A multitude of place names include *llan*, originally an enclosure with a religious building and associated structures; the name of a holy man or woman following it. Many such people remain obscure, their only record being the name of the place with which they were associated. Others, such as St David, the patron of Wales, have a national and even international reputation.

Stories of the saints and martyrs, some of them originating five or six hundred years after the events they purported to describe, were propagated to impress the faint-hearted and fortify the faithful. Many stretch credulity well beyond its breaking point, but others continue to exercise a curious fascination.

David and Patrick
Dewi Sant, St David, the water-drinking, wayfaring, sixth-century 'gipsy of God' has a number of associations with Monmouthshire. Geoffrey of Monmouth fancifully makes him succeed Dyfrig as archbishop of Caerleon, when there was no see there. More convincingly, local tradition says that David spent part of his life in prayer and meditation at a small cell or chapel which he erected at what is now called Llanthony. The name is a corruption of Llanddewi Nant Honddu, the *llan* of David on the River Honddu.

Chroniclers and poets have readily endorsed the Llanthony connection. Writing over a thousand years on, Michael Drayton evoked the emblematic leek in his lines on David's stay in the valley:

THE FOLKLORE OF MONMOUTHSHIRE

> Where in an aged cell, with mosse and Ivie growne,
> In which, not to this day the sunne hath ever showne,
> That reverend British Saint in zealous ages fast,
> To contemplation lived; and did so truly fast,
> As he did drink what crystal Hodney yields,
> And fed upon the leeks he gathered in the fields,
> In memorie of whom, in the revolving yeare,
> The Welshmen on his day that sacred herbe do weare.

After David's death, which occurred in either 589 or 601, at least two churches were founded in the area and dedicated to him; they are at Llanddewi Skirrid and Llanddewi Rhydderch. Eventually over 50 churches throughout Wales bore his name. He is the only specifically Welsh saint ever to have been formally canonised, though this did not happen until the 12th century.

David's 'aged cell' at Llanthony lay in ruins for several hundred years until a Norman knight, William de Lacy, came across it while he was out hunting. He was a kinsman and retainer of Hugh de Lacy, lord of Ewias, whose castle at Longtown is said to be linked to Llanthony by a passage beneath the Black Mountain. William, having found his Damascus road, renounced the world, repaired the cell, and embraced a regimen of prayer and poverty: 'he laid aside his belt, and girded himself with a rope; instead of fine linen, he covered himself with sackcloth; and instead of his soldier's robe, he loaded himself with weighty irons,' as a local account put it.

St David: an artist's impression

When news of such self-abnegation reached the court, Henry I and Queen Maud were deeply impressed. Maud's chaplain, Ernisius, travelled to the valley, fell under its spell, and signed on as assistant hermit. William de Lacy, summoned by the queen, suffered a moment of horror when she asked if she might put her hand in his bosom. He steeled himself to consent, and when she withdrew it she left behind a purse of gold.

Thanks to such largesse in 1108 William and Ernisius were able to build a small church, probably on the site of David's cell. The present church of St David, erected later in the 12th century stands in the same place. Its alignment is such that on St David's Day (1 March) the sun rises precisely above the altar.

Engraving of Llanthony Priory in 1777

In due course Ernisius became first abbot of the great priory constructed a short distance to the north, its own church dedicated to St John the Baptist, patron of hermits. Yet, in 1811, when the poet, Robert Southey, visited the melancholy ruins of Llanthony Priory, then owned by his friend, Walter Savage Landor, his thoughts turned to David:

> Here it was, Stranger, that the Patron Saint
> Of Cambria pass'd his age of penitence
> A solitary man ...

The patron of Ireland may also have a Monmouthshire connection. St Patrick is known to have been born at Bannavem Taburniae. The site of this settlement is untraced but the historian, Arthur Clarke, suggests that it 'was near the western sea, perhaps the Bristol Channel, and may have been in Gwent since his father, Calpurnius, was a decurion, a member of the governing class in Romanized society.' At the age of 15 Patrick was abducted by Irish pirates and kept as a slave for six years. Eventually he managed to return home, greatly changed from when he 'knew not God' in his youth. He then set out on the missionary journey which led to the conversion of Ireland.

Engraving of Llanthony Priory in 1800

Tathan and Beuno
Travelling to Wales, urged by an angel who appeared in dreams, came an Irishman of royal blood, Tathan. With a group of followers he reached the coast of Ireland and found a boat moored. Although it was without oars, sail or crew, Tathan's party went aboard, to be carried by wind and wave to a harbour 'named after the suffix of the people of the district', and therefore possibly Porth-Iscoed (Portskewett), in Gwent-Iscoed.

Caradog, king of Gwent, hearing of Tathan's arrival, invited him to found a monastic school at Caerwent. When Tathan declined, Caradog renewed the invitation in person, backed by a retinue of 24 knights. Yielding to the force either of arms or of argument, Tathan agreed to go to Caerwent, where the king gave him 'a piece of land nigh unto the city, extending from the high road to the river', which is to say from the Roman *Via Julia* to the Nedern Brook.

Tathan acquired a reputation as miracle-worker, generous host and revered patriarch. However, he cannot have been universally popular because one night some of the king's men turned 47 horses (the figure is oddly precise) into Tathan's meadow, where they spoiled the crop of hay intended for his cow. He promptly struck dead all the horses, only to restore them to life when Caradog apologised for his men's conduct.

On another occasion two men confessed to him that they had stolen a ram and murdered a shepherdess whom they later discovered was Maches, daughter of Gwynllyw (for whom, see below). The thieves' fate is not recorded, but Tathan founded a church at the scene of their crime, just over a mile from Caerwent, and called it Llanfaches. For some reason he later had the victim's body moved to his own church at Caerwent, where he himself was subsequently buried. St Athan in Glamorgan made a counter-claim to be the place of his death and burial; but in 1911 an excavation in the vicarage garden at Caerwent, just outside the Roman east gate in an area once occupied by the monastic church, turned up a skeleton which was deemed to be that of Tathan. The following year it was re-interred beneath the south aisle of the parish church which had originally been dedicated to Tathan.

Under Tangwyn (or Tangusius), Tathan's successor as abbot, a monk called Beuno studied at Caerwent. The king—by this time, Ynyr—received him warmly, gave him presents and grants of land in his native Ewias, where he established a church at Llanfeuno (or Llanveyno, now in Herefordshire). Beuno is said also to have founded the parish churches of Abergavenny and Machen, though neither is at present dedicated to him.

Not to be outdone, Ynyr himself endowed a church in gratitude at a place where he had reached firm ground after wading through a marsh—at Llanfihangel Ystern Llewern—then renounced his throne to become one of Beuno's disciples. He was succeeded by his son, Iddon, who soon faced a problem when his sister, Tegiwg (or Tigwig), either eloped with a carpenter who was working in Caerwent or was 'given in marriage to the young man lest she should have him in some other way,' as Baring-Gould notes. As the couple travelled towards the man's home at Aberffraw in Anglesey the man became increasingly ashamed and alarmed at the prospect of taking a princess to a poor dwelling. According to one account he simply abandoned her at night as she slept, and went on alone; another story says that he beheaded her, but Beuno restored her to life. A spring which gushed forth where her blood had flowed, according to the latter story, still runs at Penarth in Caernarfonshire.

After receiving news of these events Iddon rode north and implored his sister to return to Caerwent. She declined, and embraced a religious vocation in Beuno's abbey at Clynnog Fawr on the Lleyn Peninsula. Iddon, still smarting from his sister's treatment, went on to Aberffraw, where he took his sword and struck off the carpenter's head. Once more the benevolent Beuno intervened and seamlessly replaced it. Bueno died at Clynnog Fawr where he was buried.

Teilo and Dyfrig

When news came to Caerwent that a Saxon invasion was under way, Iddon decided to approach Teilo, an important monk and bishop (later saint), for help. He found him praying at Llanarth, near Usk, and the two men travelled three miles to Llantilio Crossenny where they took up a position with Iddon's army on a hillock. There, Teilo planted his cross and prayed to God to 'succour his plundered people.' The Saxons were vanquished and in gratitude Iddon gave Teilo three *modii* (27 acres) of land at the site, on which to build a church; the settlement's name meaning *llan* of Teilo at Iddon's Cross. The 12th century source of this information is dubious, but two grants of land by Iddon to Teilo of the same period (*c.*600) are documented; they are at Llanarth and Llantilio Pertholey.

Many of the early churches in Wales were indeed called after their saintly founders. A local chief would donate a piece of land, where a holy man then lived, prayed and built a simple oratory and shelter, usually of

St Teilo, from 15th-century stained glass at Plogonnec, Finistère

St Teilo's Church, Llantilio Crossenny

wood. Some saints, such as Beuno and Cybi (see below), wandered through the land with the intention of setting up churches. David and Teilo also travelled, but their churches are so numerous that they could not possibly all have been established by personal intervention. They were probably so named because they were erected on estates owned by their respective dioceses.

Teilo, who ended his career as bishop of Llandaff, was earlier a sort of missionary. When an outbreak of plague struck Wales in 547 he took his flock to Brittany, where a local magnate offered him as much land as he could encompass between sunrise and sunset. He cannily chose to ride on a stag, and so acquired many acres on which he founded Handeleau, a French version of Llandeilo.

Teilo is shown riding on a stag in a modern window of the church of Llantilio Pertholey near Abergavenny. The name's second element may mean 'muddy place' or 'defiled entrance', which could allude to the martyrdom of Christians at the site. The bell depicted above Teilo's head was presented to him to mark a pilgrimage to Jerusalem which he made

St Dyfrig, from an ancient roll, copied in one of the Dugdale MSS in the Bodleian Library, Oxford

with David and Padarn. Its ringing caused a certain mark to appear upon a perjurer and healed the sick by sounding every hour of its own accord until 'by the rash and constant handling of sinful men, it ceased from its sweet service.' Ironically, perhaps, the biggest and earliest of the four bells now at Pertholey bears the inscription, 'Sancte Georgii ora pro nobis', a request for the intercession not of St Teilo but of St George.

At one stage Teilo was taught by Dyfrig (also known as Dubricius), whose name means 'water baby'. It came about because when his unmarried mother, Ebrdil (or Efrddyl), was found to be pregnant, her father, King Peibio of Erging—the land between the Wye and the Monnow—ordered her to be tied in a sack and thrown in the River Wye. Three times she was consigned to the water; three times she floated unharmed to the bank.

On the king's command, she was then cast into a huge pyre at Matle (now Madley, Herefordshire). Next morning, men sent to recover her calcined bones found her alive and well, nursing the newborn Dyfrig. Confronted with mother and baby, Peibio had a change of heart, and welcomed them. The infant touched the king's face, and cured the affliction of constant dribbling which he had suffered for many years. Several grants of land made by Peibio to Dyfrig in the latter part of the sixth century are on record.

From such spectacular beginnings Dyfrig went on to become scholar, monk, bishop, and one of the most important early saints of South Wales. St Michael the Archangel is supposed to have appeared to him on top of Skirrid Fawr at a spot later marked by a chapel (of which a few stones still stand). On another occasion an angel told him in a vision to look for a white sow with a litter of piglets, and there found a monastery. He came across the right animals, and thus the right place. He called it Mochros ('Pigs' moor'), which is now Moccas in Herefordshire.

The college which Dyfrig earlier set up at Henllan could have been at Hentland (also in Herefordshire), where the church is dedicated to him, or at Dixton, near Monmouth, which was formerly called Henllan Tytiuc (though the second element refers to St Tedeoc). Geoffrey of Monmouth fancifully makes Dyfrig archbishop of Caerleon and in this capacity sends him with King Arthur to Bath to address the army before the battle of Badon. Later Dyfrig crowns Arthur at Silchester, and then consecrates both him and Guinevere at a glittering ceremony in Caerleon. He then resigns in favour of St David, who promptly transfers the see to Menevia (St Davids).

Dyfrig retired to a hermitage on Ynys Enlli (Bardsey Island) and died there in about 612. On the orders of Bishop Urban his remains were transferred in 1120 to Llandaff Cathedral. As they arrived, a seven-week drought came to an end.

THE FOLKLORE OF MONMOUTHSHIRE

Martyrs
Rival claims variously ascribed the foundation of Caerleon to Joseph of Arimathea, to the Silures and to the Romans. Certainly Julius Frontinus, governor of Britain from 73/4 until 77/8 AD established a base there for the Second Legion (Augusta). The Romans were still very much in charge when two Christian noblemen, Aaron and Julius, were martyred in the town—possibly by being torn to pieces by wild animals—in 279, 303 or 304, depending on the account followed.

Geoffrey of Monmouth says there were eventually three churches in Caerleon, one each for Julius and Aaron, and a third acting as the metropolitan establishment for the whole of Wales. The site of the church of St Julius, where, again according to Geoffrey, Guinevere took the veil, has been identified with St Julian's, the Elizabethan home of the Herbert family, about a mile west of Caerleon, which was demolished in the 1970s. Local tradition assigns the burial of Aaron to Penrhos, north-east of the town, where a small chapel was erected to his memory on the site of a Roman camp. In 1926, when a new church dedicated to Julius and Aaron was built in Newport some stones from St Julian's were incorporated, whilst another from Llanthony Priory became the altar.

Geoffrey also mentions a third Caerleon saint, the monk Amphibalus, of whom he gives no details other than that he 'taught Saint Alban and instructed, him in the true faith.' Amphibalus travelled to Verulamium and was given hospitality by a soldier, Alban, whom he proceeded to convert to Christianity. When the Roman authorities sought to arrest Amphibalus, he and Alban changed clothes. Dressed as a soldier, Amphibalus escaped. Alban, in a monk's habit, was arrested and put to death. After this martyrdom many people travelled to Caerleon to be baptised by Amphibalus. Enraged by such defiance, the Romans fell on the converts and slaughtered them. They took Amphibalus to Redburn, three miles from Verulamium, and stoned him to death.

Unfortunately, the account may originate in the mistranslation of a phrase in a Latin document, and therefore be fictitious. However, the martyrdom of Alban did take place, possibly in 305, in an amphitheatre outside Verulamium round which grew the present town of St Albans.

The present church in Caerleon, like 14 others in Wales and one in Brittany, is dedicated to Cadwg (or Cadoc). At Trefethin, where the church is also associated with Lleirog, grant-grandson of Caractacus, we are told that Cadwg was personally supervising construction when each

SAINTS

morning he found the previous day's work thrown down, and the masonry scattered. Suspecting satanic skullduggery, he had a great bell made and, when he judged the devil to be close by, rang it. Stung by the aural assault, Satan fled, throwing down the stones he was carrying in his apron. He thus created Garn Clochdy (Belfry Cairn), a sandstone outcrop on the mountain between Trefethin and Blaenafon.

Another bell at Trefethin, presented by Llewelyn ap Iorwerth, lord of Caerleon, and known as St Cadoc's Bell, became bewitched and killed an over-inquisitive child who climbed into the belfry. The bell was buried, and consigned to *annwn*, the land of shadows beneath the earth, whence it can be heard mournfully tolling whenever a Trefethin child meets with accidental death.

A similar story is told at Christchurch, near Newport, where a little girl was killed by a bell which then became forfeit to demons who seized it and bore it down into the earth. This, too, sounds when a child is accidentally killed in the parish.

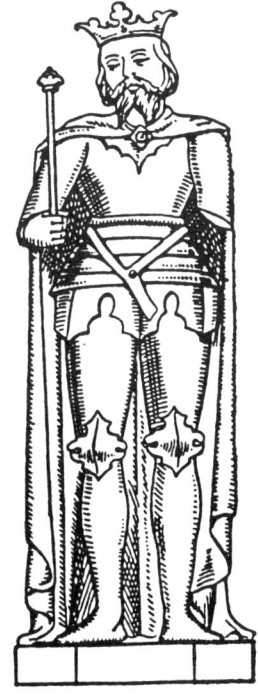

St Gwynllyw, after a window in St Woolos

Cadwg's father was Gwynllyw, whose own father, Glywys, ruled an area called Glywysing which included parts of what were later known as Monmouthshire, Glamorgan and Carmarthenshire. When Glywys died Gwynllyw inherited land between the Usk and Rhymney rivers which came to be called Gwynllwg (and still exists in anglicised form in placenames such as Peterstone-Wentloog and St Brides-Wentloog).

Gwynllyw is recorded as 'wicked, turbulent, and a maintainer of robber bands.' To this day the dock area of Newport, Pillgwenlly, takes its name from the creek or pill where Gwynllyw is reputed to have moored his pirate long boat. Gwynllyw conceived a desire to marry Gwladys, daughter of Brychan, who lived at Talgarth in the county to which he had given his own name, Brycheiniog (Breconshire). Brychan opposed the match, though he could hardly have missed Gwladys from his brood of between 12 and 63 children,

11

St Woolos Cathedral, Newport

depending on the source followed, the average number being 24 (including one, incidentally, who as St Cenedlon became dedicatee of Rockfield Church).

When his envoys were summarily ejected by Brychan, Gwynllyw gathered a force of several hundred men and marched on Talgarth. He seized Gwladys and set off homewards, pursued by Brychan, whose retainers began to harry Gwynllyw's rearguard. Meanwhile, the eloping pair ran into King Arthur, who happened to be sitting on Boch Rhiw Carn (Cheek of Stony Hill), throwing dice with Cai (Kay) and Bedwyr (Bedivere). Arthur took an immediate liking to Gwladys, and had to be dissuaded by his two knights from taking her for himself. He asked Gwynllyw on whose land they were standing. Gwynllyw swore that it was his, so when Brychan arrived in hot pursuit Arthur ordered him to retire.

Gwynllyw and Gwladys were triumphantly married, then proceeded to devote much of their life to armed violence. Eventually they were prevailed on to change their ways, either by the devout Cadwg, or by his tutor from Caerwent, Tathan, or by the fear of death brought on by advancing age. An angel appeared to Gwynllyw in a dream and charged him to build a church on a hill by a river in a place where he found a white ox with a black spot on the forehead. One day all these requirements were fulfilled, on Stow Hill, above the River Usk at Newport. Gwynllyw built there a church of 'boards and rods', the forerunner of the present entrance chapel to the cathedral of St Woolos, of which the name is an anglicised form of Gwynllyw. The church site at Kilgwrrwg, unconnected with Gwynllyw, was selected in a similar fashion: when local people disagreed, a wise man yoked two heifers and set them free to wander; the place where they rested, which turned out to be a dry tump, was chosen.

On Stow Hill Gwynllyw and Gwladys lived austere lives. Winter and summer they walked naked half a mile to the Usk to bathe. When Cadwg came to hear of this he advised his mother to move where she could bathe in the presence of 'virgins and chaste persons only.' She therefore took up residence above the River Ebbw in what is now Tredegar Park, where a pure spring ran in secluded surroundings. Its name is Lady's Well, perhaps after Gwladys, perhaps after the Virgin Mary. For his part, Gwynllyw stayed at Stow Hill. As he lay dying he was visited by Dyfrig, and subsequently buried beneath the floor of his church. However, his influence remained. When some people stole a cheese from the church, blood flowed from it when they came to break it. After pirates ransacked town and church, a great storm blew up in the Severn Sea (Môr Hafren), and the pirates saw Gwynllyw in pursuit, riding the wind. The ship foundered, and their drowned bodies were washed up on the banks of the Usk.

Cadwg continued to teach and preach. He established a monastery at Llancarfan in the Vale of Glamorgan, but it was somewhere in his late father's territory that he gave shelter to a fugitive, Ligessawc, nicknamed Llaw Hir (Long Hand), who had murdered three of King Arthur's soldiers. When, seven years later, Arthur found out where the man was, he marched to the River Usk. He paused there, chary of offending Cadwg with violence, and asked for arbitration. A panel of judges which included David and Teilo ruled that Cadwg should provide 100 cows in compensation, together with three oxen for each of the men killed. Arthur accepted, with the mocking proviso that the cows must be red before and white behind. Cadwg called for the heifers to be brought, and immediately turned their colours to suit the specification. The animals were driven across the Usk at a ford from then on called Rhyd Gwrthebau (Ford of the Rejoinders), near the present Newbridge-on-Usk. As Cai and Bedwyr grasped the beasts by the horns to pull them ashore they successively changed into bundles of fern. This event is recalled in the name of the nearby settlement of Tref Rhedynog, or Tredunnock (Ferny Homestead).

Cadwg's somewhat vindictive streak is also seen in his dealings with St Barrog (otherwise called Barry, Barnic and Barruc), a sixth century Briton of high birth who chose to live as a hermit. The church at Bedwas is dedicated to him. Barrog, together with a companion and their mentor, Cadwg, landed on an island off the Glamorgan coast. Cadwg then asked the others for his handbook, but they told him they had left it on another island. He ordered them to fetch it, using the curious sentence, 'Go, not to return'. The boat capsized and the two men were drowned. Barrog's body, cast up on the shore where Cadwg stood waiting, was buried at the spot, so giving Barry Island its name. A more prosaic explanation is that Barrog merely lived there as a hermit.

Cadwg himself met a martyr's death, either at Benevento in Italy, where he had been transported on a cloud, or at Llancarfan, where Saxon raiders fell on him as he celebrated mass. Monks who fled with his body in an elaborate coffin were pursued to Mamhilad, but however many of the raiders joined in the attempt, they were unable to move the coffin. In frustration, one beat on it with a stick, to be transfixed with horror when a bull-like bellow issued from it. Another, who cut off a golden pinnacle from the coffin, 'melted in the sight of the whole army like wax before the fire,' according to W.J. Rees in his *Lives of the Cambro-British Saints*. For good measure, the earth then trembled. It is in fact possible that the shrine of St Cadwg was indeed transferred in 1022 to a monastery at Mamhilad, though to avoid an invasion not by Saxons but by Angles and Danes.

A Saxon incursion did lead to the death of St Tewdrig (otherwise Tewdric or Theodoric), who after a career as warrior-chieftain in Glamorgan and Gwent retired to a hermitage by the River Wye on a site later occupied by Tintern Abbey. In old age he was summoned by his son, successor and fellow-saint, Meurig, to rally resistance to a Saxon force led by Coelwulph. On the eve of battle Tewdrig dreamed that an angel promised him victory, while predicting that he would receive a single blow to the skull from which he would die three days later.

The battle took place, probably in 597, at Pont y Saeson (Englishman's Bridge), which is on the hill above the Wye at Trellech Grange. Tewdrig embraced his fate, defeating the Saxons, and in so doing taking a blow to the head. He asked to be buried on Ynys Echni (Flat Holm), and was taken in that direction on a carriage drawn, say the records, by stags. Stags are unlikely animals to pull any conveyance, and it may be that the word was used with its other meaning of castrated oxen. Alternatively, in Welsh, *carw* (stag) could have been confused with *tarw* (bull or ox), particularly in transcribing a manuscript.

Wherever Tewdrig's cortege halted pure water welled from the ground to refresh him. The penultimate pause seemed to have been made at what is now called Pwll Meyric, and the last, where Tewdrig died, in a meadow not far from the Severn Sea. St Tewdrig's Well is still there, near the north-east corner of Mathern House (a name derived from Merthyr (Martyr) Tewdrig) which, after Owain Glyn Dwr's destruction of the palaces at Bishton and Llandaff, was the sole episcopal residence until 1705. Four 16th century bishops are buried in the nearby church: Miles Salley (heart only; body at Bristol), Anthony Kitchin (the only Catholic prelate to take an oath of allegiance to Queen Elizabeth I), Hugh Jones (appointed in 1574 and the first Welsh bishop of Llandaff for 300 years) and William Bleddyn (a native of Shirenewton who considered himself to be descended from Hywel Dda, king of Deheubarth). Yet another bishop, William Morgan, who in 1588 translated the Bible into Welsh, is buried in the churchyard.

At least one more bishop was a visitor to Mathern. Francis Godwin, bishop of Llandaff from 1601 until 1617, was an historian and a 'passing great lover of venerable antiquities and all good literature,' as well as the writer of the first story of space travel in English, *The Man in the Moone, or a Discourse of a Voyage Thither* (1638). Godwin describes how Tewdrig came to mind when a stone coffin was found beneath the floor of the church, and adds: 'As I was giving orders to repair this coffin, Which was either broken by chance or decayed by age, I discovered his bones, not in the smallest degree changed, though after a period of a thousand years, the skull retained the aperture of a large wound, which appeared as if it had been recently inflicted.'

On Godwin's orders the coffin was re-interred in the chancel beneath a stone tablet:

> Here lyth the body of Theodorick, King of Morganuck commonly called St Thewdrick, and accounted a Martyr, because he was slain in battle against the Saxons, then Pagans, and in defence of the Christian religion. The battle was fought at Tintern, where he obtained a great victory, but died here, being in his way homeward, three days after the battle, having taken order with Maurice his son, who succeeded him in the kingdom, that in the same place he should

happen to decease, a church should be built and his body buried in the same, which was accordingly performed in the year 600.

The first woman martyr in Britain was killed by pirates just two miles away on St Tecla's Island, just off Beachley Point. The Welsh princess, Tecla, retired to a life of prayer and meditation on the tiny island where there is still a holy well and also a ruined chapel once dedicated to her (see illustration on page 120). St Cadfan landed here in the 5th century on the way to Wales from Brittany and is believed to have founded the chapel; services were then held here for eleven hundred years.

A group of seven Welsh bishops came this way in 603 to cross the Severn from Beachley to Aust. They were to meet St Augustine of Canterbury, Pope Gregory's choice to evangelise Saxon Britain, and to try to reconcile differences between the Roman and Celtic branches of the church. As well as Gloucestershire's Aust, whose very name may be derived from that of Augustine, several other places claim to have hosted the meeting. Wherever it was, the Welsh bishops had been advised by a wise man that if Augustine rose to his feet and greeted them as brothers in Christ, they should accept his overtures; but if he remained seated and aloof, they should reject them. He failed to rise, and the Celtic church stayed independent until 768. One account of the meeting suggests that the Welsh delegation paused on its outward journey at St Tecla's Island to

Patricio Church

consult the eponymous virgin, saint and hermit. Since the reported date of her martyrdom, 47 AD, was over five centuries earlier it is more likely that the visit was simply to her chapel.

Another martyr, Issui (or Ishow), has given his name to the settlement and church of Patricio (or Partrishow), near Abergavenny. According to T. Thoresby Jones, Issui, 'an unwholesome and officious hermit,' was killed because he 'rashly rebuked some lusty pagan prince.' A different story says that he met his death at the hands of an ungrateful traveller to whom he had extended the hospitality of his cell on the bank of Nant Mair (St Mary's Stream) below the present church. Whoever did the deed is said to to have nailed Issui's skin to his cell door. Until 1900 a skin of some kind was kept nailed to the door of the church in remembrance of the atrocity. The saint's well, Ffynnon Issui, still exists just off the road, close to the stream (see illustration on page 109). People place votive crosses of tied twigs on the stone coping, and throw luck-seeking coins into the limpid water.

More Women Saints
Few of the early Welsh saints were women. To Cenedlon, Gwladys and Tecla, who have already been mentioned, one could add Govan, wife of Tewdrig, at Llangofen, near Raglan; Hiledd, daughter of Cyndrwyn, a fifth century king of Brycheiniog, though she had the misfortune of being dropped as patron of Llanhiledd in favour of the better-known (and male) Illtyd; and Mabli (Mabel), of whom nothing is known save that her name is perpetuated at Llanfapley, two miles east of Abergavenny. Llandegfedd, north of Usk, takes its name from Tegfedd (or Tecmed), mother of Teilo, who suffered martyrdom at the hands of the Saxons. When the present church, dating from the 12th century, was restored in 1875-6 a huge leg bone came to light, buried in the south wall. If this belonged to St Tegfedd she must have been eight feet tall.

The balance in favour of femininity was redressed, largely through Norman influence, with the cult of the Virgin. Well before the Normans, though—no later than 927—the monks' church at Monmouth was dedicated to St Mary. Elsewhere in Wales, 142 others followed the conquest, many giving rise to Llanfair placenames.

St Bridget (Bride or Ffraid), who lived from 454 until 521, has several dedications in Monmouthshire. At home in Ireland she rejected her father's orders to marry a chieftain. When he threatened her she reduced him to terrified silence by plucking out her eyes and throwing them on the

Carving of St Bridget on the lectern in Skenfrith Church

grass. He took to his heels, whereupon she calmly replaced her eyes and sailed away across the Irish Sea on a convenient piece of turf. She reached Anglesey, says one version of her story; another, that she arrived near the mouth of the Usk, where the village of Llansantffraid Gwynllwg (St Brides Wentloog) commemorates her landing place.

She later returned to Ireland and built a *kil* (cell) under a great *dara* (oak) at the place now called Kildare. She also established an abbey endowed with an inextinguishable flame. This, combined with acorns and oak leaves, became her emblem. All these, and the floating turf too, were carved by Richard Jack early this century on a lectern in the church of St Bridget at Skenfrith. Acorns and oak leaves recur in the sanctuary woodwork, combined with the fleur-de-lis which was the ancient badge of the princes of Gwent. The nun's head over the porch may be a representation of Bridget; and St Freide's Well is near the church. A jocular local tradition suggests that one day Bridget came in person to Skenfrith, converted the people, and went on after tea to do the same thing at Bridstow, near Ross-on-Wye. Bridstow (definitely) and Skenfrith (arguably—see chapter 8) incorporate her name.

Marching In
The Welsh did not normally 'style' saints in placenames—that is, insert the word, *sant*—though with foreigners like Bridget they made an exception. Llansantffraid, incidentally, is the smallest parish in Monmouthshire, with a church to match. As the name indicates, Llantrisant, south of Usk, has three patrons—Peter, Paul and John. There were four at Llangwm, which means Valley Church—Mirgint, Cinfice, Hui and Erneu, though at some stage they were replaced by St Jerome from the ranks of internationally known saints. St Michael himself falls into the same category.

After Mary he is the most popular patron in Wales, with almost 100 dedications, many dating from the eighth century. Ten of these are in Monmouthshire, easily recognisable as beginning with Llanfihangel (see chapter 8).

On the other hand, some Welsh saints make very few appearances. Gwennarth (otherwise Weonard or Wanner) has Llanwenarth, near Abergavenny, and a solitary church in Herefordshire. He was a monk, possibly connected with Dyfrig, and possibly martyred by the Saxons. In 1695-6 the first Baptist church in Wales was established at Llanwenarth, but its founders would have had scant sympathy with Celtic saints.

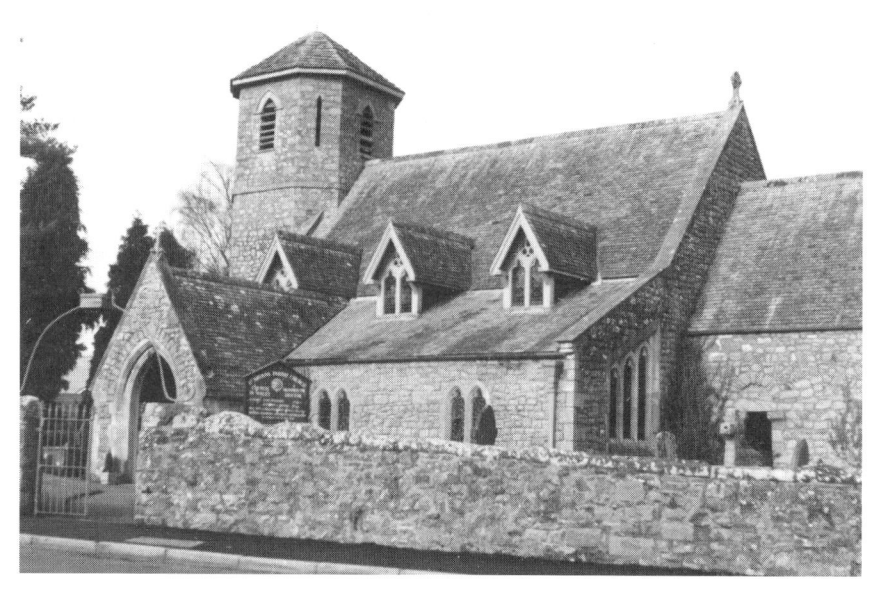

St Arvan's Church

Tysoi, of Llansoy, may also have been one of Dyfrig's disciples, but nothing more is known of him. Arfan, another shadowy figure, is thought to have been a fisherman who perished when his coracle capsized in the Wye. The sole church dedicated to him is at St Arvans. We know that it existed by 995 because in that year a labourer mowing nearby became involved in an argument with a deacon called Eli, struck him, perhaps with a sickle, and cut his finger. Eli asked the labourer to bind up the wound but as he did so, stabbed and killed him. He then took sanctuary in the church, where he in turn died at the hands of a group of men determined to avenge his victim. The violation of sanctuary was considered especially heinous and the local ruler, Nowy, whose men had killed Eli, found himself summoned to appear at Caerwent before Bishop Pater. In due course the offenders were required to be confined for six months in the monastery at Caerwent.

Even less is known of some Monmouthshire saints than of Arfan. Only the name remains of Brechfa, at Llanfrechfa, though the word could mean 'church in a speckled place', and thus exclude a saint altogether. Alternatively, it could derive from Caradoc Freichfas (Strong Arm), one of King Arthur's men. The St Dingat (or Dingad) of Llanddingad

(Dingestow) could have been the brother of Dyfrig, who spent his last years there; Dingad ap Nudd Hael, king of Bryn Buga (Usk); or Dingat, son of Brychan. In turn, the son of this Dingat, Gwytherin, is represented with his right hand raised in priestly blessing in the church to which he gave his his name at Llanvetherine (though the dedication is now to St James the Elder).

At Undy the church's patron is St Mary, but the founder, Dyfrig, is said to have dedicated it to St Gwyndaf and his wife, St Wyndaf, and called the place after them. However, the village's name may derive from the more prosaic Gwyn-dy (White house). The dedicatee at Llanelen could have been Helen Lluyddog (Helen of the Legions), wife of Magnus Maximus, who was proclaimed Roman emperor at York in 383 and executed five years later; or Helena, mother of Constantine the Great who certainly gave her name to the Atlantic island. Melon of St Mellons was born in Cardiff and died in Rouen (in 314) but his connection with Monmouthshire is unclear. One saint, Gofor, was invented, it has been suggested, by Lady Llanover, who endowed him with a spring in the village of Llanofer. Others contend that the saint in question is not Gofor but Mofor or Myfor, though he too remains elusive.

Padarn (or Paternus), a fifth to sixth century monk, may have founded Llanerch Padarn in the Tyleri valley. St Cybi undoubtedly established several churches. He was a Cornishman who travelled in his mother's land of Wales, finally retiring to a small island, Ynys Gybi, near the town of

St Gwytherin at Llanvetherine

Caer Gybi, both called after him and better known as Holy Island and Holyhead respectively. Cybi's landing in Monmouthshire is supposedly marked by a standing stone close to the River Usk near Llangybi. King Ithel, although he was the great-grandson of the saintly Meurig of Tintern, ordered that Cybi and his followers should be driven away, whereupon his horse immediately dropped dead and he himself lost the use of his eyes. Only when he went and prostrated himself before Cybi did he regain his sight and his horse's life. Ithel then presented Cybi with the land on which the church of Llangybi was built.

Something of Cybi's fierceness, alternating with a more gentle approach, is also seen in the stories of Odoceus (or Euddogwy), whose name is remembered at Llandogo, on the Wye. This saint, who lived from about 650 until 698, retired as bishop of Llandaff and came to the secluded woods by Cleddon Brook. One day, a hunted stag ran out of the trees and laid on Odoceus's cloak, which was spread out on the ground. The holy man prayed, and the pursuing men and dogs were rooted to the spot. Einon, the local lord, was so impressed that he not only adopted the reprieved stag as a pet but bestowed on the see of Llandaff all the land the hunt had covered that day. The rescue of the stag is depicted in the present church. There is no record of Einon's land-grant, though a charter of *c.*698 exists in which King Morgan returned Llandogo 'with its four weirs' to Bishop Euddogwy.

A dispute between Odoceus and Gildas, the historian, is only related in Gildas's own writings, which is hardly surprising since the latter died 80 years before the former was born. However, Gildas says that when he lived on an island in the Wye he came across some timber which had been cut for use in the saint's house. Ignoring Odoceus's objections he began to load some of it into his boat, only to desist when the saint made an awesome demonstration of his power by picking up an axe and driving it deep into a great stone. The cleft rock, called the Stone of Odoceus, afterwards featured as a landmark in descriptions of local boundaries.

Secular Piety
A much more recent story involves both justice and charity. It concerns William Jones, a poor boy from Newland in the Forest of Dean, whose story was told in 1861 by S.C. Hall. Jones worked as a boot-boy in the Kings Head at Monmouth. He fell in love with a girl above his station, despaired of winning her, and in desperation ran away, taking with him a

pair of shoes for which he had not paid. The shoemaker, Joe King, was confident that he would receive his money, and though years passed, did not change his mind.

Three decades elapsed before 'a poor man, doubled like a bow, and shaking under a ragged coat' turned up in Newland. He asked for a drink from the well where the Jones family had lived, but the woman of the house set the dog on him. He rested on a bench outside the inn (the Ostrich), but when he failed to order a drink was directed to the poorhouse. There the man declared himself to be Will Jones, a native of the parish, and asked for relief. Since he had been away for so long he was refused help, and told to go to Monmouth, from where he had fled so many years earlier.

He was taken in at Monmouth, and 'wore the pauper's dress and ate the pauper's bread.' He called on Joe King and asked whether he remembered 'Wild Will', and if so whether he still thought the longstanding debt would be paid. The shoemaker re-affirmed his belief, adding that even if he did not receive the money he would not 'sin his soul' by failing to forgive a poor fellow the value of a pair of shoes. The questioner disappeared the next day, taking with him the pauper's suit which he had been lent.

A month later a coach—this was in the early 17th century—drew up at Monmouth poorhouse. A 'fine broad-shouldered gentleman, firm on his limbs, with a back as straight as a poplar-tree' got out, and took in a bundle which contained the missing clothes. Then he drove to Joe King's and convinced him with some difficulty that he and the pauper were not only the same person, but that he was also William Jones. He left behind on the table a heavy purse of gold.

In 1615 he founded a free grammar school in Monmouth, and endowed almshouses. 'He did intend to have done for little Newland what he did for great Monmouth, but never quite forgave their turning him over to Monmouth parish—how could anyone forgive *that*?' Yet he did leave £5,000 to the poor of Newland, 'with directions about their having the gospel preached—to teach them charity.'

In 1628 Walter Powell noted in his diary: '18 August. Sent my five sonnes altogether to Monmoth free scoole, viz. John, Wm., tho:, Rich: & Charles.' Three centuries later (in 1917), Leonard Clark, then a poor boy from the Forest of Dean, and later to be known as a writer and poet, went to what had become Monmouth Grammar School on a William Jones Scholarship. The present buildings date largely from the 1860s, at which time the original schoolroom was demolished. Beneath its floorboards were found coins which had escaped from the pockets of schoolboys during the course of 250 years.

Sadly, the scholarships endowed by William Jones are no more, but his memory lingers. His deeds would surely have won the approval of St David.

CHAPTER 2

Soldiers

The peaceful atmosphere of east Monmouthshire's rolling fields and luxuriant woods belies a troubled past, though gaunt castle ruins readily evoke the conflicts of yesteryear. Romans, Saxons, Normans and English passed this way as invaders, not without resistance. Civil war came with Owain Glyn Dwr and with 17th century battles between king and Parliament.

In earlier times the bleak moors and mountains to the west of the county were sparsely populated. They too, with their rugged valleys, saw a massive invasion of a different kind during the industrial revolution. The resulting struggles and tensions (partly covered in chapter 9) helped, to motivate the Chartist movement and its ill-fated 'rising' of 1839 at Newport.

This chapter sets out, not to re-tell all this history, but to examine its echoes in terms of tales and traditions, ballads and beliefs.

Romans, Arthur and Countrymen
When the legions of Emperor Claudius invaded Britain in 43 AD resistance was led by Cunobelinus, better known as Shakespeare's Cymbeline. When he died his son, Caradoc (Caratacus) fought on, meeting the Romans in some 30 battles until he was forced to flee to south-east Wales. Possibly through the mediation of the Druids he was welcomed by the Silures, a fierce tribe whose members worshipped a feline deity which survived into early mediaeval literature as Cath Palug. Although the Silures strongly resisted the Romans, in 51 AD Caradoc lost a decisive battle against forces led by Ostorius Scapula, and was captured shortly afterwards.

In the view of one historian, Peter Salway, the battle took place at Newtown in Shropshire. The Herefordshire Beacon near Malvern also has its adherents, including Edward Elgar, whose opera, *Caractacus*, is set there. Further south still, local tradition places the capture of Caradoc (if not the battle) at Heston Brake near Portskewett, just over a mile from the Severn Estuary.

Sudbrook Camp, a short distance away, was thought to be the site of the Silures' last stand against the Romans, which took place over 20 years after Caradoc's defeat. The same tribe occupied Llanmelin Camps, from which, after finally accepting Roman hegemony, it moved in the 70s AD to the newly-established town of Caerwent—though the thickness of walls there may indicate that sporadic hostility towards the Roman garrison lasted for many more years.

The town's name, Venta Silurum (Market-place of the Silures) in due course became Caer Guent (Fortress Venta), and so supplied a designation for the whole land of Gwent. Some 2,000 years after the Romans' arrival a thoroughfare near Rhymney is still known as Y Fordd Rhufeinig (The Roman Road). Local tradition also claims as Roman roads Clwyd y Sarn (The Causeway Gate) at Blaenau and Y Sarn Hir (The Long Causeway) on Bedwellty Mountain. The Romans, it is said, built the first bridge over the Afon Lwyd at Pont-hir (which means Long Bridge), so that their troops could march dryshod from Caerleon to a hill camp at Candwr Lane.

The Romans unwittingly contributed to the Arthurian legend at Caerleon, where their huge amphitheatre came to light only after a major excavation carried out by Mortimer Wheeler in 1926-7. Previously, when it had simply appeared to be a green hollow in a field known as King Arthur's Mead, it was considered to be the site of the Round Table.

A Norman castle mound also added to the story as the supposed place either of Arthur's burial or of his palace. A tower there was pressed into service as the vantage point used by Guinevere when she gazed across the River Usk in hopes of seeing Geraint and Enid's return. So said Tennyson in *The Idylls of the King* (1859). The poem was partly written at the Hanbury Arms in Caerleon, where for many years Tennyson lingered in the memory as the man who sat with feet on the mantelpiece, smoking a black clay pipe.

A Caerleon man once supposedly found his way into the Mynde, as the castle mound is called, where he saw Arthur and his knights feasting. They made him welcome, and gave him a purse of gold. His being found dead drunk on the road outside the mound made people dubious of his tale, but from that day he drank no more. He protested his veracity for the rest of his life.

Another story, written out in Gwentian Welsh for Sir John Rhys by a Mr Craigfryn Hughes, tells of a Monmouthshire farmer. He consults a wise man who takes him to an underground chamber beneath a wood (perhaps Wentwood), where he sees hundreds of men lying asleep, each with his hand on the stock of a gun. Despite the modernity of the arms, these were 'Arthur's thousand soldiers sleeping till the Cymry have need of them.' Sworn to secrecy for a year and a day on pain of death, the farmer never sees the wise man again, nor does he succeed in finding the cave entrance.

The death of Arthur, from a 19th century engraving

A different account places the sleeping warriors—a persistent theme—in a cliff cave beneath Chepstow Castle. A potter by the name of Thompson stumbles in and sees Arthur and his knights asleep. He takes a bugle from the wall and picks up a sheathed sword, but in doing so rouses some of the sleepers. As he flees in fear a voice calls after him:

> Potter Thompson, hadst thou drawn the sword or blown the horn,
> Thou wouldst have been the luckiest man ever born.

Other versions of the same encounter place it below Richmond Castle in Yorkshire, naming Thompson but not Arthur; and at Sewing Shields Castle near Hadrian's Wall, with the king but without the potter.

Arthur and his men are supposed to awaken when calamity threatens the Cwmry, yet despite many terrifying crises in the last thousand years they have apparently not done so. However, according to S.P.B. Mais they did rouse themselves in 1914, when they were seen riding through St Julian's Wood between Caerleon and Chepstow.

The 6th century Welsh historian, Gildas, who wrote in Latin, does not mention Arthur, though he describes a leader known as Ursus—the Bear in Latin, Artos in Celtic and Arth in Welsh. However, Ambrosius Aurelianus, whom Gildas does chronicle, may have been succeeded by Arthur as leader of a confederacy of princes warring against the Saxons. A modern historian of Monmouthshire, Arthur Clarke, believes that Arthur was a Roman-educated Briton who knew the value of cavalry: 'he may have organised a mobile force (hence the mediaeval tradition of knights) which was able to crush the Saxons, who never became horsemen.'

In the lives of early Welsh saints (see chapter 1) Arthur's image is far from heroic: he is brutal, dissolute, and something of a bully. Perhaps this was the true picture, but it is completely at variance with the more common one of the chivalrous prince, son of Uther Pendragon, crowned at the age of 15 by the saintly Dyfrig. In the origin of these versions, Geoffrey of Monmouth's *History of the Kings of Britain*, written in Latin and finished in about 1136, he wields the sword, Caliburn, against a whole series of enemies: Picts and Scots, Saxons and Norwegians, Irish and Gauls, and also a Spanish giant he meets on the Mont St Michel. He holds a triumphant plenary court at Caerleon and is re-consecrated there with his queen, Guinevere, 'the most beautiful woman in the whole island.'

Remains of Monmouth Priory, showing 'Geoffrey of Monmouth's Window' to the left of centre, with the church of St Mary behind

While Arthur is away fighting in Gaul his nephew, Mordred, seizes power, taking both kingdom and queen. On Arthur's return Guinevere retires in disgrace to the nunnery of St Julius the Martyr at Caerleon. In 542 Mordred dies in the battle of Camlan but Arthur also retires with a fatal wound to the Isle of Avalon.

Geoffrey of Monmouth is a shadowy figure. His signature appears in six different documents, all connected with religious houses in or near Oxford. He became bishop of St Asaph in 1152, though he probably never visited the see. He may have died in 1155. Lewis Thorpe writes:

> To have called himself *Galfridus Monemutensis* he must have had some vital connection with Monmouth, probably that of birth. Everything in his writings and his thinly-sketched autobiography points to his having been a Welshman, or perhaps a Breton born in Wales. There must have been some biographical reason for his constant preoccupation with Caerleon-on-Usk ...

Others have speculated that Geoffrey had a Norman father and a Welsh mother, and that he was educated at the Benedictine priory in Monmouth. 'Geoffrey's window' in the room where he is supposed to have written his book is still pointed out in a surviving fragment of the priory, now a youth hostel.

Detail of the balcony to 'Geoffrey's Window'

Geoffrey's narrative has been dismissed as fanciful, but its importance is not as history—though Thorpe adds that 'history keeps peeping through the fiction'—but as story. Indeed, as E.T. Davies has observed, it was 'the main channel through which the Arthurian legend became included in the mainstream of European literature.'

Of the many additions to the cycle, some sought to cut Arthur down to size. Others, such as those in the *Mabinogion*, reinforced his heroic stature. One of these, dating from about 1100, deals with the Twrch Trwyth, a king's son who has been turned into a gigantic, malevolent boar. Arthur undertakes to hunt down the Twrch and his pack of companion boars, and to retrieve three treasures he carries entangled in the bristles of his head: a comb, a razor and a pair of shears.

After a series of running battles across much of Wales the beast is brought to bay off Beachley Point, or, according to another interpretation, between the mouth of the Wye and St Pierre Pill. Arthur's men seize the razor and shears but the Twrch escapes by land to Cornwall. The chase continues and the comb is recovered. The Twrch, pursued by Aned and Aethlem, the fastest hounds in the world, swims out to sea. None of them is ever seen again.

SOLDIERS

Many sites claim Arthurian associations, or did so. Above Abergavenny a rock formation on the Sugar Loaf was once called Cadair Arthur (Arthur's Chair) and a great square stone on Skirrid Fawr was known as Cist Arthur (Arthur's Chest). Arthur's legend undoubtedly continues to hold the imagination, and commercial considerations have their part to play, as anyone visiting Caerleon quickly learns.

The Norman Yoke
Some 500 years after Arthur's time, Gruffydd ap Llewelyn ruled Wales, until his murder in 1063. His head was sent to Harold (later the last Anglo-Saxon king of England), who promptly married Gruffydd's widow, Ealdgyth. There is a tradition that Harold planned the first castle at Caldicot, though the earliest record, dated 1120, gives Walter FitzRoger as founder.

In 1065, Harold did apparently supervise the construction of a lodge at Portskewett for Edward the Confessor but as soon as he left, Gruffydd's son, Caradog, moved in and destroyed both buildings and servants. Harold's retainers were unlucky, for more of them were killed soon afterwards. Tostig, jealous of his brother, Harold's, standing with the king, and furious at being banished himself from the royal presence, attacked Harold's servants in Hereford, 'lopped off the hands and legs of some, the arms and legs of others, and threw them into the butts of wine and other liquors that were put in for the king's drinking.' So, at any rate, said a contemporary account.

At the time of the Norman Conquest the Three Castles—Skenfrith, Grosmont and White—were held by sons of Prince Gwaethfoed. Bach, the eighth and presumably youngest, was at Skenfrith. The sixth son, Aeddan, lord of Clytha as well as of Grosmont, founded churches at Clytha, Bryngwyn and Bettws Newydd. He loved the red roses which grew so plentifully at Grosmont, and in some records the church there is called Rosllwyn (Rosebush). When Edmund, earl of Lancaster, received the Three Castles from Henry III in 1267 he took the red rose as the symbol of his house.

Another of Gwaethfoed's sons, Gwyn, held Llantilio Castle, which may have been called White after his name, though the present structure, or what remains of it, dates only from about 1184-5. Even when Gwyn became old and blind he still loved hunting, but one day he returned from an expedition to find a Norman baron installed in his stead. He appealed to the king—by this time, William Rufus, who reigned from 1087 until

1100—to let him fight fairly for his castle in single combat. This was agreed. A duel, which for the sake of fairness took place in a darkened room, was won by Gwyn who killed his opponent and resumed his lordship. So runs a most unlikely story, given the savagery of the times, of which a clear example comes from nearby Abergavenny.

The castle there, which reputedly stood on the site of the giant Agros's stronghold, was captured in 1173 by Seisyll ap Dyfnwal during King Henry II's absence in Normandy. Two years later, so as to make his peace with the king, Seisyll accepted the advice of his brother-in-law, Rhys ap Gruffydd, to restore the castle to its Norman lord. William de Braose took possession, and at Christmas in 1176 organised a feast to which he invited Seisyll, his son and other Welsh chieftains.

When the celebrations were in full swing de Braose abruptly demanded that all the Welsh should swear to travel unarmed in future in Upper Gwent. They indignantly refused, and were promptly massacred—to a man, says one account; with the sole exception, says another, of Iorwerth of Caerleon, who managed to escape. For good measure, de Braose sent men to Seisyll's castle, Castell Arnallt, which they destroyed after murdering his seven year-old son, Cadwaladr, and abducting his wife, Gwladys.

In 1182, the surviving sons and grandsons of the victims of the massacre, led by Iorwerth, took advantage of de Braose's absence at Dingestow to storm Abergavenny Castle and burn down most of it. Then they went on to Dingestow in search of de Braose. There, too, they took and burnt the castle which was under construction by Ranulf Poer, the sheriff of Herefordshire, but de Braose narrowly escaped.

Writing only some six years after these retaliatory actions, Gerald of Wales comments on the qualities of the men of Gwent, who 'have much more experience of warfare, are more famous for their martial exploits and, in particular, are more skilled with the bow and arrow than those who come from other parts of Wales.' During the assault on Abergavenny Castle arrows penetrated an oak door 'almost as thick as [the width of] a man's palm'; and Gerald adds in what seems to be an eye-witness comment that 'as a permanent reminder of the strength of their impact, the arrows have been left sticking in the door just where their iron heads struck.' Many modern visitors must have read Gerald, because, according to the curator of the castle museum, they often enquire whether the arrow heads are still to be seen.

SOLDIERS

Abergavenny Castle, with the Sugar Loaf in the background to the right

Despite his reverses at Abergavenny and Dingestow de Braose flourished for the best part of another 30 years. In 1206 he was given the lordship of the Three Castles by King John but fell from favour four years later. He fled first to Ireland, then to France, where he died as a beggar in 1211.

His wife Maud de St Valerie and one of their sons fell into John's hands. They were imprisoned in Windsor Castle and deliberately starved to death. Like her husband, 'the Ogre of Abergavenny', Maud was detested by the Welsh, who told terrible stories about her. Long before the days of William Tell she is reputed to have forced a chieftain called Madog to shoot an apple from his son's head. Maud, popularly known as Moll Walbee, is thought to be depicted in effigy in St Mary's Church at Hay-on-Wye, and a huge stone supposedly thrown by her is preserved at Llowes. Two de Braose sons did survive their parents. One, Giles, became bishop of Hereford and, for a time, lord of the Three Castles.

Civil Wars

Almost 600 years after his death, Owain Glyn Dwr remains perhaps the most famous single figure in the whole of Welsh history. Strange portents accompanied his birth, at least according to Shakespeare, who makes him say: 'The front of heaven was full of fiery shapes', 'The frame and huge foundation of the earth/Shaked like a coward', and 'I am not in the roll of common men.'

The Welsh saw him as *y mab darogan*, the son of prophecy, whilst he traced his descent from all three princely dynasties of mediaeval Wales. He was well-to-do, cultivated, a patron of poets, and also a soldier. Between 1400 and 1409 he led the last major Welsh rebellion against the English, controlled huge areas of Wales, and threatened parts of England. For a time an independent Wales with its own church, universities and native prince seemed possible.

In August 1402, Glyn Dwr raided Abergavenny, Usk, Caerleon and Newport. Two years later his men were defeated at Campston (or Camstwn) Hill near Grosmont by an English force led probably by Richard Beauchamp, earl of Warwick. Glyn Dwr himself narrowly escaped capture; his standard was seized from its bearer, Ellis ap Richard. However, a Welsh victory followed shortly, at Craig-y-Dorth, after which the English were chased to the gates of Monmouth Castle.

In March 1405, Rhys Gethin, one of Glyn Dwr's lieutenants—said to have sacked Grosmont five years earlier—invested the castle there with a strong force of Gwent men. An English detachment sent from Hereford made a surprise attack on the besiegers and routed them. Prince Henry the future Henry V, who was born at

Usk Castle

SOLDIERS

Monmouth—is held by tradition to have commanded that day but in fact he remained at Hereford, from where he wrote:

> My most redoubted and most Sovereign Lord and father, I sincerely pray that God will graciously show His miraculous aid towards you in all places, praised be He in all His works, for on Wednesday the eleventh of this present month of March, your rebels of the parts of Glamorgan, Morgannok, Usk, Netherwent and Overwent, assembled to the number of eight thousand men, according to their own account, and they went on the same Wednesday, in the morning, and burnt a part of your town of Grossmont within your Lordship of Monmouth and Jennoia [?]. Presently went out my well beloved cousin the Lord Talbot and the small body of my household, and with them joined your faithful and valiant knights Edward Newport and John Greindor, the which formed but a small power in the whole; but true it is indeed that victory is not in the multitude of people, and this was well proved there, but in the power of God, and there by the aid of the Blessed Trinity, your people gained the field, and vanquished all the said rebels, and slew of them by fair account in field, by the time of their return from the pursuit, some say eight hundred, others a thousand, being questioned upon pain of death ...

Even if, as one historian suggests, these figures should be divided by ten, the loss was nevertheless significant. The question arises as to where the dead might have been buried. A likely site was thought to be the corner of a field which generations of Grosmont farmers had traditionally left unploughed, but an excavation in the early 20th century revealed not a victim of 1405 but the remains of a Roman soldier.

The Welsh cause suffered a further heavy blow two months after Grosmont. Glyn Dwr's oldest son, Gruffydd—one of 11 children, not counting illegitimates—was leading an expedition against Usk Castle when his force met defeat at the hands of an English army on the hill of Pwll Melyn (Yellow Pool). The site has not been identified, though it must have been near Usk. The rebels fled into Monkswood Forest, where Gruffydd was taken prisoner. He spent the rest of his life as a captive in the Tower of London or Nottingham Castle. Of the 300 men who surrendered, most were massacred in front of Usk Castle. Glyn Dwr's brother and constant companion, Tudur, died in the fighting; so did John ap

Hywel, muscular Christian and abbot of the Cistercian monastery of Llantarnam. A friar who had promised that all who fell that day would sup in heaven was bitterly taunted as he slipped away from the field when the cause seemed lost. He replied that as he was fasting he must deny himself the prospect of a meal.

On the English side at Pwll Melyn, according to one source, was Dafydd Gam, red-haired, flamboyant and a possible model for Shakespeare's Fluellen in *Henry V*. His patronymic was ap Llewelyn. His nickname means 'squinting' and Glyn Dwr is said to have made up an impromptu verse, beginning *O gweli di wr coch cam* (If you see a red-haired squinting man) and going on to say that Gam's house would be burnt down.

Dafydd had previously gone to Machynlleth, where Glyn Dwr had summoned a parliament, and tried to stab him. On giving a promise (which he failed to keep) of supporting the Welsh cause in future, Dafydd was allowed to go free. If the story were true it seems likely that he would have been summarily killed when Glyn Dwr's men ambushed and captured him in 1412. Instead, he was ransomed, on the orders of Henry IV, for 200 or 700 marks (just over £133 or £366), depending on the source followed.

According to local tradition, the ambush, Glyn Dwr's last recorded act of defiance, took place near Llantilio Crossenny, where Dafydd Gam had a house called Hen Gwrt (Old Court). It is still said in the village that his children were so numerous, that if they joined hands they could span the half mile from the house to the church. That Dafydd was indeed lord of the manor is confirmed by a stained glass inscription preserved in the church, which was moved there in 1930 when Llantilio Court was demolished. This had superseded Hen Gwrt of which the moated site, empty but impressive, remains.

The inscription, in a window in the north wall of the nave, reads: 'Dav Gam Eqv Avr Manor [Davidus Gam Eques Auricomus Dominus Manoris] Llantilio Crossenny Occisus in Campo Agincourt Ano 1415'—David Gam, golden-haired knight, lord of the manor of Llantilio Crossenny, killed on the field of Agincourt in the year 1415'. On the eve of the battle, Gam, sent by Henry V to estimate the enemy's strength, reported: 'An't please you, my liege, they are enough to be killed, enough to be taken prisoner, and enough to run away.' On the day, he threw himself forward to take a sword thrust intended for the king, who knighted him as he lay dying.

Kentchurch Court with 'Owain Glyn Dwr's Tower'

By this time Owain Glyn Dwr was probably dead, too. Though his great rebellion failed, he was never betrayed, never captured. His last years remain a mystery. According to the chronicler, Adam of Usk, he was 'hiding in the open country and caves and in the thickets of the mountains.' There are strong traditions that he died in western Herefordshire: on Lawton's Hope Hill, between Leominster and Hereford; in Harewood Forest, between Hereford and Ross; or in Haywood Forest, three miles south of Hereford. Three of his daughters, married to Englishmen, lived in the area: Janet at Croft Castle, Margaret at Monnington-on-Wye, Alice at Kentchurch.

A cupboard off a bedroom at Kentchurch Court is said by some to have been his hiding place. In the same house, just on the English side of the Monnow, is the striking portrait of an old man with penetrating eyes, a long, lined, ascetic face, a high forehead and a determined mouth. This is taken to show Sion Cent, an eminent poet, contemporary with Glyn Dwr, whose chaplain he may have been. Though it lacks the wart he had under the left eye, it could also depict Glyn Dwr himself, whose presence at Kentchurch could have passed unremarked if he had assumed the persona of Siôn Cent.

Until well into the 20th century stories of a wizardlike character called Jack of Kent circulated on both sides of the Monnow, and indeed further afield (see chapter 3). They may reflect the belief in Glyn Dwr's lifetime which attributed supernatural powers to him. 'I can call spirits from the vasty deep / And teach thee to command the devil', says his Shakespearean incarnation.

The awful weather in 1402 which negated the efforts of the army led against him by Henry IV was certainly thought to owe something to uncanny influence. The same held for Glyn Dwr's ability to appear in unexpected places and to elude capture, though these were the skills of a fine guerrilla leader rather than of a wizard. Glyn Dwr did have his own soothsayer, Crach Ffinnant, but captains and kings of the time regularly sought the advice of such men.

Engraving of 1800 after the painting at Kentchurch Court, possibly showing John of Kent or Owain Glyn Dwr

There is still a firm belief that Glyn Dwr died at Monnington-on-Wye, where a flat broken stone by the church porch is said to mark his grave. This was apparently opened in 1680 and a body 'whole and entire and of goodly stature' found inside. Yet Adam of Usk wrote that after Glyn Dwr's body had been buried at night the grave was discovered by his enemies, so it was re-interred by his own people, 'but where his body lies is unknown'. It is possible that the re-burial took place at the isolated hamlet of Monnington Straddel, eight miles roughly south-west of Hereford, where the manor was owned by Alice's husband, John Scudamore. Near a mound there, a chapel stood. It is now gone, though the adjacent Chapel Farm recalls its existence. Efforts to find Glyn Dwr's resting place have continued until as recently as 1997 but they remain fruitless.

SOLDIERS

There are reminders of him such as at Llanfihangel Crucorney where people say that he rallied his troops on the cobbled forecourt of the Skirrid Inn before using the mounting block to bestride his horse and ride off to attack Pontrilas. At Newcastle a venerable oak tree was said to have been planted by him (see chapter 3).

More spectacular tales emphasise how Glyn Dwr, having died a hero, survived as a legend, entering what R.R. Davies has called 'one of the most exclusive coteries of Mediaeval Europe, that of the sleeping kings ..., popular political heroes who would return one day to save their peoples.' Like Arthur before him, Owain sleeps in a cavern with his men in armour, spears against shoulders, swords at hand, waiting for the country's call.

Some nationalist movements of the late 20th century have drawn inspiration for the great rebellion of earlier history. One of them, Meibion Glyn Dwr, is thought to have taken its name from a poem written in 1974 by Michael Raven, and set by him to the tune of a Welsh funeral hymn.

Sons of Glyndwr

Owain Glyndwr the king is not dead;
He lies asleep in the sons he bred.
Ring, bugles, ring, your rallying cry,
Long live the king who cannot die.

Murmuring streams and whispering trees
Bid you awake and heed their pleas:
Leave you the hills, the mine and the fire,
Drive you the foe from every shire.

THE FOLKLORE OF MONMOUTHSHIRE

> Mourn for your dead, their blood it ran red;
> Speak you the word long gone unsaid.
> Ring, bugles, ring, your rallying cry,
> Long live the king who cannot die.

After their fierce struggle for independence in the 15th century the Welsh, during the Civil War of over 200 years later, overwhelmingly took the side of the English king. Monmouth itself was for Parliament, but even so when Oliver Cromwell visited the town 'he narrowly escaped assassination at the hands of one Evans, who attempted to shoot him', says tradition, in the Queens Head Inn (see also chapter 3).

The reception proved much more cordial at a farmhouse near Gilwern Hill. There Cromwell and his men were hospitably fed on brown bread and milk. The jug used was treasured as 'Cromwell's Cup' in a house at Clydach until the end of the l9th century.

Other local traditions tell of a skirmish on the slopes of the Blorenge after which ten casualties were buried in Llanelen Churchyard, and a battle between Llanishen and Trellech where blood splashed up to the horses' fetlocks and left a permanent reminder in the name of the ground, Bloody Fields.

Grosmont Castle is said to have been bombarded by Parliamentary forces, though this may have been a convenient way of explaining earlier damage. At Llangybi a local magnate, Sir Trefor Williams, took first the Parliament then the Royalist side. Prisoners of both categories were held at different times in the cellars of the White Hart, an ancient inn once owned by the Knights of St John.

More famous captives were imprisoned at Chepstow Castle. During the Commonwealth, Bishop Jeremy Taylor, the saintly author of *Holy Living* and *Holy Dying*, languished there for a time. At the Restoration, Henry Marten, one of those who had sat in judgment on Charles I and signed his death warrant, was confined in the castle tower which now bears his name. Conditions were scarcely rigorous, for Marten's wife, daughter and servants were allowed to live with him in the castle. He frequently dined out in the neighbourhood, his witty conversation standing him in good stead. Far from the conventional puritan, he confessed to being 'a great lover of pretty girls' and published correspondence with his mistress, Mary Ward, under the title of *Familiar Letters to his Lady of Delight* (1662).

SOLDIERS

Chepstow Castle, with Marten's Tower in the centre

Nevertheless, he remained a staunch republican, later categorised by Thomas Carlyle as 'a right hard-headed, stouthearted little man, full of sharp fire and cheerful light; sworn foe of cant in all its figures: an indomitable little Roman pagan if no better.' But his visits to the mansion of St Pierre as a dinner guest came to an abrupt end when he told his host, Mr Lewis, that if he could have his time over again he would behave exactly as he had before. 'I do not think', he said on another occasion, 'one man wise enough to govern us all.'

His sentiments are confirmed in the epitaph in the form of an acrostic which he prepared for himself:

> Here or elsewhere, all's one to you or me,
> Earth, airs or water gripes my ghostless dust,
> No one knows how soon to be by fire set free.
> Reader, if you an oft tried rule will trust,
> You'll gladly do and suffer what you must.
>
> My life was spent with serving you and you,
> And death's my pay, it seems, and welcome, too,
> Revenge destroying but itself, while I
> To birds of prey leave my old cage and fly.
> Examples preach to the eye; care then (mine says)
> Not how you end but how you spend your days.

Marten, who died in 1680 at the age of 78, was buried in the chancel of the parish church at Chepstow. A later vicar, Reverend Thomas Chest (for whose own epitaph, see chapter 7), objected so strongly to a regicide being given such an honoured place that in 1702 he had the remains moved to the north aisle. A further transfer took them to the entrance porch, where they are now. Interest in the stone has been so great that it has worn out and been replaced several times, but Marten's wise words are still there.

Henry Marten, from an old print

According to tradition, Charles I visited many houses in Monmouthshire during the Civil War. He was twice entertained by the High Sheriff of the county, Nicholas Moore, at the Manor House, Caerwent. He also spent some time at a gabled house at Tregare called Llwyn-y-Gaer. After his disastrous defeat at Naseby, in July 1645, he stayed at Llangattock Lingoed in a stone farmhouse called Great Campston; at Tredegar House, where all that now remains of the building of that time is the old hall; and at Raglan Castle. There he occupied the state apartments to the north-east of the courtyard, and played bowls with Walter Pritchard of Treworgan on the green, whose attitude was much too egalitarian for the historian Bradney's liking since he told the king that 'Bowles had the same virtue in them that the Foot-balls had, viz. to make all fellowes.'

In visiting Raglan Charles may not have been aware of gloomy prophecies such as:

SOLDIERS

> Pam ddel y brenin i Rhaglan,
> Yna bydd diwedd i'r Cymry,
> (When the king shall go to Raglan,
> Then shall Welshmen be finished.)

Another, even darker, predicted that the crowned son of Anne—and Charles's mother was Anne of Denmark—would be dragged by his teeth all over the kingdom and finally slain by an axe.

While Charles was at Raglan his host, William Herbert, earl of Worcester, received a visit from Reverend William Swift, future grandfather of the author of *Gulliver's Travels*, and vicar of Goodrich, 10 miles away in Herefordshire. 'I am come', announced Swift, 'to give his majesty my coat.' When the earl, albeit pleasantly, remarked that the coat seemed to be of little worth, Swift responded 'Why, then, take my waistcoat.' It turned out that into the coat's lining were sewn 300 gold coins which the vicar had raised by mortgaging some of his land. Clarendon later wrote in his great *History of the Rebellion* that 'the king received no supply more seasonable or acceptable during the whole war than these 300 broad pieces, his distress being at that time very great and his resources altogether cut off.'

Raglan Castle, from an engraving of 1800

Looking across the bowling green to the keep at Raglan Castle

Some mansions were of course occupied by Parliamentary forces, including Wonastow Court, another Herbert property, and Trostrey Court, where dispatches and letters written by Cromwell turned up in the 1940s. Ironically, this was the home of the ardent royalist, Major Charles Hughes, whose tomb in Trostrey Church records that he fought in 'King Charles ye firsts Army against ye rebells.'

In August 1646, General Fairfax, in the dining room of his headquarters, Cefntilla Court at Llandenny, accepted the surrender of Raglan, the last castle to hold out against Parliament. The Court is still owned by Lord Raglan, who is so designated because the earls of Worcester were raised to the marquisate by Charles II in recognition of their prolonged resistance during the Civil War.

It was perhaps after his stay at Raglan in 1645 that Charles found himself followed by Parliamentary troopers. He rode through Shirenewton and Crick (where he left Crick House by the back door as pursuing horsemen entered at the front) to Portskewett, then took the New Passage Ferry from Black Rock across the Severn Estuary to Chisell Pill in Gloucestershire. When the boatmen returned they found troopers waiting to cross whom they realised were on the king's trail. They had no choice but to ferry men and horses but they set them down on a reef called the English Stones, close to the Gloucestershire side, telling the soldiers they could easily wade the rest of the way. In fact a deep channel separated reef from shore; the tide was rising rapidly, and all the troopers drowned.

When he learned the news, a furious Cromwell suppressed the ferry, which was owned by the Lewis family of St Pierre, Henry Marten's future hosts. It resumed operations only in 1718 and, just over a century after that, returned to its old crossing route from Beachley to Aust. The Black Rock Hotel went out of business, then became a private house, and was eventually demolished, its site now a public picnic place from which one can look across to the treacherous English Stones as well as the great modern bridges which have superseded the old ferry.

It is always a pity to allow the facts to spoil a good story, but the New Passage drama may never have taken place. Charles certainly intended to take the ferry on 24 July 1645; however, according to his attendants' diaries he changed his mind and went off to Newport. Even more conclusive is the fact that from 25 to 29 July he was the guest of Sir Philip Morgan at Ruperra Castle, beyond Newport.

The 60 Parliament troopers pursuing Charles on 24 July may well have thought he had crossed the Severn, and forced the boatmen to take them over from Black Rock. Early in the next century, during a Chancery case between the Duke of Beaufort and Thomas Lewis of St Pierre, Giles Gilbert stated in evidence that as a boy, an hour after seeing the king pass through Shirenewton he observed Cromwell's troopers riding hard near Portskewett, and later heard that they had compelled the ferrymen to take them across the river.

On the other hand, different witnesses testified that the king and 26 others made the passage, after which 12 Royalists compelled the boatmen to put out again when the tide was too low. The king's men were landed on a bank called the sandbed and told to ride to Chisell Pill, but as the tide rose they were all cut off, and drowned. According to one version of the story Cromwell himself watched this from the shore with malign glee.

Other actions by Cromwell were remembered, often inaccurately, in oral tradition. He is said to have destroyed Grosmont Castle, though this was done on the orders on Edward IV, some 200 years earlier; to have taken Raglan Castle, which fell to Fairfax; to have irreparably damaged Chepstow Castle, though for many years after the Civil War it continued to be garrisoned, and therefore viable. Cromwell House in Bridge Street is supposed to have lodged him on the night after the capture of Chepstow, 25 May 1648.

Cromwell did indeed order the slighting of Newport Castle. There is a story that when the Parliamentary forces were encamped on Fairoak Hill at Christchurch, $2^1/_2$ miles from Newport, a man approached Cromwell and offered, for a suitably large reward, to reveal an underground passage leading into the castle. After taking the castle, Cromwell had the traitor hanged from the nearest tree. He is also said to have stayed at Murenger House and to have directed that the head of the statue of Jasper Tudor, Duke of Bedford and uncle of Henry VII, in a niche of the tower of St Woolos, be shot off by a canon ball.

Monmouth Castle changed hands several times during the Civil War before finally falling to Parliament in 1645. After this, a man called Evans is supposed to have levelled a musket through a parlour window with the intention of shooting Cromwell, only to be restrained by the townspeople. Another story (see page 87) places the assassination attempt in the Queens Hotel.

Much of the stone from the demolished castle was used in 1673 to build Great Castle House. Cromwell's face is supposed to be included in the ornate plaster ceiling of a room on the first floor, having been quietly inserted in the design by an admirer.

Two prehistoric sites near Monmouth, a tumulus near Dixton Church in a field called the Clappers, and earthworks at Buckholt Camp, were both thought to have been used by Cromwell's gunners as vantage points from which to bombard the town. Only within the most recent memory did the supposed deeds of this formidable man begin to fade.

Here lie the valiant

> John Frost in Wales a-hunting went, and well knew how to ride;
> He had a fine bred Chartist horse but got on the wrong side.
> If he had held the reins quite firm in his own hand,
> They'd ne'er have hunted him into Van Diemen's Land.

So runs a London street ballad of the mid-19th century. John Frost's fame—or notoriety—derived from what was variously called a demonstration, a riot or a rising in Newport, after which he and two fellow-leaders, Zephaniah Williams and William Jones, were found guilty of high treason.

Frost, born in 1784 at the Royal Oak Inn, Thomas Street, Newport, became a successful draper in the town's High Street. A keen interest in civic affairs led him to serve as councillor, magistrate, harbour commissioner, poor law guardian, and on four occasions as mayor of Newport. He became involved in politics, stimulated no doubt by hearing William Cobbett speak at the Kings Head, Newport, in 1830, and joined the

Chartist movement. In 1838, members from Pontypool, Caerleon and Newport elected him as their delegate to the People's Convention in London.

Williams, born in 1795 at Argoed near Blackwood, was a master collier and mineral agent widely known for radical politics and atheist ethics. The Royal Oak Inn at Blaenau, which he ran with his wife, Joan, provided a favourite meeting place for local Chartists.

Jones, born in Bristol in 1806, trained as a watchmaker, then worked for some time as an actor before settling down to practise his original trade in Pontypool. He acquired a considerable reputation as a Chartist speaker.

'John Frost (The Chartist)', lithograph by Edward Morton in the National Portrait Gallery

In May 1839, the colliers and ironmakers of Monmouthshire were incensed when three Newport men and Henry Vincent, a Chartist 'missionary' and fiery orator, were sentenced at Monmouth to a year's imprisonment on a charge of conspiracy to disturb the peace. A plan emerged for a great march on Newport. Columns led respectively by Frost from Blackwood (men of the Rhymney and Sirhowy valleys), Williams from Ebbw Vale, and Jones from Pontypool, were to rendezvous at Cefn at midnight on Saturday-Sunday 3rd-4th November before marching the last two miles to Newport together.

Appalling weather and confused planning led to delays. Jones and half of his 2,000 men did not arrive at all. Even so, some 5,000 men armed with sticks, pikes, mandrells (double-edged coal picks), swords and guns massed in front of the Westgate Hotel soon after 9 a.m. But the authorities had been forewarned, and the mayor, Thomas Phillips, stood ready in the

*The attack of the Chartists on the Westgate Hotel, Newport
(Newport Museum and Art Gallery)*

hotel with a party of special constables and soldiers. Firing began, and left 22 Chartists dead. Of these, 10 were later buried by night in unmarked graves on the north (and unfavoured) side of St Woolos's Churchyard. The rest of the crowd dispersed.

Many were arrested later. Frost was taken on 5 November in Newport at the house of a friend, Jones a week later in a wood near Crumlin. Williams was discovered at Cardiff on a vessel waiting to sail to Portugal.

Their cause was not necessarily helped by anonymous letters like this, addressed to the Newport magistrates:

> Ye serpents and generations of vipers, why seek ye the life of Frost? You may succeed, but what think ye of the mighty millions? If ye can escape the bullet, who can escape the match? There are Samsons in Cambria and foxes in the street. It is true ye may escape, but where are your children? ... Consider this, O ye Philistines! and be wise in time.

In January 1840, the three Chartists stood trial at Monmouth and were sentenced to be hanged, drawn and quartered. After spending some time in cells they learned that their sentences had been commuted to penal transportation for life. They left on the steamer, *Usk*, from a place on the

Place of the Chartists' embarkation at Chepstow (now the Wye Knot Restaurant)

bank of the Wye at Chepstow now marked by a plaque unveiled in 1985 by Alexander Cordell, the advocate of trade union rights whose historical novels feature the Chartist movement. After a 15-day voyage to Portsmouth, they spent a week on a prison hulk, before sailing for the dreaded Van Diemen's Land—Tasmania. A vigorous campaign for their release was already in progress.

Thomas Phillips received a knighthood for his part in the affair. He died at Llanelen in 1867, not far from the Old Vicarage, which was later to be the home of Cordell. In 1854, 14 years into their sentence, the Chartists were released when it was deemed safe to do so. Williams and Jones elected to remain in Van Diemen's Land, whilst Frost returned, via America, and immediately started campaigning against the evils of transportation. Two lectures he gave in 1856 were published as a pamphlet, *The Horrors of Convict Life*. He settled across the Severn from his native Monmouthshire at Stapleton, near Bristol, and died there in 1877 at the age of 92.

As was usual in the days before mass newspapers, the events of 1839 were the subject of ballads printed for sale by street hawkers. Some of the sheets were hostile to the Chartists, others sympathetic. In a 'Cân Newydd' (New Song) published at Llanrwst, Ywain Meirion takes umbrage as much at the Chartists' choice of day as at their deed:

> This was, indeed, a frightful business,
> Spreading fear throughout the land;
> That they should rise up on the Sabbath
> 'Gainst the law to make their stand.

He ends with a resolutely quietist assertion:

> 'Tis better to submit than argue,
> For fear that hate this kingdom taint;

THE FOLKLORE OF MONMOUTHSHIRE

> In parliament men speak with wisdom,
> And hear in peace each just complaint.

Frost himself is made to express a regret which he certainly did not feel in a sheet entitled 'The Trial, Lamentation, and Farewell, of the Unfortunate John Frost', printed by W. Bear of Swansea:

> Oh, in Newport Town I once did dwell,
>   In harmony and peace,
> Where with my wife and children dear,
>   All blessings did increase,
> Until treachery and rebellion,
>   My spirits did inflame,
> Caused me from virtue's paths to stray,
>   And bring myself to shame.

What appears to be a more genuine feeling of sorrow at exile and loss of liberty characterises 'The last Farewell to England [sic] of Frost, Williams and Jones', issued in Shrewsbury by J. France and in Birmingham by T. Watts:

> At Monmouth we were tried for treason,
>   And we were condemned to die,
> Great and small throughout the nation,
>   For to save our lives did try,
> England, Ireland, Wales, and Scotland,
>   Manifold for us did strive,
> And through a deal of perseverance,
>   Government did spare our lives.
>
> Sad was the day we drew together,
>   Thousands of men from far and near,
> Which caused grief and consternation
>   In every part of Monmouthshire.
> That fatal day we'll long remember
>   Which caused distress on every mind,
> It was the third of last November,
>   Eighteen hundred and thirty-nine.

SOLDIERS

The Trial, Lamentation,
and Farewell, of the Unfortunate
JOHN FROST,

Who his now taken his Trial before The Right Honourable N. C, Tindal, Knight, the Honourable Sir J, Parke, Knight, and the Honourable Sir J. Williams, Knight, and C. Bateman, Sheriff. Monmouth, For High Treason, and Sedition,

The Court opened on Tuesday and the Day was spent in selecting the jury, and the court adjourned at half-past five o'clock till nine o'clock the following morning. On Wednesday the court opened and the Clerk of the Arraigns Read the indictment against Frost, who pleaded not guilty, and he said it was now their duty to proceed and find the truth of that plea.—After opening the case for the prosecution and given a long address to the Jury, the Council for Frost Objected to the present mode, stating that the prisoner had not had the list of witnesses and jury delivered ten days previous, according to the Act.—Which took up much time and the court Adjourned. On Thursday the court opened and commenced examining the Witnesses againt Frost, which continued on Thursday, Friday, and Saturday, and the Sentence deferred, and the legality of the Trial, for the decision of the Twelve Judges. It is expected to be transportation.

Come all you tender Christians,
    That dwell both far and near,
Unto my Lamentation,
    I pray you lend an ear.
With grief and woe I am oppressed,
    Sorrow absorbs my mind,
My aching heart beats in my breast,
    My sighs invades the wind.

Oh, in Newport Town I once did dwell,
    In harmony and peace,
Where with my wife and children dear,
    All blessings did increase,
Until treachery and rebellion,
    My spirits did inflame,
Caused me from virtue's paths to stray,
    And bring myself to shame,

Its for the crime of treason
    For which I am to blame
Come listen for one moment
    While I relate the same,
On the fourth day of November last,
    It was the fatal day.
The bare remembrance of the same,
    It fills me with dismay

With pikes and swords and pistols,
    We most of us armed were
When we got to the Westgate Inn,
    Some one fired at the Mayor,

It was a shocking sight to see,
    The blood run from the wounds,
But what was much more malancholy,
    Was the dead bodies on the ground.

I quickly apprehended was,
    Examined then with speed,
And to await the assizes,
    To Monmouth was conveyed,
There to await our trials,
    All at the bar to stand,
And to appear before the Judges,
    To hear their dread command.

Before the sentence on me is past,
    The judges to me do say,
You must now prepare to meet your doom
    Without the least delay,
That others may take warning
    By your unpleasant fate,
And shun the crime that you have done,
    Before it is too late,

Farewell my wife and children dear
    I bid you all farewell
What pain I feel on your account
    No human tongue can tell
May God be your protector
    while in this world you stay
And may I meet you with sins forgiven,
    Upon the Judgment day,

W. BEAR, PRINTER, SWANSEA

Ballad Sheet
(Newport Museum and Art Gallery)

The Chartist dead were not forgotten. On Palm Sunday in 1840 their graves at St Woolos were decorated with flowers and placarded with this verse:

> May the rose of England never blow,
> The Clyde of Scotland cease to flow,
> The harp of Ireland never play,
> Until the Chartists gain the day.

The following year a newspaper reported from Newport:

> Sunday week, being Palm Sunday, the graves in our churchyard were decorated with flowers and evergreens. The most conspicuous were those in which the men in the late Chartist riots were buried; and at the head of each grave were placarded the following lines written on a large sheet of paper.

> Here lie the valiant and the brave,
> That fought a nation's rights to save;
> They tried to set the captives free
> But fell a prey to tyranny!
>
> Yet they shall never be forgot,
> Though in the grave their bodies rot;
> *The Charter* shall our watchword be
> Come death or glorious liberty!

The Chartists are still remembered. Civic recognition came for John Frost with the naming of a square after him in Newport. Other scraps of information have been handed down over the years by word of mouth—the Chartists' predilection for blue waistcoats of good Welsh cloth, their gatherings at various public houses including the Coach and Horses Inn at Blackwood, their secret meetings at 'the Chartists' Cave' on the mountain near Duke's Inn at Dukestown. And it is still said that at St Woolos snow will never lie on their graves.

CHAPTER 3

Spirits

For centuries, beliefs in beings with supernatural powers inspired feelings of apprehension and dread. Even when such sentiments weakened, through a willing suspension of disbelief, stories including a sprite, witch or devil continued to command an audience, much as horror films do now. Some earlier narratives still produce a genuine frisson, and logical explanations for certain reported phenomena remain elusive.

Over 200 years ago a formidable Monmouthshire minister, Edmund Jones (1702-93) was anxious to give credence to accounts of omens, witches, apparitions and fairies because he considered that to deny such things led to irreligion and atheism since 'the next step is to deny the being of God, who is a *Spirit*, and the *Father of Spirits*.' Strangely enough, it seems that although religious observance and also belief have greatly decreased since Jones's day, credence in paranormal phenomena remains strong. An ICM poll of 1,000 people carried out across Britain in 1998 produced the response that 64 per cent believed in psychic powers, 38 per cent in ghosts, 34 per cent in poltergeists and 26 per cent in alien visitations. At the same time, however, the numbers of those claiming personal experience of paranormal activity are decreasing.

The Old Prophet
Edmund Jones, characterised by D. Parry-Jones as 'the last native collector of ghost and fairy stories in Wales, who at the same time really believed in them', was born at Pen-llwyn in the big, sparsely-populated upland parish of Aberystruth in the north-west corner of the old Monmouthshire. By the age of nine he could read the Bible in Welsh and

as a young man he became assistant pastor at Penmaen, one of the earliest Independent chapels in Wales (built in 1694). In 1740 he moved to the Tranch, near Pontypool, and stayed there for the rest of his long life. He died in his 92nd year, and was buried at the Ebenezer Chapel, which he had founded in Pontnewynydd. He had insisted that if he died before his wife, she should not afterwards be buried in the same grave lest she prove an obstacle to his rising on the day of resurrection.

Pen-llwyn Uchaf, the birthplace of Edmund Jones

When Jones founded his chapel he chose the name Ebenezer because he asserted that his successor would be so called; and, 50 years on, the next minister turned out to be Reverend Ebenezer Jones. Other predictions by Edmund Jones came true during his lifetime, and founded his reputation as Yr Hen Broffwyd, the Old Prophet.

He walked many miles to preach. Wrapped in a voluminous cloak (a gift from the countess of Huntington), and supporting himself on a great staff, he travelled as far east as Stroud in Gloucestershire and as far west as St Davids in Pembrokeshire. One day in the mountains he took off his shirt to give to a starving vagrant. When his wife complained, he answered: 'The Lord will provide.' Next day he received a roll of flannel sent as a gift by a Mynyddislwyn woman.

Stories of Jones continued to be told within living memory, some of them paralleling those of the saints and their churches a thousand years earlier. For example, he was called to Llangattock, near Crickhowell, where members of the Bethesda Chapel who had been meeting in a barn could not decide between two sites offered for a new building. They called in Jones. He arrived, to find the congregation assembled. The elders explained their dilemmas and how they had decided to appeal to him.

'Appeal to me', he roared. 'Did ye not think of appealing to the almighty?' With an imperious glare he ordered: 'On your knees, all of you,' before starting to pray. Three-quarters of an hour later, one elder, whose knees were suffering on the bare floor, asked: 'How long, Edmund Jones, how long?' 'Until I receive a revelation from heaven.'

A good half-hour later, Jones suddenly stood up and thundered: 'Follow me, ye lost sheep of the House of Israel.' They all followed him out of the barn, half a mile up the hillside, then half a mile down again. The manoeuvre was repeated three times, when the question was asked again: 'How long, Edmund Jones, how long?' 'Until I receive a sign from above,' he answered.

On the next circuit, as Jones passed beneath a tree a starling flew down and perched on his shoulder. He stopped, and triumphantly called: 'Blessed shall be the Lord God of Israel. Where this tree now stands shall the trumpet of the Lord sound forth within this land. The sign is given: ye have but to obey.' The site turned out to be neither of those previously favoured by the contending factions and so proved acceptable to all.

Jones believed fairies to be 'evil spirits belonging to the Kingdom of Darkness.' In his book, *A Relation of Apparitions of Spirits in the County of Monmouth and the Principality of Wales*, first published in 1767, he states that he has 'no reason to question the truth' of the many accounts he quotes. Under the heading 'On Apparitions, Fairies and other Spirits of Hell', he devotes to the same subject a chapter of his later book, *A Geographical, Historical, and Religious Account of the Parish of Aberystruth in the County of Monmouth* (1779).

He was taxed with credulity by later writers, including Parson Kilvert, who considered there to be 'a ludicrous naïve simplicity about his reflections and conclusion.' Yet, as late as 1918, a soldier on leave walking home from Pengam over the mountain to Ynys-ddu reported this encounter on the crest of the ridge above Blackwood:

> There, standing by a gate in the bright moonlight, was an elderly man, apparently enjoying his last pipe before turning in for the night. He directed me on my way, but, on finding he was Welsh speaking, I paused to have a short chat with him. I found him quite an interesting person, well acquainted with local lore and familiar with the *straeon cefn gwlad* [country stories] about Edmund Jones.
>
> 'But you do not believe in fairies like the Old Prophet?' I enquired. 'Indeed I do, or at least, I used to,' he replied, 'and to tell

the truth, that is why I am up here tonight. When I was a child,' he added, 'on such a brave moonlight night as this, my mother used to take me up here to watch them at their revels.'

Fairies

Many of the accounts quoted by Jones are second hand, though such a term is perhaps unduly disparaging: after all, he was relating what people had personally told him of their encounters with *Bendith eu Mamau* (their Mothers' Blessing) or *Y Tylwyth Teg yn y Coed* (the Fair Family in the Wood), as the fairies were euphemistically called. However, in at least one passage Jones himself is the eye-witness:

> If anyone thinks I am too credulous in these relations and speak of things of which I have no experience, I must let them know they are mistaken; for when a very little boy, going with my aunt Eliza, my mother's sister, in the day time, somewhat early in the morning, but after sun-rising, from Hafodafel towards my father's house at Penyllwyn, at the upper end of the field of Kae y Keven [Cae y cefn, ridge field], by the wayside which we were passing, I saw the likeness of a sheepfold ... and within the fold a company of many people, some sitting down, and some coming in and going out ... It seemed to me as if they had lately been dancing, and that there was a Musician among them. Among the rest, over against the door, I well remember the resemblance of a fair woman with a high crown Hat and a red Jacket, who made a better appearance than the rest, and whom, I think they seemed to honour.

The fairies' love of music and dancing recurs in many stories. Edmund Jones tells how a Llanhiledd man, Rees John Rosser rests in a mountain barn early one morning after feeding his oxen. He hears music, then sees 'a large company' come in and dance. 'He lay there as quiet as he could, thinking they would not see him, but in vain; for one of them, a woman, appearing better than the rest, brought him a striped cushion with four tassels, one at each corner of it, to put under his head.' A cock crows. The dancers leave, taking their cushion.

In this case they do not try to persuade the onlooker to join in, but often they do. A Mrs Habbakkuk (born in 1802) passed on from her grandmother, who lived at Pwll Farm, Llangwm, the tale of two farm-workers walking home late, who heard music and saw fairies dancing.

SPIRITS

Plucked from the fairy circle, by T.H. Thomas

One joined in; the other went home. When the first man failed to appear for work next morning his friend consulted a conjuror or wise man who said nothing could be done for a year and a day. When this time had elapsed the villagers would have to form a circle round the fairy ring and pull the man into it as soon as the fairies appeared. This was done, but the bemused farmworker could say nothing of any significance about his experiences, though he expressed surprise at discovering that he had been away for so long.

Another man, taken into a fairy ring near the ruined Capel Newydd at Llanofer Uchaf, not far from Blaenafon, was also absent for a year and a day. A Mrs Gardner, who related this to the folklorist John Rhys in 1883 when she was 90, said she had been instructed as a child that although adults who joined in fairies' dancing were likely to be detained, the young might dance without fear of jeopardy.

In the 1870s, Polly Williams of the Ship Inn, Pontypool, told how as a child at Trefethin she was on her way home from school one day when she saw fairies dancing in a dry place beneath a crab tree. She joined in, and continued to do so on similar occasions for several years, always first removing her *ffollachau* (clogs) so that, like the fairies, she could be noiseless. When finally she decided to give up dancing with them, they retaliated: one of her legs was dislocated.

At Basaleg another girl, Ann Francis, was punished for greed. One evening as she gathered wood she heard music and saw fairies dancing beneath an oak tree. She filled a bucket with clean water and placed it near them so that they might quench their thirst. When she went back for the pail she found a shilling (5p.) at the bottom. By repeating her act of kindness she eventually amassed the sum of 21 shillings. When her mother found the nest-egg, she urged the girl to go more often with her pail of water, but the fairies sensed a change of motivation, and the supply of shillings came to an abrupt end.

The mention of money recalls the statement made in 1831 by W. Howells: 'In some places, particularly in the lower parts of Monmouthshire, there existed till lately a notion among the dairy maids, that the fairies paid occasional visits to their dairies, but were not so liberal as in former days, when they never skimmed their milkpans without remunerating them with a *silver penny*, which was placed in some conspicuous place for the maid.'

Writing in 1904, Margaret Eyre tells how 'about 40 years ago' a girl at Penallt 'used to go out every night by her bedroom window to dance with the fairies, always at a certain time, and was back at a certain time.' Another girl at Trellech told her that the fairies danced by the Parkhurst rocks, 'which shows their good taste, for it is a lovely place.' They also danced round the Virtuous Wells (for which, see chapter 5), especially on All Hallows' Eve (31 October), drinking the water out of harebell cups. In the Wye Valley, wood sorrel was known as fairy bell, and throughout Wales the foxglove as *menig* or *maneg ellyllon*, elf glove. A Trellech farmer who 'didn't like all them silly tales' dug up the fairy ring by the wells, to find them dry next day—but only to him. 'He went again in the morning, hoping to find some water collected, and found instead a little old man sitting there, who told him that he was very much displeased at

The Newcastle Oak, as it was (Chris Barber)

the ring being dug up, and that the sods must be put back at once. When this was done the water came again, but not before.'

Such powers of reprisal undoubtedly helped to make people fearful. As recently as 1936 there were newspaper reports of the awe inspired by rings such as the 'green circle of the dimensions of a large flywheel ... in a field at Abercomin, near Llanhiddel [Llanhiledd] Church' and a similar circle on the mountain top between Cwmtillery and Waunafon. Various artificial mounds and hillocks (*twmpathau*) were also thought to be among the fairies' preferred spots. For example, William Coxe wrote that the castle mound at Newcastle, near Monmouth, was 'supposed by the common people to be the haunt of spirits.'

The fairies also favoured certain trees, particularly the hazel and the oak, especially the 'female' oak. The expression is rather mysterious, especially as the oak was called *Y Brenin Bren*, the King Tree, but it may mean simply a fine specimen. Many believed it dangerous to lop or cut down a female oak in a pleasant, dry place, lest they were afflicted by a lingering and possibly fatal pain. The few woodcutters inclined to do such work believed that the ache in their arms which resulted could be remedied only by bathing them in the water of certain wells.

Coxe was told by a villager that the ancient oak, 27 feet in girth (now gone) near the Wellington Inn (now a private house) at Newcastle, enjoyed the protection of invisible spirits and that misfortune befell anyone who

The site of the sapling which has replaced the Newcastle Oak

harmed it. One man who climbed the tree to chop off a branch, fell and broke his arm. Another tampering with it fractured his leg, and a third 'perished shortly after his sacrilegious enterprise by an untimely death.' When the ancient tree's last branches came off in a great gale those who collected them for kindling all managed to set their houses on fire.

Fairies also ventured into people's houses, especially during stormy weather. Monmouthshire farm doors were seldom locked or bolted at night, and a bowl of milk was left on the hob for the fairies. Care was taken that no object likely to offend them, such as a sharp knife, was anywhere near. One of Lady Llanover's gardeners, William Williams, aged 70, told John Rhys in 1883 of a family living locally whose ancestors, four generations earlier, used to leave a basinful of bread and milk every night by the fire which was always empty by the following morning. One night an ill-disposed servant left a bowl of urine instead. The fairies sought him out and told him that as a punishment there would always be an idiot in his family. The curse stuck. Williams knew the name of the man who originally offended and that of the current sufferer among his descendants. Today we would perhaps say that the family was unfortunate enough to have a faulty gene.

Another gardener on the Llanofer estates, wrote Rhys, 'remembered that the fairies used to change children, and that a certain woman called Nani Fach in that neighbourhood was one of their offspring.' Beatrix Wherry, staying in Monmouthshire in 1903, met at Trellech a Mrs Pryce, 'a weird-looking figure in her heavy cloak and cottage bonnet,' who told her of fairies 'about the size of a six year-old child, with beautiful white skins, dressed in a short white garment, no shoes or stockings, and having white eyes and white hair.' 'They liked the babies of we country folk,' she added, 'as being fine and solid-like, and they used to rear them up with their own.'

William Jenkins, schoolmaster at Trefethin in the late 18th century, worked some land near the Trefethin Oak. Somewhat rashly, he dug up the circle round the tree on which the fairies danced. He stopped short of cutting down the tree but piled kindling round it and destroyed most of it by fire. Nothing happened immediately, but a month later Jenkins's wife woke one morning to find the baby by her side was not her own. No trace of her own daughter, Gwenllian, could be found. Mrs Jenkins refused to have anything to do with the changeling, which was adopted by the sexton's wife.

Mrs Jenkins became distraught. She wandered through the *eithin* (gorse) at nights, and prayed by the remains of the old oak. A year and a day later she found Gwenllian by her side once more. The girl grew up to be taciturn and morose, 'not like other maids', possibly because she was not allowed out of her mother's sight in the daytime, and she had to sleep with her bedroom door firmly closed at night. There seems to be no record of the changeling's fate; perhaps she stayed on with the sexton's wife, who had no children of her own.

As recently as 1936 a newspaper article mentioned Moses Thomas, son of Parson Thomas of Llantrisant, who used to tell the story of a mother haymaking at Llanvetherine. She left her baby peacefully asleep in the shade of a tree, but when she heard crying she went over to find the child gone and another in its place. She refused to deal with the changeling, and for some reason her own baby was brought back: perhaps because a wagon loader had seen a fairy 'creep silently and stealthily along the hedge' to make the original substitution. The child seemed none the worse, and the haymakers—especially the mother—were overjoyed.

It may be that the notion of changelings was an attempt to explain sickly or handicapped children. If so, such stories help to understand the fear which 'the fair family' could engender in the credulous.

The Pwca

We know this mischievous sprite as Puck, from *A Midsummer Night's Dream*. There is a tradition that Shakespeare, after hearing local stories from his friend, Sir William Price of Brecon, visited Cwm Pwca near Clydach to see for himself. Indeed, as late as the 19th century some believed that he had written the *Dream* while staying there. Not far away, at Winchestown near Nant-y-glo, a house called Ty Pwca still exists. The name recurs by the Dowlais Brook, above Henllys.

It is said that a Welsh 'peasant', when asked to illustrate the appearance of Pwca, *drew this with a piece of coal*

Y Trwyn, a lonely farmhouse high in the Gwydden Valley near Mynyddislwyn acquired undying fame from the pwca who took up residence there from a few days before Christmas until Easter Wednesday, some time in the 18th century when Job John Harry was the farmer. The spirit, described by Edmund Jones as 'a thrower of stones and a stroker of persons' moved there in a jug of barm (yeast) collected by a servant; or alternatively he inserted himself in a stray ball of yarn and rolled up hill and down dale until he reached his destination.

The creature knocked at doors, spoke (in Welsh) out of an oven by the hearth, and played his host's fiddle for hours on end at night. He also made himself useful on the farm, where he plashed (laid) hedges, cut firewood, milked cattle and moved wagons. He expected to be treated well in return. A servant girl regularly put out 'Master Pwca's' evening snack of a slice of white bread and a bowl of fresh milk. One night, though, she drank the milk herself and ate most of the bread, leaving only the crust. Retribution swiftly followed. Soon afterwards, as the girl passed the spot where she had previously left the food, she was seized under the armpits by invisible hands and subjected to an (unspecified) 'castigation of a most mortifying character' and at the same time given 'in good set Welsh a warning not to repeat her offence on peril of still worse treatment.'

Pwca left just as abruptly as he had come. He or his fellow then turned up at a house near Tredegar and upset it so effectively that it became known as Ty Trist (Sad House). Many years later a nearby colliery adopted the name.

In a more benevolent mood, in return for his nightly bowl of milk, a pwca cleaned the hearth, polished kettles, washed dishes, milked cows and harnessed horses at Molly Rosser's farm on Stow Hill in Newport. The story was still told in the early 20th century. Some 30 years earlier, Wirt Sikes, US consul in Wales, visited Trwyn Farm and reported that 'you cannot find a Welsh peasant in the parish but knows all about the Pwca'r Trwyn.'

It has been suggested that the Pwca tales at Trwyn and elsewhere were put up to screen the presence of a proscribed Welsh nobleman, Yr Arglwydd Hywel (Lord Hywel), who fled for his life after being defeated in battle by the English in medieval times. Once when servants at Trwyn or Pant-y-garreg were comparing hands a voice from the room above said: 'The fairest and smallest hand belongs to the bwca.' The servants asked to see it; a floorboard was moved and

SPIRITS

Hywel's small, fine hand with a gold ring on the little finger came through the aperture.

Another possible origin emerges from a narrative quoted by John Rhys in his famous book, *Celtic Folklore*:

> Long ago there was in service at a Monmouthshire farm a young woman who was merry and strong. Who she was or whence she came nobody knew; but many believed that she belonged to the old breed of *Bendith y Mamau*. Some time after she had come to the farm, the rumour spread that the house was sorely troubled by a spirit. But the girl and the elf understood one another well, and they became the best of friends. So the elf proved very useful to the maid, for he did everything for her—washing, ironing, spinning and twisting wool; in fact they say that he was remarkably handy at the spinning-wheel. Moreover, he expected only a bowlful of sweet milk and wheat bread, or some flummery, for his work. She took care to place the bowl with his food at the bottom of the stairs every night as she went to bed. It ought to have been mentioned that she was never allowed to catch a sight of him; for he always did his work in the dark. Nor did anybody know when he ate his food: she used to leave the bowl there at night, and it would be empty by the time when she got up in the morning, the *bwca* having cleared it.
>
> But one night, by way of cursedness, what did she do but fill the bowl with some of the stale urine which they used in dyeing wool and other things about the house. But heavens! it would have been better for her not to have done it; for when she got up next morning what should he do but suddenly spring from some corner and seize her by the neck! He began to beat her and kick her from one end of the house to the other, while he shouted at the top of his voice at every kick: 'Y faidan din dwmp yn rhoi bara haidd a thrwnc i'r bwca' (The idea that the thick-buttocked lass should give bread and piss to the bwca).
>
> Meanwhile she screamed for help, but none came for some time; when, however, he heard the servant men getting up, he took to his heels as hard as he could; and nothing was heard of him for some time. But at the end of two years he was found to be at another farm in the neighbourhood, called Hafod yr Ynys, where he at once became great friends with the servant girl: for she fed him like a young chicken, by giving him a little bread and milk all the time. So he worked willingly and well for her in return for his favourite food. More especially, he used to spin and wind the yarn

for her; but she wished him in time to show his face, or to tell her his name: he would by no means do either. One evening, however, when all the men were out, and when he was spinning hard at the wheel, she deceived him by telling him that she was also going out. He believed her; and when he heard the door shutting, he began to sing as he plied the wheel: 'Hi wardda'n iawn pe gwmpa hi, / Taw Gwarwyn-a-throt yw'm enw i' (How she would would laugh, did she know / That Gwarwyn-a-throt is my name). 'Ha! ha!' said the maid at the bottom of the stairs; 'I know thy name now.' 'What is it then?' he asked. She replied, 'Gwarwyn-a-throt'; and as soon as she uttered the words he left the wheel where it was, and off he went.

He was next heard of at a farmhouse not far off, where there happened to be a servant man named Moses, with whom he became great friends at once. He did all his work for Moses with great ease. He once, however, gave him a good beating for doubting his word; but the two remained together afterwards on the best possible terms: the end of it was that Moses became a soldier. He went away to fight against Richard Crookback and fell on the field of Bosworth. The bogie, after losing his friend, began to be troublesome and difficult to live with. He would harass the oxen when they ploughed and draw them after him everywhere, plough and all; nor could anyone prevent them. Then, when the sun set in the evening he would play his pranks again, and do all sorts of mischief about the house, upstairs, and in the cowhouses. So the farmer was advised to visit a wise man (*dyn cynnil*), and to see if he could devise some means of getting rid of the bogie. He called on the wise man, who happened to be living near Caerleon on the Usk; and, the wise man, having waited till the moon should be full, came to the farmer's house. In due time the wise man, by force of manoeuvring, secured the bogie by the very long nose which formed the principal ornament of his face, and earned him the name of *Bucar'r Trwyn*, 'the Bogie of the Nose'. Whilst secured by the nose, the bogie had something read to him out of the wise man's big book; and he was condemned by the wise man to be transported to the banks of the Red Sea for fourteen generations, and to be conveyed thither by 'the upper wind' (*yr uwchwynt*). No sooner had this been pronounced by the cunning man than there came a whirlwind which made the whole house shake. Then came a still mightier wind, and as it began to blow the owner of the big book drew the awl out of the bogie's nose; and it is supposed that the bogie was carried away by that wind, for he never troubled the place any more.

The Devil

Two intriguing objects are preserved in the Skirrid Inn at Llanfihangel Crucorney: the jug in which each night, as the last customer left, a drink was put out for the *pwca*; and the pot kept above the great fireplace for the devil's brew of ale. When official religion came to reject a belief in fairies it continued to accept the existence of devils and of *the* devil. Back-sliders risked if not divine then diabolical retribution.

Sikes was told that 'to William Jones, a sabbath-breaker, of Risca, the devil appeared as an enormous mastiff-dog, which transformed itself into a great fire and made a roaring noise like burning gorse.' The famous warning inscribed on a stone at Llanfair Discoed that the devil will take those who play ball games on Sunday (see page 239) was probably the work of a mason influenced by William Wroth, whose hell-fire sermons drew big crowds. From 1600 until 1642, Wroth was rector of Llanfihangel Roggiett and Llanfaches, where he is buried.

The Skirrid Inn

He would unquestionably have intervened if the devil had attempted the kind of behaviour reported from earlier times. A farm at Llanishen called Llanfair is said to take its name from an attempt to build a church there which failed because the devil pulled down by night whatever was constructed by day.

At Aberystruth parishioners disagreed over the siting of their church. Some favoured a place on the mountain, Mynydd Carn y Cefn; others preferred a field on a farm in the Tylery Valley. Work began at the first site—later called Lle'r Eglwys (Church Place)—but was abandoned when anything built by day disappeared by night. Construction then started at the second site, which seemed to be proven as acceptable when a white horse arrived with a bag of money on its back and imprinted its hoof on a slab of rock. This place, later called Ty Llawn Bwrn March (House of the Fully-Laden Horse), was in turn deserted when arguments arose as to who should take possession of the horse when building finished. The animal 'kicked up its heels, threw off its shoes, and vanished in a flame of fire'— returning, so people concluded, to its master, the devil. Finally, a strange light seen playing over the confluence of the Ystruth brook with the Ebbw Fach river was taken to indicate the definitive site which became known as Cwm yr Eglwys (Church Valley). The magician Merlin—held by some to have been born in Basaleg—prophesied that the first bellringer in the new church would be a bull. On the day before the formal opening a bull calf did indeed get in and tangle himself in the bell ropes, so making an unholy jangle. Perhaps this was a bad omen, for the church eventually burned down and had to be re-built on the same site in 1857.

Early Christians began erecting their church at Pontllanfraith in a place which overlooked a grove where pagan ceremonies had been held. Twice in the night the masonry collapsed and a voice intoned: 'Myned is llwyn' (Go below the grove). Such oracular advice could not be ignored: the place so prescribed is where the church still stands.

Another move to a more favoured site took place at Mathern. Building originally began in a field about a mile from Chepstow which was afterwards called Old Churches. However, every night all the stones laid during the day disappeared and were later found where Mathern Church now stands. After a short spell of fruitless effort, the builders had the good sense to comply with the insistent and invisible directions.

On the other hand, malign influences had to be resisted. In the 16th century a priest at Usk detected that the cause of a destructive tempest was demonic activity. Praying as he went, he led parishioners in procession through the town in a column of threes. Eventually the chief demon was cornered on a rock in the river near the bridge. The priest drew a circle on the ground, ordered him to appear in it, and forced him to desist from harming the town.

Later in the same century, in 1589, to be precise, a Welshman imprisoned in the Tower of London wrote a letter, still in existence, to the Lord Treasurer, Burleigh, offering in return for his freedom to deliver treasure buried beneath Skenfrith Castle. 'The voyce of the country', he wrote, 'goeth there is a dyvill and his dam in this castel; one sets on a hogshead of gold and the other upon a hogshead of silver.' He undertook 'by the

Skenfrith

grace of God and without any charge to the Quene or your lordships' to eject the pair, adding:

> If the treasure be there I will look for something at your hands, for the country saith there is great treasure. No man in remembrance was ever seen to open in, and great warrs hath been at it and there was a place not far from it whose name is Gamdon, which is as much to say the *game is doun*.

So far as can be ascertained, the game failed even to start, because Burleigh did not take up the offer.

The devil and his dame are mentioned in connection with another room in Skenfrith Castle, where they were supposed to be seen dancing when the moon was full. So said the centenarian Miss Pritchard (born in 1799; see also chapter 7). She also told the (unconnected) tale of a Hereford bull which escaped from Part-y-Seal, climbed the castle wall, walked round it, and came safely down.

The devil and his wife feature once more in a story taken down in 1907 by Mrs E.M. Leather from William Colcombe of Weobley in Herefordshire:

> There was a rectory near Grosmont so very badly haunted that when a new person [parson] came, long ago, he could not stay one night through. He offered a reward to anyone who would be brave enough to watch all night there and find out what was wrong. Two

sailors offered to do this, and were promised five pounds each, a roast goose for supper, and as much cider as they could drink, if they could rid the house of its visitors.

They made up a good fire in the kitchen, and at ten o'clock one sailor went down to the cellar to draw a jug of cider, but there was the devil himself sitting on top of the hogshutt [hogshead]. The candle went out, the sailor fainted. As he did not come back his companion also lighted a candle, and descended to see what had happened. He was not at all dismayed by what he saw, but his candle went out.

He went upstairs to the kitchen and relighted it, returning to the cellar only to have it blown out again. But the third time it kept alight, he called out bravely, 'By your leave, a jug of cider I must have.' Drawing it, he took up the fainting sailor, and returning again to the kitchen succeeded in reviving him. When asked why he fainted, he said he had seen the devil, 'and he was all great big eyes.'

Soon they wanted a faggot to roast the goose. The brave sailor going down to the cellar to get one, found the Devil sitting on the faggots. 'By your leave, a faggot I must have', he said, and calmly took one, returning a second, a third, and fourth time, as the wood burnt away, till the goose was nearly done. Then came a loud noise in the chimney, and down came the Devil's wife, calling out to her husband: 'Mr Longtuth, Mr Longtuth, the goose is nearly ready!' The undaunted sailor answered her, 'Done or not done, there's none for thee!' at which his unwelcome visitor departed again up the chimney.

The men ate the goose and went to bed, the timid one taking the side next the wall. They had not been asleep long when they were re-awakened by a great noise in the room. Still knowing no fear, the brave sailor, concluding that the 'Owd un' and his wife were having a game of football, hurried on some clothes and kicked out in the dark, shouting that he would join the game. He soon found it much too hot for him, so he called out 'Two to one's not fair, here is one for my landlord', and kicked the football straight through the window, smashing it. The devil and his wife immediately vanished like streaks of fire after the ball, which turned out to be a bundle of old deeds, torn to bits in the scrimmage. This, or something contained in them, had caused all the disturbance, for nothing has been heard or seen at that house since, and the sailor was held to have well deserved his reward.

SPIRITS

The language used here suggests a re-telling of the tale by Mrs Leather, but another story of a brush with the devil reminiscent of Prospero's books or *The Sorcerer's Apprentice* employs the words and phrases of the speaker, Mrs Pryce of Trellech. She and her two brothers, one of them with toothache, go to see a healer called Jenkyns (for whom, see also chapter 6). The pain is quickly charmed away, then:

> When the toothache was gone, Jenkyns went out o' the kitchen to fetch a drop o' cider, an' me brother see'd a big, big book on the corner of the table, an' began to look at it. Jenkyns hollers out from the other side of the house, 'Don't you touch that books or it'll be the worse for you!' When 'e came back me brother says, 'You must have got the Old Man 'imself about 'ere to have such like goings on', says 'e. Just then there came a great noise in the room above, bowling about the floor, like as if a great ball were rollin' about. 'All right', says Jenkyns, 'if you don't look out, you'll have him a bit closer.'
>
> With that 'e takes a candle an' blows into it, puts it on the table, an' draws a circle round it. Then the light all burnt dim an' blue, and the whole room got cloudy an' misty. Presently, we see'd a little old man sittin' in a chair next to Jenkyns, 'e was rockin' 'imself to and fro, squeakin', 'Jenky, Jenky, Jenky!' an' again, 'Jenky, Jenky!' Then Jenkyns blew into the candle agen, an' the dim blue light went away, an' the candle burned clear, an' lo an' behold! that little old grey man was vanished.
>
> 'There!' says Jenkyns; but me brothers didn't wait to hear any more; they just took to their heels an' set off home as if the Old Man was after them, leavin' me to follow as best I could. But I believe to this day 'twas the Old Gentleman himself as we saw.

Others who reputedly had dealings with the devil were Emmanuel Rogers of Cwmtillery and Shams Phylip of Blaenafon, who crossed the intervening mountain to meet in each other's home to practise black magic. Even during storms one or other might be seen on Coity Mountain, and damage caused by lightning or high winds came to be attributed to them. They were also thought to poison springs and brooks so that animals which drank from them sickened and sometimes died.

One night at Phylip's home the two men quarrelled. Rogers rode off on his pony, declaring 'I am going home. No more of your devil's work for me. Come what will, I shall never see you again.' When he had passed

Twyn Gwrhyd Farm he began to sense that something was amiss. As he neared his own farm he saw his favourite mare in the meadow on her back, legs in the air, and foaming at the mouth. Powerless to treat or to pacify the animal, he could do nothing but ride back over the mountain. 'Oh', said Phylip, 'I thought you were never coming to see me again.' Rogers begged him to help. He received advice, and went back home for a second time, to find the mare back on her feet. Next morning she was as well as ever, but Rogers sold her a few weeks later, at Caerleon Fair. Thereafter he referred to Shams Phylip as *Dyn y Diawl* (the Devil's Man), and their friendship never resumed.

Terrifying though diabolical powers might be, reassurance could be drawn from the 'Old Gentleman's' inability to avoid being tricked. A limestone outcrop in Tintern which looks down from the Gloucestershire bank of the Wye, acquired the name of Devil's Pulpit because the devil used it as a vantage point from which to harangue monks working below in the abbey fields. One day he went down to talk at close quarters, and cheekily suggested giving a sermon from the rood loft inside the abbey. The wise Cistercians readily agreed but as soon as the devil set foot in the church they showered him with holy water, which to him felt scalding hot. He fled in great anguish to Llandogo, whence he jumped back across the river to England, leaving the marks of his talons on a stone. The tale seems to be relatively recent since, as Ivor Waters, Chepstow's local historian, points out, in an age which disliked anonymous landmarks there is no record of the Devil's Pulpit prior to 1769.

Battles of wits often revolve round the building of bridges. No explanation seems to have survived as to why a bridge over the Sirhowy River at Argoed, Pont Syr ap Hywel or Pontsyrpowel, came to bear one of the classic names of the *pwca*, Hywel or Howell. However, when the same name occurs some 10 miles east as Hen Bont ap Hywel, the original bridge over the Afon Llwyd between Pontypool and Trefethin, there is a story.

Dafydd ap Hywel, a strong man and over seven feet tall, was a parson who liked preaching and teaching, but also singing and drinking. His parishioners, who could cross the river only on stepping stones, pestered him to build a bridge. Somewhat pessimistically, he was musing one night that since most of the people crossing the bridge would be going to hell the devil ought to build it, when the devil appeared by his side. Dafydd tried to persuade him, without success. Then the two agreed to hold a trial of strength, after which the loser would build a bridge and give it the winner's name.

SPIRITS

Standing one on either side of the river, they pulled. The first round went to the devil, who managed to drag Dafydd to his own side. Stung by this, Dafydd summoned up all his strength and won the second pull. The third and deciding struggle lasted for three hours until at last parson triumphed over devil. Next morning, as good as his word, the devil sent a team of masons to build a bridge which he called after the victor of the contest. Etymologists assert that Pontypool (Pont-y-pwl) simply means bridge of the pool—the pool being in the Afon Llwyd—but the tale of the epic tug o' war lingers in the imagination.

'As Newcastle teems with tales of sprites and elves', wrote Archdeacon Coxe in 1801, 'so Grosmont rings with the achievements of John of Kent.' A century later another clergyman T.A. Davies of Llanishen, described the same personage as 'the Robin Hood of the banks of the Wye.' He appeared as early as 1595 as a character in Anthony Munday's play, *John a Kent and John a Cumber*, and remained famous, at least in parts of Herefordshire and Gloucestershire as well as Monmouthshire, until within living memory. As a boy he is reputed to have made a compact with the devil in exchange for his soul after death, whether his body were buried in or out of a church. John (or Jack) did not hesitate to trick or cheat the devil, and the bridge over the River Monnow between Grosmont and Kentchurch is the subject of several stories concerning their jockeying for mastery. Jack undertook to build the bridge with

Monnow Bridge, near Grosmont

the help of the devil, who was to bring stones from Garway Hill. The devil had to work under cover of darkness, and one night when the cock crowed to signal dawn he had to jettison an apronful of stones, thus creating (according to the variant adopted) rocks on Garway Common, the Seven Sisters at Symonds Yat, or the Devil's Lappit in the Oak Wood just above Tintern.

When the bridge was finished the devil claimed the soul of the first to cross. Jack outwitted him by rolling a loaf of bread over. A little dog chased it; but animals have no souls, so the devil was thwarted. A different twist is that Jack agreed to cross first; but he argued that his shadow had preceded him in the moonlight so the devil had to be content with that, and Jack stayed shadowless for the rest of his days.

Great feats of strength and agility are attributed to Jack. Like some primeval giant, he is supposed to have leapt from the Sugarloaf to the Skirrid, and left his heelmark on landing. A Mrs Briton, a farmer's wife from Trellech, continues:

> An' when he got there he began playing quoits, he pecked [threw] three stones as far as Trelleck, great big ones, as tall as three men (and there they still stand in a field), and he threw another, but that didn't go quite far enough, and it lay on the Trelleck Road, just behind the five trees, till a little while ago, when it was moved so as the field might be ploughed; and this stone, in memory of Jack, was always called the Pecked Stone.

Trellech is 12 miles from the Skirrid. The five trees (now reduced to three) mark the meeting point of four parishes, Trellech, Cwmcarfan, Mitchel Troy and Penallt. The Pecked Stone, alternatively explained as a building stone

The three which remain of the five trees

rejected by the devil, is also called Packing Stone, from the packmen who rested their burdens on it.

A variant of the story of the three thrown stones is that they featured in a contest between Jack and the devil. From the top of Trellech Beacon, a mere mile away. Jack threw first and reached the outskirts of the village. The devil tried next, and managed a little further. Then Jack made an even longer throw, and the devil gave up in disgust. In either form the story purports to account for the three great standing stones which may have given Trellech its name (see also chapters 4 and 8).

Worsted at stone throwing, the devil unwisely chose to take on Jack at mowing. During the night before the contrast Jack liberally stuck harrow tines in half of the hay field due to be cut by the devil. As a result the Old Gentleman had to keep stopping to whet his scythe. He thought the problem was burdocks, and kept muttering, 'Burdock, Jack! burdock, Jack!' Of course, he lost.

Another crop, another problem:

> One day the Devil and he [Jack] were passing through a field of potatoes. Jackie told Satan to choose tops or bottoms. The Devil chose the tops and so Jackie got the potatoes. Passing through a field of wheat, the Devil, having first choice, thought this time he would choose the bottoms, and so Jackie got the wheat. Going further through a third field, Satan still had first choice, and, as it was swedes, of course he chose the tops, and Jackie had the roots. Jackie was always getting the best of it, and the Devil was evidently looked upon by countryfolk as somewhat of a simpleton, which, indeed, he is.

In another story the devil and John or Shon (Siôn in Welsh) co-operate:

> Once Shon, for some reason, was amusing himself by keeping crows out of the corn. He shut them in a roofless barn, and when he wanted to get a drink he persuaded Satan to turn himself into a great crow and stand on the barn wall and watch them. The farmer asked him, 'How about the crows?' Shon replied, 'They are all in the barn.' The farmer retorted, 'Then I'll take my bow and shoot them.' 'Very well,' said Shon, 'but don't shoot the crow on top of the wall.' The farmer approached and tried to fire, but the bow would not act and he could do nothing. That's the reason why the barn has never had a roof since.

Grosmont Church

A variation on this tale is that Jack confines the birds in the roofless barn while he goes to Grosmont Fair. 'Sure enough', an old woman told Coxe, 'they were there, for they made a terrible clatter, and did not fly away until Jack himself came and released them.'

At times, Jack did work. Once he was filling a dung cart when the devil appeared and offered to do the job himself. The condition was that if he could both fill the cart and catch Jack before he got to the fold gate 'he would have him altogether.' Jack ran hard, but the devil worked even harder, and caught him by the coat tail just as he vaulted over the gate. Fortunately, the cloth parted, so Jack made good his escape.

He is supposed to have owned horses 'with the speed of Lapland witches' on which he hunted on Sundays, forcing people to join in. Once he left a fiery animal in a barn from which no one dared move him. Three weeks elapsed, then Jack came by, and the horse sprang out to join his cavalcade. Many people believed that such horses could fly through the air. Mrs Leather was told at Grosmont that Jack set out at dawn from Kentchurch with a mincepie for the king and reached London in time for breakfast with the pie still hot. This was despite a delay when Jack caught his garter in a church weathercock as he flew over. The cellar at Kentchurch Court which allegedly served as a stable for Jack's horse was shown to visitors until about 1900, together with Jack's bedroom, where on stormy nights a ghostly figure issued from a recess in the panelling.

At least six candidates, including John Kemp, archbishop of Canterbury in 1452, have been put forward as the historical prototype for Jack. Some of these are shadowy figures, like Dr John Gwent, a Fransiscan friar with a reputation for working miracles, who was born near Chepstow, lived at Grace-Dieu near Dingestow, and died in 1348. Of John Kent, said to be a mischievous trespasser, we know only that he lived on the Herefordshire border in the 15th century. Of the same period were Father John of Kentchurch, doctor of divinity, Oxford professor and Welsh bard; Dr John Kent of Caerleon, astronomer and author of a book on witchcraft; and also Siôn Cent, a Welsh priest and bard patronised by the Scudamores of Kentchurch Court to whom he became chaplain.

No doubt aspects of these figures—involving witchcraft, miracles, mischief—were amalgamated into the mythical Jack Kent, but many have favoured Siôn Cent as the original. He was rector of Kentchurch in the 1380s, sympathised with the reforming Lollards, and mentioned the rebellious Sir John Oldcastle in one of his poems. A portrait preserved at Kentchurch Court is thought to show Siôn Cent, or Owain Glyn Dwr (see page 38). Indeed, Owain is said to have adopted the pseudonym of Siôn Gwent at one stage, and some believed that they were the same person.

We shall never be sure. At least in tradition the personage was buried at Grosmont. He cheated the devil by arranging to be interred beneath one of the church walls, and so neither in nor out.

Witches
'The Old Prophet', Edmund Jones, firmly believed in witches, and also feared them, as is shown by a story related about him by Edgar Phillips. When a certain old woman lay dying at Crumlin, Jones refused to pray at her bedside, so convinced was he that she had sold her soul to the devil. He grudgingly agreed to sit on the doorstep while a chapel elder went into the house to pray. When Jones heard the man's fervent entreaties he soon began to call *amen* or *bendigedig* (blessed) at the top of his voice. To his horror, though, a great black mastiff appeared at the window, put his paws on the sill, and howled mournfully. Jones stared in panic, then jumped to his feet and shouted, 'Come on, Thomas *bach*. Old Nick has come to fetch her!' The elder went to the door, to see Jones running away down the steep street, followed by a mastiff as frightened and bewildered as him.

Belief in witches lingered long after Jones's time. In the 1870s a seller of straws from Beaufort was widely considered to be a witch. One would like to know how she acquired her nickname, for she was called Mari Can Punt: Mary Pound of Flour. Miss Pritchard (see above) of Skenfrith told how as a child she and seven companions had to cross a wire bridge over the Monnow to attend the only available school, run by the vicar in the vestry of Garway Church. They had to pass the cottage of a reputed witch, by the well at the bottom of Hell's Wood (otherwise called Ellis's Wood),

*Skenfrith Bridge, with the Bell Inn on the left,
from a woodcut of 1800*

where each child in turn spat and cursed the witch because 'her eye was upon them.' The woman received the blame for every calamity in the neighbourhood. When the landlord of the Bell Inn put a sack over her head and beat her, fish died in the river and ducks drowned.

Witches could at will impede the accomplishment of routine tasks, or so people believed. One who lived at St Arvans for some reason cursed the baking at Yew Tree Cottage; the bread would not rise until she was placated. According to an article published in 1936 in the *South Wales Argus* a witch known as Mari'r Gwrhyd (Mary from Gwrhyd), who lived in Gelli'r Crug (Heather Grove) at a hamlet called Two Houses, went one day to ask for bread at Hendre Gwyndir. The farmer's wife gave her a loaf but when she got home she found it contained barley flour as well as wheat, which she considered an insult. Next day the farm milkmaids set about churning butter, but with no success, even though they worked long into the night. Two more days they laboured in vain; still no butter. In desperation, to avoid wasting the cream, they tried to use it in making cakes, but the dough ran all over the place or clung to their fingers. In the end they gave up in disgust and fed the mixture to the pigs, who were sick for several days as a result. Mari never called at Hendre Gwyndir again.

A few miles away, at Cwm Celyn, near Blaenau, a woman known as Old Ann could also sabotage the butter making if her requests for bread were refused. Robert ap Watkin, one of her neighbours, was a mule driver: his animals were used to take loads of coal to the canal at Gofilon, and to bring back limestone from Llanelli Hill and Clydach to Blaenau, Nant-y-glo, Ebbw Vale and Blaenafon. Overnight they were turned out to forage on the mountain. One morning he searched for them in vain until he recollected that he had refused to lend one of them to Old Ann. He decided to confront her:

> At the outset the old witch denied all knowledge of the mules, but after a good deal of cajoling she told him, 'Ewch i'r ffynnonau oerion yng Ngwmtyleri' (Go to the cold springs at Cwmtillery). 'I have been there this morning, and they were not there,' said Robert. 'Go there again and you will find them.'
>
> Ffynnonau Oerion were well known to Robert, and to the local inhabitants. They were reputed to possess healing powers; the water was always cold and the springs were full during even the driest summer. The location of the springs is still marked on ordnance maps, but the cool waters have vanished with a general subsidence of this colliery area.
>
> Robert crossed Mynydd Shams [Mount James], or 'Cock and Chick' as it is known today, from Blaina, and there, browsing near the springs, he found his eleven mules. Robert became more convinced than ever that Old Ann was possessed of powers beyond the natural. One morning he called at her shack, but failed to get an answer. He peeped through the window and saw the old woman stretched out on the hearthstone, where two hounds were mauling her. He ran away, and a day or two later he returned and found her dead in a pool of blood. The hounds had disappeared. Robert never lost his mules after that.

It was even dangerous for a man to cross his wife if she were a witch. The following story, set in the Wyeside parish of Penallt, was told early in this century to Beatrix Wherry by Mrs Briton of Trellech:

> It 'appened when Mr Mason was livin' at the Argoed. 'Is gardener was very partic'ler 'bout havin' turf from the 'ill, an' they 'ad ter

bring it across the river in boats, an' old Tom Griffiths an' Jacob Jones, they was 'elpin'. Well, on the last day, when they'd got it all up, Mr Mason's gardener, 'e left some money down at the Boat Inn, so they should 'ave some beer, 'cause 'e was pleased they'd brought the turf up so quick. So Tom, when 'e went up to tea, 'e says to Sarah, 'e was goin' down for an hour, 'cos they was goin' to 'ave some singin' down at the Boat; but Sarah, she said, 'Thee shassent go down theer; thee'st better stay at 'ome an' 'ave thee's supper.'

Well, Tom, 'e wouldn't stay, so she said, 'If thee goes down theer, thee bisn't comin' 'ome tonight.' An' she began to curse an' swear, an' she wished the devil 'ud run off with 'im if 'e went down, but still 'e went. Well, 'e was comin' up again, about ten, with old Jacob Jones, an' Jacob was a little way in front; 'e was tellin' me about it arterwards. 'E said, 'It's as true as my hand's there,' 'e said, 'I felt myself goin' up, an' it took my breath away, it was so swift, an' I went up right over the hedge.' It were one of those 'igh 'edges all over dog-briars an' blackberry branches. An' 'e went right over, sheer down into the meadow the other side. Presently 'e 'eard some swearin' close by, an' 'e said, 'Tom, is that thee? What t'devil art doin' theer?' An' Tom said, 'Jacob, is that thee? What t'devil art doin' heer?'

The Boat Inn

> An' then they tried to get out, but they couldn't, an' they was all scrat about, an' bruised, an' cut, an' try as they might they couldn't get out, they was so buried in briars an' brambles. They lay there swearin' an' talkin' to one another till half-past five in the mornin', when they 'eard Dan an' Tom, their two boys, comin' up home from the tinworks. Then Jacob 'e called out, 'Lord bless thee, Dan, is that thee? Coom an' get us out o' this!' An' them two boys 'ad the greatest difficulty in gettin' 'em out, an' when they got 'ome, there was old Sally boilin' the kettle, an' she said, 'I telled thee, Tom, thee oosn't come 'ome, an' thee didn't.'

The tinworks mentioned was probably at Redbrook, across the river from the Boat Inn. The Argoed (a word meaning 'edge of the wood'), the biggest house in Penallt, was built in about 1580. Between 1800 and 1860 it was let to tenants, of whom the Mr Mason of the story must have been one. Later, when Beatrice Webb's father was the owner, visitors included George Bernard Shaw.

A short way down the Wye, at Whitebrook, a witch swore that a woman who denied her something should lose all her cows. Now she had no cows, but so strong was the curse that she went mad and wandered distraught through the woods in search of animals she did not possess. Even men of the cloth, like Edmund Jones, could retreat in the face of such threats. Earlier this century the vicar at Llantilio Crossenny proposed moving the headstones from the churchyard to form a boundary wall. The blacksmith, whose wife was reputed to be a witch, objected. 'If the vicar disturbs the family grave,' he said, 'I shall disturb the vicar.' The headstones were left in place.

Stories of the witches' ability to fly, once commonplace, have long ceased to command credence. However, in the early years of the 20th century T.A. Davies noted this classic tale:

> An old inhabitant of the Narth [near Trellech] told me that long ago a labourer, tired out with tramping and out of work, called at a cottage on the moor and begged a night's shelter. An old woman answered the door, and said he was quite welcome, but she had only one bedroom with two beds. Only too glad of any shelter he went to bed immediately.
>
> Late at night the old woman came up, and, thinking him asleep, went to a box, and taking out a short stick, went to the window,

opened it, and said, 'Out I go', and out she flew. The man got up and dressed quickly—for he was not asleep—went to the box, found another similar stick, went to the window, and said 'Out I go', and flew after her, catching her up on the way to a large country mansion not far off. When they got to the kitchen door, putting out her stick she said 'In we go', and into the kitchen they went, and regaled themselves with a good supper. Then, remembering that the wine cellar was underneath, she pointed her stick in that direction and said, 'Down we go', and they were in the cellar and enjoying good wine.

Drinking too much they got fuddled, and when they tried to get out they bumped their heads against the ceiling, roused the occupants, and were taken prisoner. In those days burglary meant hanging. On the morning when the man was about to be hanged his mother—really the old woman—approached the hangman and asked to be allowed a few minutes' talk with her son. When she got near him she handed him the magic stick, and saying, 'Up we go', they were over the prison wall in no time and there was no hanging.

Davies comments on witches' perceived ability to change themselves into the form of various animals. A shepherd told him how as a young man at Llandenny, near Raglan, he spotted a rat in a barn, battered it with a stick and left it for dead on a pigsty. It disappeared, but a few days later he heard that an old woman, reputed to be a witch, was ill in bed nearby, covered with bruises. She died soon afterwards.

Another story related by Davies concerns the riding of horses by witches. A carter goes into the stable one morning and finds his horses loose, and covered with sweat. He notices a straw on the back of one animal, picks it off, and throws it out of the door. Then he sees a long straw on a second horse. This, too, he picks up, doubles, and throws out of the doors which he shuts. Then he hears a voice outside saying 'Come along, Hannah, we must be going.' A second voice replies: 'I'm afraid I can't walk as I'm fairly doubled up.'

A more frightening tale concerns a barn at an old dairy farm at Penrhiwellech, near the former Marine Colliery at Cwm. People believed that witches and wizards met there at Hallowe'en to ride the horses and terrify the neighbourhood. Again near Cwm, at Llandafal, a woman was thought to be able to concoct potions which would turn her into a cat or a rabbit.

SPIRITS

As recently as 1955 Fred Hando took down from a Mr Reynolds of Trellech the classic story of a witch from Pont-y-Saeson. A hare is repeatedly started on Trellech Moor but never caught because it seems to disappear close to a witch's cottage. A fast greyhound bitch is brought in for the hunt. She, too, fails to catch the hare, but she does manage to nip one of its legs. The witch is not seen for weeks, and when at last she comes out she hobbles on a bandaged ankle. This belief in the ability of witches to change into animals was so widespread that, according to Marie Trevelyan, when a hare was difficult to skin women said, 'This one was a bad old witch,' and when it took a long time to cook, 'This old witch has many sins to answer for.'

In the Vale of Ewias an old woman clad in a black shawl once eked out a living by selling flowers and telling fortunes. She punished those who crossed her; two farm workers at Pandy claimed that she conjured up a storm over the Black Mountain which ruined the crops of a farmer south of Wiral Wood who had set his dogs on her.

Some children from Llanthony were playing in Wiral Wood when the Old Hag, as she was called, happened along. The children, hidden among the trees, began to shout 'Old witch' and 'hag', but as she came nearer they fled towards the ruins of Walter Savage Landor's house. Soon, a crow landed on one of the walls. The children were so frightened by its resemblance to the old woman that they ran again, this time towards Llanthony Priory, with the crow diving and swooping round them. From the shelter of the ruins they looked towards the wood and again saw the black-clad figure of the old woman.

Another time, a shepherd driving his flock down the mountain chased the Old Hag from his path with harsh words. She said nothing, but fixed him with a long stare. From then on, whenever he took his sheep down the same path they were harried by a huge crow which flapped about them. Nothing he or his dogs could do was of any avail until they crossed a stream north of Wiral Wood, at which point the crow would fly of off to the west.

One night the rector at Llanthony saw her standing in his churchyard at the centre of a circle of figures which he took to be those of the dead. The moonlight shone straight through them. He crossed himself and went home to put a lighted candle in the window, and also tied a red ribbon round his baby daughter's cradle to keep evil at bay.

The hallowed precincts of Llanthony Priory must have given some protection against witchcraft; so did the stream's running water. The clergyman's sign of the cross, candle and red ribbon must also have helped. Sticking a knife or a tenpenny nail into a witch's tracks also worked, but first the tracks had to be found. A cross of whitethorn or birch over the door gave some protection; sprigs of mountain ash or elder over stable doors prevented witches from riding and ruining the horses. Even the simple act of spitting could help as we saw at Skenfrith. More drastic action involved drawing blood from the witch.

A very elaborate strategy came into play at the Narth near Trellech when a mare's death was attributed to witchcraft. The animal's heart was cut cut, stuck with needles and pins, and stitched back into the body. This procedure should have revealed the identity of the witch responsible, but the heart merely disappeared—perhaps stolen by the witch when surveillance faltered. However, at the Panta, a farm near Devauden, a similar attempt with the heart of a pig—this time boiled for a day and a night after being transfixed—succeeded in unmasking a witch and in preventing other pigs from dying in unexplained circumstances.

An earlier age was more direct, and more brutal. In 1649, when a witchfinder arrived at Newcastle, near Monmouth, a bellman announced that any woman denounced as a witch would be tried 'by the person appointed.' What seems like a large number of 30 women were arrested. They were stripped, and the witchfinder then attempted to prick with a pin every part of their bodies in the hope of finding a spot insensitive to pain. The discovery of such a place, called a witch-mark, was taken as an infallible proof of guilt, and the woman would then be burnt. There seems to be no record of the fate of the women of Newcastle.

Ghosts

Even after their deaths, it seems, certain witches continued to seek fresh victims. Edmund Jones, always ready with a lugubrious story, tells how the figure of 'a poor old woman, with an oblong four-cornered hat, ash-coloured clothes, her apron thrown across her shoulders, with a pot or wooden can in her hand' would appear in front of people on the road over Llanhiledd Mountain, especially in misty weather, 'sometimes crying "Wow up".' Anyone who saw or heard her would be sure to lose his way. Jones says that the 'Old Woman of the Mountains' was the spirit of 'one Juan White'—his anglicisation of Siwan Gwyn—'who lived time out of mind in these parts.' Wirt Sikes adds that a friend born in Monmouthshire in about 1850 wrote to him: 'Juan White is an old acquaintance of my boyhood. A cottage on the Lasgarn hill near Pontypool was understood by us boys to have been her house, and there she appeared at 12 p.m., carrying her head under her arm.'

A more tenuous figure, that of a classic White Lady, haunts a pool at Llanfihangel Crucorney. She is thought to be Eleanor Thomas, who drowned there in the 15th century. She is known as the Lady of the Ring, from an iron band she was forced to wear on her wrist to nullify her powers of witchcraft. Alternatively the ring is thought to have been used to secure her during bouts of madness. Either way, her appearance betokens an imminent death in the neighbourhood.

The Old Woman of the Mountain, as visualised by T.H. Thomas in 1880

Another White Lady walks in the same village, at Llanfihangel Court, from the hallway of the house to the Lady Wood, nearby, where she vanishes. A Mr Bennett, who lived at the Court in the 1940s, gave this account to Edmund J. Mason:

> There were several ghosts, he said, but his favourite was the White Lady, who on a particular night of the year, came down the hill behind the house, passed through a certain room and out at the front, with a bloodcurdling scream. He said they had become so used to this ghost that if they were aroused from their sleep, they would look at their watches, remember the date and go to sleep again.

THE FOLKLORE OF MONMOUTHSHIRE

Llanfihangel Court

Two ghostly duellists were also seen engaged in a fight on the stairs. The loser's blood is said to have left an indelible stain. This conflict might have accounted for the lady's distress, though another possibility could be the skeleton with bullet embedded discovered beneath the terrace at the point where she screams.

An entirely benevolent Grey Lady, thought to have been a member of the Lewis family which owned the mansion (now a golf and country club) at St Pierre, appeared there at intervals until at least the 1950s. Grosmont Castle has its own Grey Lady, as does Cefntilla Court at Llandenny. Lewis Browning of Blaenafon recalled a White Lady (*Lady Wen*) whose reputation kept the peace in a particular area during turbulent times: 'The workmen and their families dwelling here never used to have their slumbers disturbed by night rioters, the fear of meeting the White Lady keeping such at a respectable distance.' Until recent road widening obliterated it, the Mare Pool by the wall round Piercefield between Chepstow and St Arvans sheltered a spectral lady who rose from the water on moonlit nights on a white horse's back and flew over Piercefield's grounds, always in the same direction, that of Porth Casseg (Mare's Gate).

Other figures are very vague, such as the shape clad in long white robes seen in Raglan Castle during the Second World War, or the grey, hooded form of a monk, kneeling as though in prayer, which has been repeatedly sighted at Tintern Abbey. More spectral monks cross the road nearby at the foot of the Cefn Hills and walk into Chepstow Park Woods.

Few ghost stories are told at first hand, but in her book, *A Monmouthshire Christmas*, Mrs Maria Hubert relates an experience of her own in December 1970 at Usk Priory, which she was thinking of buying to live in. On visiting the house she reacted very favourably, save for a sudden feeling of fear which prevented her from going up a certain staircase. A little later she looked out of a window and saw five nuns walking from the house towards the church; she felt disappointed because she took them to be other potential purchasers. When she mentioned the nuns to a local man he responded: 'Oh, they old biddies won't buy, they bin there long enough already.' She discovered that the five nuns had been pensioned off well over 400 years earlier when their priory as suppressed in the time of Henry VIII.

There are far more ancient ghosts than these. Since its re-discovery in the 1920s the great amphitheatre at Caerleon has often echoed to the sound of Roman soldiers' feet. Newport's Norman castle is apparently haunted by its founder, Robert FitzHamon, in the shape of a fierce giant which vanishes as soon as mortal eye falls on it.

An extraordinary number of phantom carriages and coaches has been noted in Monmouthshire. There are several round Monmouth itself. On the road to Rockfield one apparition crashes on stormy nights into a wall at Croft-y-Bwlla, thus re-enacting an accident in which three passengers lost their lives. At the same place women rounding up cows in the early morning for milking often gave them a slap on the rump if they failed to move. Sometimes their hands passed straight through, and they recognised animals which had died years earlier. During the Second World War Land Girls refused to enter these fields before daylight.

More phantom coaches have been seen west of Monmouth travelling through woods on White Hill, on the road between Trellech and Bigsweir; and on the old towpath along the Wye between Redbrook and Monmouth, the last one reported by a teetotal Methodist who saw a coachman whipping his horses and a woman peering out of the vehicle.

Between Devauden and St Arvans, especially at Hallowe'en, horses and men—all headless—have been seen. At Glyn, near Devauden, in the 1920s a farmer was shaving, one Sunday morning, when he noticed outside in the yard a ghostly coach and horses. He put the phenomenon down to his sabbath-breaking action, and never shaved again on a Sunday in his life.

Certain stretches of road enjoyed a particularly eerie reputation. A tall, cloaked figure seen between Cwm and Aberbeeg has been identified as the ghost of a policeman killed in a brawl in 1911. A top-hatted man encountered in 1980 carefully looked at a watch, then walked away, casting anxious looks behind, before vanishing. The apparition seemed to be associated with a woman's screams which came from a nearby wood.

In his book on Tintern, W.H. Thomas observed the consequences of a local belief that the road to Livox was haunted:

> Many a neighbouring villager, surprised by night, performs a circuit to avoid this lonely place during the reputed hours of a spirit's walk. It is said that during the last [18th] century, an innocent peasant girl was the victim of seduction and murder, her ruthless violater thrusting her alive down a chasm in the rock. Some time ago, on blasting it for lime, her skeleton was discovered.

A frightening encounter between Trellech and Penallt was described by Mrs Briton in the early years of the 20th century:

> One night about twelve o'clock I was goin' along the road down to Mitchel Troy, where we used to live; I was just nearin' the Potash [a house] when I heard like a lot o' people talkin' in the air. First I thought 'twas the gypsies, but as I was comin' by the hedge in the field I saw a sort of a black cloud comin' through the gap, an' I heard a sound o' clankin' chains, but all at once I knowed it wasn't gypsies 'cos they weren't there, an' I heard voices all round. I ran, an' ran, I was so frightened till at last I fell right into a sand pit at the bottom of the hill.

Public houses frequently boast phantoms, which can be by no means bad for trade. The Cross Keys at Usk had an unquiet spirit which lifted the latch or opened and closed the door of Room 3. A connection was suggested with the suicide of a servant girl there, some years before. At the Gockett Inn (Tafarn y Grugiar Ddu) near Trellech, the ghost of a woman weeps for her sailor sweetheart, lost at sea, and watches for his return. The landlady, Mrs Hazel Short, told me in 1997: 'I saw her 18 months ago in the Still Room, in an old part of the house. Late one night when everyone had gone she appeared out of the wall—a tall, blonde woman dressed in white, and then went back in again. I'd never have believed it.'

SPIRITS

The Gockett Inn

During the 1980s at the Carpenters Arms, Shirenewton, crashing noises from the cellar, objects flying round the bar, and the presence, sensed but unseen, of a young woman, were attributed to the crime of a former landlord, who had murdered his daughter, Catherine, and walled up her body in the snug. The Skirrid Inn at Llanfihangel Crucorney is haunted by the ghost of a one-eyed man who stabbed himself, rather than suffer hanging after being sentenced to death by Judge Jeffreys in the late 17th century. The presence of Jeffreys is not authenticated but a room at the inn did serve as a courts and hangings were carried out on the premises.

The Queens Hotel at Monmouth has a room with bullet-pocked beams where an attempt was made to kill Oliver Cromwell when he was spending a night there, or so it is said. The would-be assassin's ghost continues to haunt it. In the same town, just over the Monnow the former Rising Sun, now re-named Riverside Hotel, has (or had) a record of poltergeist activity coupled with rumours of a customer who died on the premises (albeit peacefully, as he nodded off after a drink), and also a suicide.

Poltergeist happenings also took place at the Three Horseshoes, Pentwynmawr, near Pontllanfraith, in the 1920s but they ceased when the landlord of the time died. Not far away, the Cross Oaks Inn at Penmaen still feels the influence of a former landlady, Aunty Polly Cummings, as lights and alarm systems switch themselves off, kettles move, and a mysterious gentle breeze springs up.

Some unexplained phenomena seem to be connected with injustices, violent deaths or tasks left unfinished in life. Part of Mynydd Coety (Coity Mountain) behind Coalbrookvale, called Cefn Coch, is haunted by the ghosts of Scotch Cattle (see chapter 9), early trade unionists who went disguised in animal hides to persuade or even coerce fellow workers.

A more banal story, with echoes of the sentimental song, 'She was poor but she was honest,' comes from Ebbw Vale, where the ghost from Victorian times of a young woman with babe in arms walks along the mill stream towards St John's Church. The woman fell in love with a man well above her station, the son of wealthy farmers, who wished him to marry a sea captain's daughter. In the meantime he courted the poor woman, who refused to submit to him unless they were first married. He deceived her by means of a bogus ceremony, to abandon her shortly afterwards, unaware that she was carrying his child. When the baby was born even the man's father wished him to marry the mother. However, he insisted on pursuing the match with the captain's daughter despite his father's solemn curse. Just before the wedding, the rejected woman made a last, desperate appeal—unsuccessfully. She and her baby were later found drowned—perhaps murdered—in the mill stream. The father's curse proved to be effective, for the faithless lover died at sea, leaving his new wife with a fatherless child.

Will the Fiddler died through suicide. He was an itinerant musician based at Cwmbrân. As his repertoire ran to only eight tunes, he was called Wil Wyth Tiwn, Eight Tune Will. Even so, only four of the titles of his tunes have been remembered: 'Dafydd y Garreg Wen' (David of the White Rock), 'Ap Siencyn' (Son of Jenkins), 'Y Deryn Pur' (Pure Bird) and 'Bugeilo'r Gwenith Gwyn' (Tending the White Wheat).

The last of these tells of the shared but unrequited love of two young people, Ann Thomas, the Maid of Cefn Ydfa, and Wil Hopcyn, writer of the song. In fact, both were fictional, and the words were written by Iolo Morgannwg to a tune previously called 'Yr hen Gelynen' (The old Enemy), see opposite above.

Will the Fiddler earned a precarious living by playing at festivals such as the *mabsant* (see chapter 11) and at public houses. But he fell upon hard times, perhaps as he grew old, and did away with himself. As a suicide he was buried according to custom, at a crossroads, by night (at Lower Llanfrechfa). Rumours soon circulated that he was haunting the spot, farmers claiming that their horses shivered as they passed it. One night, they dug up the body and re-buried it well away from any road, near the Mountain Air Inn. Until the 1930s local people pointed out the supposed grave of Wil Wyth Tiwn, marked by a particular pattern of stones.

Money, goods or even tools hidden during life could cause unquiet spirits to seek them after death—or so it was believed. In about 1900 a psychic cyclist visiting Tintern became convinced that the shade of a Saxon soldier had made contact with her. Having been killed and buried without ceremony, the soldier could not rest until two masses were said for his soul. The lady made the necessary arrangements, and a message of thanks came back from the grateful Saxon spirit.

A ghost tormented by unexpiated guilt summoned a coachman travelling at midnight near Trosnant to meet him exactly a week later. The man felt a compulsion to comply. His friends fervently prayed for his safety, two of them even electing to accompany him to the rendezvous, but unaccountably losing him. The ghost led him to a spot near a nail works and told him to move some old iron. Underneath this he found a bar of bright metal which, on the ghost's orders, he threw into Glyn Pond, between Pontypool and Hafodyrynys (off the present A472).

A variation on the same story came from Henry Jones, living at Pontypool in 1870, who had earlier worked as a miner near Cwmynyscoy.

A ghost confronts him in the pit and tells him to go the following night to a place on the mountain near Crumlin. He ignores the summons, but the ghost, visible to him though not to others, insists until he accepts. The miner's friends try to intervene but the ghost spirits him away to a place where he has to move a heap of stones, then dig up a bar of gold. They fly through the air again, and the man drops the gold into Glyn Pond. 'Now I can rest at last,' says the ghost, and leaves the man at Croes Penmaen.

A surprising number of similar narratives is on record. A mower on his way home after reaping at Llandegfedd, east of Cwmbrân, is confronted by an apparition which he recognises as the ghost of a former owner of Graigwith Estate. The spirit guides him to a ruined building and asks him to remove some stones from a wall. In the cavity he finds a bag which he judges from its weight to be full of gold; the ghost tells him to drop this in Graigwith Pond. He does so, collapses on the doorstep when he arrives home in the early hours of the morning, and dies two weeks later. The pond is dragged, but no bag of gold comes to light.

At Nantycelli Farm, Wolvesnewton, a manservant is told by a ghost to be in a certain room at midnight the following day. He complies, but as nothing happens, he begins to walk downstairs only to turn back when he hears rapping. He sees the ghost, which tells him to put his hand behind a beam—the room has no ceiling, and is open to the rafters—and take out an old stocking containing 12 guineas (£25.60p.). 'I got this for some sows and pigs I sold at Usk market,' says the ghost. 'I swore the devil should have the money before my wife laid hands on it. Take it to Cae Byndra brook and throw it over your head into the water.' The man does as he is told. When the story gets out people search the brook but find no gold.

Thomas Cadogan, owner of a big estate at Llanfihangel Llantarnam, removes some landmarks and dishonestly obtains land belonging to his neighbour, a widow. After he dies his ghost meets another local woman by a stile, who questions him as though he were alive. He explains about the markers and she moves them back to their proper position, upon which he vanishes. Only then does she remember that he is dead, and falls into 'a state of extreme terror.'

In a book published in 1831 William Howells tells the story of two workmates at Crumlin. One dies and his ghost commands the other to go with it, one cold, snowy night, to a great boulder. The man, to his surprise, lifts it with ease and retrieves a mattock from underneath. At the ghost's behest he takes it to a river and, standing with his back to the water, throws it in. For some time afterwards he is 'out of his senses, and the superstitious class strongly condemn the practice of hiding anything, relating this as an instance of the evil of doing so.'

Some stout-hearted people refused to help ghosts in this way. Edmund Jones writes of Halter John Harry, a Quaker who lived at Ty'n y Fid (House in the Hedge) on the north bank of the Ebwy Fawr river close to the Victoria Bridge. One night he is in bed with his wife when he sees a light coming upstairs. He tries to wake his wife by pinching her but fails, and the ghost of a former occupant, a weaver called Morgan Lewis, appears. Walter John boldly asks: 'Morgan Lewis, why dost thou walk this earth?' The ghost explains that it seeks some bottoms (skeins) of wool hidden in the house. Walter John gives a stern rebuff: 'I charge thee, Morgan Lewis, in the name of God that thou trouble my house no more.' Lewis meekly complies.

Jones also relates the case from Panteg, near Pontypool, of Margaret Richard who was expecting a child and went to church to marry the father, Samuel Richard. When he failed to turn up Margaret knelt and prayed that he might 'not have rest in this world nor in that which is to come.' Shortly afterwards, Samuel sickened and died. Then he took to haunting Margaret, so much so that people started calling her Marged yr Yspryd (Spirit Margaret). Eventually, a friend advised her to forgive Samuel. Soon afterwards she found the ghost waiting for her by a stile next to a footbridge and asked what it wanted. 'I want nothing,' it said, 'but do thou forgive me, and I shall be at rest, and never trouble thee any more.' She did so. They shook hands, and parted for ever.

Not all ghosts proved as accommodating. Mrs Leather reports that a man at Longtown, having heard a Baptist minister preaching against superstitions and belief in ghosts, retorted: 'I know what I have sin [seen]. I helped myself to turn a man in his grave, up at Capel-y-ffin; he come back, and we thought to stop him, but after we turned him he come back seven times worse. He was a hurdle maker, and you could hear him tap, tap, tap, choppin' wood for his hurdles all about the place where he used to work. No use of him [the preacher] tellin' *me* there's no ghosts.'

Another recourse was a full ceremony of exorcism involving 12 parsons. One account of this comes from Margaret Eyre:

> Old Mrs Pirrett lived in Monmouth whilst her husband was away fifteen years at the Peninsular War, and got her living by brewing,

The church at Capel-y-ffin

etc. She had to go and brew at a big house which stood where the Grammar School stands now, by the Wye Bridge. She had to go in the middle of the night, so as not to use the copper when the cook wanted it. She was crossing Wye Bridge shortly after midnight when a coach and four dashed past her, coachman and horses alike without heads, and rushed straight into the river. She went on as well as she could, her knees shaking with terror, and went to the front door, the way she always had to get in at night. A clergyman came and opened it, in a bath of perspiration and said to her in furious tones, 'What do you want here?' then, 'Come in, for heaven's sake, quick!' As she passed towards the back of the house she saw a lot of gentlemen standing in a circle in one of the sitting rooms. 'An' when she came to think of it she saw as how they must have been laying the ghost she met.'

A successful exorcism caused a ghost to appear, then to shrink in size so as to be put in a tiny container which was then consigned to a river or pond. The process could be a terrifying battle of wills, as the agitation of Mrs Pirrett's parson showed. The furious phantom of a rich, tyrannical man, known as the Great Giant of Henllys, was summoned to the church by three parsons with book and candle. It rampaged about like a roaring lion, a raging bull and a battering wave of water before submitting and entering a tobacco box in which it was thrown into Lynwyn Pool, to remain there for 999 years.

Three attempts were made before the spirit of Tom the Lord was successfully confined. Tom, a riotous drunkard one night fell into a reen (dyke) at Redwick, and was drowned. Soon afterwards a local farmer called Thorn began to find the taps of his cider barrels open in the mornings. He took to leaving a mugful of cider ready outside each night before goin to bed, which placated the mischievous spirit, and the barrels were left alone. If he forgot the cider would flow again, and in addition 'shords' (gaps) were made in the farmer's hedges. At apple time Tom appeared high in the trees and pelted pickers with fruit—and cider apples are very hard.

The minister of the village chapel attempted to lay the ghost, but failed—for lack of faith, said some. A second attempt was equally unsuccessful, so 12 ministers gathered and with due process before the assembled population of Redwick they laid the ghost. People say that each spring at the place of exorcism a coffin-shaped bed of white violets blooms. The place of the ghost's confinement is not remembered but an orchard pool is thought likely by some, a fitting place for one so devoted to the juice of the apple.

Not far away, another troublesome spirit is recalled. In the 1960s Reverend Henry Morgan of Holy Trinity Church, Newport, told the story of Eve Roberts, daughter of the Whitson postmaster who died at the Farmer's Arms, Goldcliff. How she met her death is not recorded, but afterwards people at the inn began to be troubled at nights by the sound of moving furniture, rattling crockery and clanking fireirons. The figure of a woman in white was seen to leave the inn and walk to the church close by, so a ceremony of exorcism was organised. At the name of Eve Roberts, the ghost appeared and fled northwards, pursued by some of the villagers. Past Nash it went, until it reached the outskirts of Newport. There, in Batchelor Street, it plunged into a well, and was seen no more. Ffynnon Efa—Eveswell—as it became called, gave its name to the whole district.

Other people, it seems, are happy to accept peaceful co-existence with ghosts. To this day the Old Rectory at The Bryn, a tiny village a few miles

Goldcliff Church

south-east of Abergavenny, has a friendly apparition. In his book, *Haunted Gwent* (1995), Alan Roderick has documented many more ghosts of recent times, some of them benign, and appearing in ordinary houses to ordinary people.

One has to concede, though, that some who see ghosts are deeply shocked by the experience. Lower Bailey Pit, near Monmouth, an unusual name for a house, may derive from the Welsh, Cad y Put (Battle Pit). Until its destruction by fire in 1973 the building was perhaps the most haunted place in the whole of the county. In the 1960s an unseen man with a wooden leg stamped round the upper floors. A plumber who came to turn off water in the derelict house left hurriedly when doors inexplicably slammed behind him. Three young couples ventured inside one night, only to feel a pervading atmosphere of evil. As they left one man shone a torch back at an upper window; he saw there, as he thought, the father he had never known, since his father had died when he was a baby. The whole party regained its composure only after starting to sing 'Bread of Heaven', so as to ward off an overwhelming sense of dread.

A new house now stands on the site. It is peaceful.

CHAPTER 4

Earth

The unknown can inspire both fear and curiosity. Mysterious spaces beneath the surface of the land such as caves and passages readily aroused such feelings. Buried treasure provided another powerful attraction.

On the surface, unusual tumps and bumps provoked puzzlement or awe. Standing stones, too, engaged the imagination, and were sometimes felt to be almost animate. The bare hills and high mountains so abundant in Monmouthshire added their due share of fascination.

Underground, Overground
There is no doubt that many people had an atavistic perception of perils lurking below the ground. After all, one might stumble on sleeping warriors (chapter 2) or supernatural beings (chapter 3). In many parts of Britain there are persistent tales of a fiddler who sets off to explore a cave or passage, playing as he goes so as to stay within hearing of his friends on the surface. Just such a tradition holds that a fiddler became lost in a cave at Trellech and failed to return, though his music could be heard for years afterwards. A variant of the story says that people hear music beneath a certain meadow, dig down and find a cave in which two aged men are playing, one a harp, the other a fiddle. It turns out that they have been there for many years, taking turns to go out at night in search of food, and are both persuaded to leave the cave, but they die soon afterwards.

The garrison at Chepstow Castle could reputedly send and receive messengers through secret passages. Raglan Castle had its supposed underground link with the village and another—improbably, to say the least—with Trevella, six miles to the south. Pencoed Castle, between

Llanmartin and St Bride's, had similar links with Tre Garn on one side and Cillwch Farm on the other; and also with Garn Fawr, via Chapel Farm at Llandevaud and Kemeys House. The last details were heard by Olive Phillips in the White Hart at Llangybi, which claims a tunnel of its own, to the nearby church. Magor boasts a reputed underground link from Manor Farm to the church.

At Machen the Elizabethan manor house, Plas Machen, is supposed to be connected by underground passage with Ruperra Castle, almost a mile away in Glamorgan. From Skenfrith Castle, where the government apparently discounted stories of buried treasure in 1589 (see chapter 3), a tunnel allegedly ran below the Monnow to a convent (now gone) on the Herefordshire side of the river. The nuns are thought to have embroidered the sumptuous cope still preserved in the church. It was said that 'Great wealth was conveyed and received' through the tunnel, and until at least the 1920s local people believed that treasure lay buried somewhere in the castle ruins.

Ty Coch, a mansion at Llantarnam, is believed to have an underground passage to the abbey. The monks of Llanthony are supposed to have dug a tunnel three miles long beneath the mountain ridge to Longtown, presumably to be used in troubled times or when weather conditions ruled out the overground track called Rhiw Cwrw, Beer Path. In the same area, castles at Longtown and Oldcastle, four miles to the south, were thought to be joined by a tunnel, the mid-point of which was marked by a watch-tower on the hill (which must have been near Ty Mawr).

Along the ridge above Llanthony runs the long distance path opened in the early 1970s which roughly follows the remains of Offa's Dyke, cut some 1,200 years earlier to mark the boundary between Wales and England. Subsequent generations, unaware of the dyke's purpose, were inclined to see it as the devil's work, as they did with other structures they found difficult to comprehend. Alternatively, it was felt that a giant could have been responsible.

It was certainly believed that Ithel, a giant who lived at Llanhiledd, set about collecting stones from Cefn Grib above Hafodyrynys to build himself a house. One day as he was returning with a load in his apron, the strings broke and the stones fell to the ground. He left them where they lay, to form the mound which can still be seen next to St Illtyd's Church.

On the southern edge of the Mynydd Maen (Stone Mountain), a short distance from Risca, is a tumulus which has been variously called Tumberlow (in Speed's map of 1557), Twm Barlwm and Twyn Barllwm.

EARTH

Twmbarlwm on the skyline on the right

In 1796, David Williams wrote, 'The artificial Hillock upon the high mountain near Risca, is commonly called Tom Barlam; I conjecture this name to be a corruption of Tum-ulus Berthlan, some mighty Potentate in Wales, but know nothing about him.' One suggestion is that Bran, the father of Caradoc was buried there. In 1830, a band of navvies determined to solve the mystery by digging into the tump but every time they took pick or spade in hand lightning flashed and thunder rolled, so they abandoned the project.

Another contention is that wizards held court here, and when a wrongdoer was sentenced to die he was thrown into the valley below: hence its name of Dyffryn y Gladdfa, Valley of Burial Place. Much more recently when Europe was in turmoil in 1848, the year of revolutions, fierce fights between wasps and bees were observed on Twmbarlwm.

More recently still, by a stream on the east side, sounds resembling unearthly organ music have been heard from time to time. One little girl who went to look for its source disappeared for ever, though a member of a local family did manage to make a recording of the so-called music. The phenomenon still lacks a conclusive explanation. Perhaps it is part of the enchantment which Arthur Machen described in his autobiographical volume, *Far Off Things* (1922): 'As soon as I saw anything I saw Twyn Barlwm, that mystic tumulus, the memorial of peoples that dwelt in that region before the Celts left the Land of Summer.'

THE FOLKLORE OF MONMOUTHSHIRE

Not far away is Twyn y Calch (Hill of the Lime), with its distinguishing white scar. A baron returning from the wars plans to build a church to expiate the evil deeds he has committed. But whilst stone is plentiful, lime for mortar is lacking and in desperation the baron calls on the devil for help, without mentioning the building he has in mind. He finds a huge sack which the devil agrees to fill with limestone and carry down the mountain for him. As he stands watching the devil at work he accidentally lets fall the plans for his church, whereupon the devil instantly drops the sack and makes off, leaving the huge patch of lime which can still be seen.

Some ancient tumuli were used as sites for churches, at Basaleg and Llantilio Crossenny, for example. Others, when their purpose for burial was forgotten, served as landmarks. The Gipsy Tump near Newbridge could have shown the way to a ford across the Usk; another at Bedwas stands at the junction of two ancient trackways.

The generic name given to the hillforts and enclosures of pre-history was Tai'r Hen Bobol (Houses of the Ancient People) or Cytiau'r Gwyddeloch (Irishmen's Huts). At Mynyddislwyn a tumulus near the church is called Twyn Tudur, after the saint believed to be buried there, together with treasure. Local people felt that any attempt to dig there would call down a heavy thunderstorm. Another belief was that the bodies of Roman soldiers slain in battle by the Silures were buried in the mound. Stone from the whole area, wrote Marie Trevelyan, was regarded as 'curative and almost sacred.'

Tump Terrett, Trellech

EARTH

At least two former castle mottes of the middle ages were assimilated into the tales commonly applied to more ancient tumuli. At Trellech the mound of a former de Clare castle, known as Tump Terrett, was locally believed to be the burial place either of a British prince or of Welshmen killed while fighting King Harold's army. Anyone digging there could expect drastic consequences, though, somewhat incongruously, a summer house once stood on the top.

The mound at Newcastle was shunned for another reason: within, it was believed, dwelled the spirits of dead people who wished to atone for wrong done in their lives. In fact it may have been the site of Castell Meirch (Stallion Castle), a mediaeval outpost of the Monmouth garrison. Nearby, the Newcastle Oak (see chapter 3) was felt to enjoy supernatural protection, and in addition local tradition held that it had been planted by Owain Glyn Dwr.

Standing Stones

Some of the many standing stones in Monmouthshire were erected as long as 3,500 years ago. One, Langstone, has given its name to the village, five miles from Newport, where it lies, rather than stands.

Some which might seem mysterious are straightforward enough. The Pecking Stones near the old church at Penallt were conveniently placed so that packmen could rest their burdens after their steep climb from the Wye ferry at Redbrook. Others were markers for travellers though some acquired a sinister reputation. 'A peasant pointed out to me,' wrote W. Sikes in 1880, 'on a mountaintop near Crumlyn, Monmouthshire, a crossroads stone, beneath which, he attested, a witch sleeps by day, coming forth at night.' A century earlier a stone at Bwlch y Llwyn on the Mynydd Mulfraen above Nant-y-glo, which guided travellers from Abergavenny, had a smaller stone at its base which purported to have the miraculous print of a lamb's foot.

The massive Druidstone, over 10 feet high, in the grounds of a house near Castleton, may also have been a Guiding Stone or Maen Gobaith. Its edge points towards an ancient trackway leading to Pen-y-lan and Caerleon, while its shadow at true midday falls towards Twmbarlwm. Another possibility is that this was a sepulchral stone, perhaps part of a burial chamber. Either way, a local tradition asserts that when a cock crows at midnight the stone goes down to the River Rhymney for a bathe. According to a similar belief at Llanfihangel-y-Fedw, the Carreg y

Derwydd (Wizard Stone) there goes to water to swim when a cock crows at night.

The name of Druidstone indicates an assumed association which was no doubt more comfortable for people than remaining completely in the dark as regards its origins. However, the stone was once known as Gwâl-y-Filiast (Lair of the Greyhound Bitch), which links it with the story of a princess turned for her sins into a wolf or greyhound and giving birth to twin cubs. She suffers for a long time until King Arthur seeks her out and orders that she and her offspring be restored to human form. The hound involved could also be Sirius, known to the Romans as Canicula (Little Bitch), which eternally chased Lepus (the hare) through the sky.

The so-called Devil's Quoit at Llanfihangel Rogiet was certainly a marker. Its name comes from the notion that the devil threw it—from Somerset, or merely from the adjacent Gray Hill. Still remembered in the village, if no longer believed, is the assumption that anyone moving the stone would forfeit his life. Under ancient Welsh law this was indeed the case with both marker and boundary stones.

Stones were among the landmarks followed when parishes beat their boundaries, usually at Rogationtide. At Llanfair Discoed after a peramubulation in May 1722 the next recorded was in September 1937. The circuit began at 'the pimple stone', on which certain participants were bumped as an aid to memory. From Cross Palmer the procession went successively to Windmill Wood, Five Lanes, Cas Troggy Brook, and through Wentwood to the Foresters' Oak (where forest laws were upheld, justice dispensed, and sheepstealers hanged—the

Base of a wayside cross a mile south of Trellech on the road to Parkhouse

EARTH

last in 1829). From there the walkers returned to the village after covering 10 miles. Pennies were strewn for children, and the vicar, Reverend H. Sowden, read the appropriate collects. Further perambulations were held in 1977 and 1995, the last taking the form of a sponsored walk to raise money for the renewal of the church roof.

Churchyard and wayside crosses were also once the goal of processions which would deck them with garlands on festival days. People liked to be buried near churchyard crosses, perhaps because they were a centre of activity: the parish clerk proclaimed news from them, and the lowest step provided a seat for the village elders. Bargains struck and engagements undertaken at the cross were regarded as particularly binding.

Standing stone on Gray Hill

In 1643, Parliament ordered that all such monuments should be destroyed and only the bases of some 80 churchyard crosses remain in Monmouthshire. Whilst some have been restored, only one—at Kilgwrrwg—retains its ancient head. There are 30 known sites of wayside crosses, of which just over half still have some masonry. Again, only one is complete: Croes Llwyd (Grey Cross), on a farm of that name near Raglan. These crosses had certain melancholy associations, since suicides were once buried beside them.

THE FOLKLORE OF MONMOUTHSHIRE

Y Garn Llwyd

The colour grey is often associated with ghosts and death in Wales and Brittany. Gray Hill (Mynydd Llwyd), with its monoliths and stone circle, preserves its ancient *gravitas* despite the ceaseless surge of the distant M4. Fred Hando has suggested that the complex of stones here had as one of its functions the indication of the precise positions of sunrise and sunset on Midwinter Day.

The Grey Cairn (Y Garn Llwyd)—in fact the remains of a burial chamber in the parish of Newchurch—has been claimed as the relic of one of the contests between Jack Kent and the devil (see chapter 3). So have the three famous monoliths at Trellech, which are also locally known as Harold's Stones, said to commemorate the English king's victory in battle. John

Harold's Stones, Trellech

Williams, an experienced dowser from Abergavenny, told Janet and Colin Bord—authors of *The Secret Country*, a study of ancient sites—that when he placed his hands on one of the stones he was flung back from it. He described the force involved as 'spiral-like, building up through the body.' The significance of the stones is unclear. Whether they were boundary markers or had a commemorative or ritual role will probably never be known, but they are venerable monuments with a powerful presence.

Similar remarks may well be made in a few thousand years from now about the four monoliths at Waun-y-Pound, above Tredegar. They were in fact erected in 1972 as a tribute to Aneurin Bevan and as a mark of his association with the three towns of Tredegar, Rhymney and Ebbw Vale. Bevan, who often addressed open-air meetings at Waun-y-Pound, was the MP for Ebbw Vale from 1929 until his death in 1960. He is best known as the architect of the National Health Service, for which he partly drew inspiration from the Tredegar Workmen's Medical Aid Society. Some 2,000 people gathered by the stones on the bitterly cold evening of 15 November 1997 to commemorate Bevan's birth at Tredegar a century earlier.

Bevan Monument

Hills and Mountains

The Black Mountains shared by Breconshire, Herefordshire and Monmouthshire are so called because of their appearance from afar, though they are made of red sandstone. To the south of the *massif* is an outlier near Abergavenny, the Sugar Loaf, so named from its conical shape, though its old Welsh name is much more poetic: Moel Fannau, Bare Beams. Across the River Usk is the Blorenge or Blorens, of which the name derives from *blawr* (grey) and *eisen* (rib), which in turn reflect

The Sugar Loaf

the mountain's grey-ribbed appearance when it is streaked with snow in winter. A depression known as the Punch Bowl used to be the venue for bouts of fisticuffs between men who worked in the neighbouring collieries and ironworks.

Further south and west is the Gray Hill, mentioned earlier, one of whose twin peaks is called Mynydd Allt Tir Fach (Mountain Height of the Small Land), ludicrously anglicised to Money Turvey. Its earlier name was Allt y Blaidd (Wolf's Height), though some applied this to the Gray Hill as a whole.

On the Mynydd Maen, as it drops towards Cwmbrân, there is a reedy hollow which in winter fills with water and is called Pwll Trachwant, the Pool of Greed. A fine house once stood nearby. One day an impoverished cousin knocked at the door to ask his affluent relatives for some food for his wife and children, but was met with a peremptory refusal. Under lowering skies he set off in despair to return home. He had not gone far when he felt the ground shaking under his feet, and turning he saw the house engulfed by a huge landslip. Ever since then, on certain stormy nights, the cries of those who perished have been heard by the pool, a warning against greed.

Some have perceived malevolent powers at work on mountains, as in the accounts of the Old Woman of Llanhiledd (see chapter 3). On the other hand, Mrs E.M. Leather passed on the story of 'a helpful and beneficent spirit':

EARTH

A few years ago a man was driving a lady from Longtown to Llanveyno, and she, being a stranger, questioned him concerning the 'Apparition of Our Lady' at Llanthony. He replied that he did not believe it at all; there were indeed spirits to be seen on the mountain, but they were different. He had seen, and he knew. Once he went to see friends at Llanthony, and was returning directly over the mountain to Longtown, when a fog came on suddenly, and he lost his way. He was standing, quite at a loss, when a man came towards him, wearing a large, broad-brimmed hat and a cloak. He did not speak but beckoned, and the man followed him, until he found himself in the right path. Turning round, he thanked his unknown friend, but received no reply; he vanished quickly in the fog. This seemed strange, but he thought no more till, on visiting his friends at Llanthony later, they asked if he reached home in safety that evening, as they had been anxious. When the stranger in the broad-brimmed hat was described they looked at each other in surprise. 'What,' they said, 'tell us exactly what his face was like.' He described the stranger more minutely. 'It was T-- H --, for sure,' they cried, 'he knew the mountain well, and he has been dead these two years.'

The sign of The Skirrid Inn

The most famous mountain in Monmouthshire is the Skirrid—Ysgyryd Fawr, Big Rough—otherwise known as the Holy Mountain because its great fissure was believed to have opened at the precise time of the crucifixion. At the same moment a spring with holy and healing water gushed forth.

People set great store by earth from the Skirrid. Farmers took handfuls to scatter on their fields for fortune and fertility. It was also sprinkled on the coffins of the dead and in the foundations of churches. Pilgrimages were made, especially on Michaelmas Eve (28 September), to St Michael's Chapel, which stood on the highest point, where Archdeacon Coxe arrived with 'animation and lassitude, horror and delight,' though it is merely 1,600 feet high. Only a few stones of the chapel now remain.

The cleft in the Skirrid, seen from the summit

Arthur Machen cherished the memory of looking out as a boy from the vicarage of Llanddewi Fach and seeing this 'mountain peak in a fairy tale' which shone 'a clear blue in the far sunshine.' Another writer, H.J. Massingham, recorded his impressions in memorable terms:

> I do not see how any sensitive person could fail to be drawn into the mysterious orbit of the Skirrid when he catches sight of it, as he will, from so many points of the compass among the Western Marches. Its hunched shoulders or bowed head overpeers the high places in so many different directions that I have seen it not far from Pandy, below where the Olchon and Escley mountain brooks join the Monnow, slowly emergent from a cloudburst, the vapours washing off it like the waves from the back of a risen sperm whale and looking so stricken and forlorn through the riot of the tempest that it appeared to be the high seat of grief and bereavement. Though it often changes from the various angles of vision, it is recognisable as *the* Holy Mountain.

CHAPTER 5

Water

In Wales as a whole some 1,200 natural springs once had an odour of sanctity. Pagan veneration of such places made them a target for Christians who adopted them for their own rite of baptism. Converts who moved from the darkness of heathenism to the light of faith took the symbolic power of the water to be literal, and so there grew up a belief in its medicinal properties which in some cases was no doubt justified by the chemical content. Monmouthshire had over 60 springs of this kind, some of which enjoy a continuing reputation for physical or mental healing.

The old county had four main rivers. Between the Rhymney to the west and the Wye to the east were the Ebbw and the Usk, of which Edward Thomas wrote that they 'cut across my childhood with silver bars and cloud it with their apple flowers and their mountain-ash trees, and make it musical with the curlew's despair and the sound of the blackbird singing in Eden still.'

Rivers and their tributaries were workhorses, too, powering mills and foundries, bearing goods and people, and supplying fish. They led inevitably to the Severn Sea, and the great oceans beyond.

Springs and Wells
Springs of pure water welling eternally from what seemed to be another, mysterious world excited feelings of awe and veneration in early peoples. The Christians were quick to take over sites associated with what they considered to be heathen cults, and they used springs for baptism. Many centuries elapsed before the rite moved into churches, some of which were built near springs and shared their dedications to particular saints, as at

Bedwas (Barrwg), Bedwellty (Sannan), Bryngwyn (Peter), Gofilon (Patrick, the only such instance in the whole of South Wales), Llangybi (Cybi) and St Maughan (Maughan). Skenfrith had three springs, St Bride's, near the church of the same saint; St Noe's (or Noye's), by the chapel which once stood to the west of the village; and the Priest's Well in Darren Wood, which gave rise to a stream whose water was thought to be particularly beneficial.

A strong local tradition suggested that the stones by this well owed their red colour to the blood of a man decapitated there 'for the £5 reward which was offered for the head of any Catholic priest found in the country after Queen Elizabeth's orders for all to depart by St John's Day [24 June] 1559. or to change the Missal for the book of Common Prayer.' Franciscan friars who lived near Rockfield must have subscribed to the belief because they made a yearly pilgrimage to the well. A similar tradition of stones stained by a martyr's blood also applied in Rockfield itself, at St Michael's Well.

The Priest's Well, near Skenfrith

Several other martyrs are associated with particular wells. At Partricio people still place votive crosses of tied twigs on the coping of Ffynnon Issui (see also chapter 1), and throw luck-seeking coins into the limpid water. Pwll Meurig, near Mathern, enjoyed the reputation of bringing about miracles. In addition, the Welsh historian, Nennius, writing in about 800 AD, had this to say about it:

> There is a spring by the wall of Pydew [Pwll] Meurig, and there is
> a plank in the middle of the spring and men may wash their hands

Ffynnon Issui (St Issui's Well)

and their faces, and have the plank under their feet when they wash. I have tested it and seen it myself. When the sea floods at high tide, the Severn spreads over the whole shores and touches it, and reaches to the spring, and the spring is filled from the Severn Bore, and it draws the plank with it to the open sea, and it is cast about in the sea for three days, but on the fourth day it is found in the same spring. Now it came to pass that a countryman buried it in the ground to test it, and on the fourth day it was found in the spring, and the countryman who took it and buried it died before the end of the month.

Nennius mentioned 20 marvels, of which 13 were associated with water.

The 12th century *Liber Landavensis* (Book of Llandaff) relates another. As Rhiwallon ap Tudfwlch was riding off after plundering churchgoers at St Maughan a great fish leapt from Ffynnon Oer (Cold Spring), startling his horse and making him break his arm. He was so impressed by the incident that he not only gave up his booty but made a grant of land to the diocese. The well became a landmark on one of its boundaries. 'The fish represented the pagan spirit of the well,' writes Francis Jones, 'and here, under clerical influence, it has been metamorphosed into a guardian of the Church.'

Many wells were widely believed to possess medicinal properties. People filled bottles to take home at Skenfrith's Priest's Well. St Cadoc's at Penrhos and St Issiu's at Partricio were thought especially efficacious. Perhaps because he objected to those who tramped over his land to reach it, a farmer substantially destroyed Ffynnon Wen (White Well), otherwise known as Ffynnon Illtyd, near Argoed Farm at Brynithel. Edmund Jones remarked that Ffynnon y Rhiw Newydd (Well of the New Hill) near Blaenau was 'deserted, as if it had lost its virtue' after being 'demolished by a malevolent drunken man.' Many other wells disappeared in the mining areas of Monmouthshire because their water drained into pit shafts and headings.

Ffynnon y Cleifion (Well of the Sick) near Usk, and another of the same name at Dingestow, are thought to have been favoured in mediaeval times by sufferers from leprosy. Later the water, like that of many other wells, was used to treat inflammation and other troubles of the eyes. The former is said to have run red after a battle, as did Ffynnon Gwaed (Blood Well) at both Mynyddislwyn and Upper Bedwas.

Very cool water was particularly prized. Ffynnon Angoeron, a cold well on the flank of Lasgarn Mountain above Llanofer, was usually strewn with bent pins, buttons and other small objects which people dropped in when they made a wish, keeping silent lest the spell be broken. The Ffynnonau Oerion (Cold Wells) to the east of Cwmtillery not only had medicinal powers but slaked the thirst of passing huntsmen and also gave their name to a mountain.

Llangattock Vibon parish had a well which was said to cure the king's evil, scrofula. This was also the case with the Fairy Well of Llwyndu (Dark Grove) near Abergavenny, which could in addition help with diseases of the joints and general debility. One wonders whether it would be effective with today's M.E. The fairies responsible for this well's powers, which included restoring the bloom of youth, could sometimes be seen there in the early morning. Unfortunately, the last sighting was over 100 years ago.

Newcastle's reputedly sacred well, 'in summer much frequented by invalids', wrote Archdeacon Coxe, was thought good for rheumatism. A century later, in 1904, Joseph Bradney visited and found young people there who threw in pins and silently wished as they did so. A similar procedure was followed at Mamhilad's Holy Well; at least three others bore the same name: near Caldicot, between Mitchel Troy and Wonastow, and near Monmouth. More sacred wells were at Trefethin (Ffynnon Wenog) and Abergavenny (Ffynnon y Garreg).

The nine wells (some say seven) grouped in a circle in Llanofer Park and known as Ffynnonau Ofor were greatly prized for their healing qualities at least until the end of the 19th century. Coxe heard that at times crutches were left hanging from nearby trees as a testimony to cures achieved. Under the title of 'Ffynnon Ofor' Jane Williams published, in 1844, a tune taken down 'from an old man near Llanover who said he had learned it by ear in his youth':

Nine more springs, now reduced to four, made the famous Virtuous Well, sometimes known as St Anne's Well, at Trellech. Its water, drunk on an empty stomach in the morning, was thought to be good for particular ailments. According to Edward Lhuyd (?1660-1709) these included 'the scurvy, collick and other distempers.' Writing in 1839, W.H. Thomas was full of rational enthusiasm:

> The medicinal celebrity of this spring is not dependent on the veracity of monkish traditions or vulgar tale, but it possesses in itself the evidences of its fame. To all with a debilitated constitution, especially to sufferers from dyspepsia, hypochondriasis, and amenorrhagia [absence of menstruation], these waters, with proper management, would prove an effectual relief. Little does the proprietor of this neglected fountain, over which the wisdom of our

The Virtuous Well, Trellech

ancestors built a devotional shrine, know the treasure which the Almighty has deposited in his hands or he would gratefully rebuild its ruined walls, cleanse out its channels and invite guests to a festival of health.

Others were more fanciful. Charles Harper claimed in the late 19th century that 'love-lorn maids were used, in byegone times, to come and drink the waters of the Virtuous Wells, as in some sort, a love-philtre.' 'They are wiser now,' he added. Fairies were thought to dance by the well on Midsummer Eve (23 June) and drink its water from harebell cups the following morning. A farmer once blocked access, only to be confronted by a little old man who told him his land would be completely waterless until he relented and so it proved.

Posies were thrown into the well as offerings. Pins and other bright objects were deposited for luck and to foretell the future. Pebbles were dropped in, and the resulting bubbles anxiously watched: no bubbles meant that a wish would not be granted; a few, that it would be delayed; many, that it would be achieved.

Belief in the well's power decreased as modern medicine became more effective and more widespread. In 1951, the stonework, in fulfilment of W.H. Thomas's hope of over a century earlier, was restored to mark the

Festival of Britain, but visitors came less for therapy than for the picturesque. However, in 1998, candles and flowers could be seen in niches of the stonework. Neighbouring trees were festooned with pieces of cloth tied there and left in a revival of a practice going back 200 years in Wales, the rags representing the survival of a belief that disease will be discarded along with a token of the sufferer's clothing. They may also embody the hope that a deeply-felt wish or longing will be satisfied.

Streams and Rivers
The description of Monmouthshire as 'well watered' is something of an understatement in view of its complex and abundant network of powerful streams and rivers. The Rhymney—once called Afon Eleirch, Swan's River—defined much of the western boundary with Glamorgan and gave its name to the Cardiff suburb of Rumney to the south and to the town of Rhymney to the north. Near the town, fossilised marks in the river's bedrock were popularly thought to have been made by the hooves of Norman horses or even by those of the steed of a much earlier visitor, Mari Lwyd, the Blessed Mary. The poet, Michael Drayton (1563-1631), mentions the Rhymney in connection with the 'gallant nymphs of Gwent' which he imagined besporting themselves in it.

The Ebbw's name (Ebwy in correct Welsh) may mean 'talking or gushing water' or 'river as wild as a horse,' either of which would be entirely appropriate. It is a tributary of the Usk, like the Afon Llwyd (Grey River), which was once called Torfaen, the stone-breaker, a name now applied, perhaps rather strangely, to the area of a new unitary council set up in 1997.

The Usk runs for 60 miles through Monmouthshire before joining the Severn Sea below Newport. Arthur Machen, like Edward Thomas, celebrated the peacefulness of its valley, but its waters can be treacherous. Pencarreg Farm at Llanbadoc claims to have been flooded as many as 13 times in a single season. In the same village there was a public house called the Bell Inn; the hillside above is Twyn Bell and a stretch of the river, Bell Pool. Apparently, a bell from the church tower fell into the water and was miraculously recovered, but further details are lacking,

Further downstream, at Llantrisant, a young girl who went too near the river narrowly escaped being dragged in by a gnarled hand which surfaced from the water and grasped her dress. She ran home in terror, to be reminded of the cautionary verse:

> Nicky, Nicky, Nye,
> He pulls you down
> Beneath the water
> To drown, drown, die.

Parents repeated it to reinforce the message that children should avoid the greedy, fast-flowing waters of Monmouthshire's many rivers.

The names of the Usk and Wye both derive from forms of an ancient word for water, *gwy* and *wysg*. That of the Wye's tributary, the Monnow (Mynwy), means simply Little Wye. This in turn gives Monmouth (Trefynwy, Monnow Town). The first syllable of both Monnow and Monmouth is locally pronounced *Mun*, which is closer to the Welsh than to the English form of the words.

Monmouth from the Wye, 1861.
The vessel in the foreground is a trow

Discussions of the main rivers' respective merits for fishing go back at least to the 12th century, when Gerald of Wales wrote that 'the Wye has more salmon and the Usk more trout,' and added that 'in winter salmon are in season in the Wye but in summer they abound in the Usk.' Some 400 years later in his long poem, *The Worthiness of Wales* (1587), Thomas Churchyard offered these comments:

> A Pretie towne, calde Oske neere Raggland stands,
> A river there, doth beare the self same name:
> His christall streams, that runnes along the sands,
> Shewes that it is, a river of great fame.
> Fresh water sweete, this goodly river yeelds,
> And when it swels, it spreads ore all the feelds:
> Great store of fish, is caught within this flood,
> That doth indeed, both towne and countrey goode.
>
> A thing to note, when sammon sailes in Wye,
> (And season there: goes out as order is)
> That still of course, doth sammons lye,
> And of good fishe, in Oske you shall not mis.
> And this seemes straunge, as doth through Wales appere,
> In some one place, are sammons all the yeere:
> So fresh, so sweete, so red, so crimp [crisp] withall,
> That man might say, loe, sammon here at call.

During the second half of the 18th century the Wye began to attract a large number of visitors. John Byng (later Viscount Torrington), who made something of a hobby of travelling, arrived in Monmouth in 1781, found the boat fare to Chepstow of 1½ guineas (£1.55½p) too steep, and hired a horse. He spent the night at Tintern's Beaufort Arms, where he remarked that 'bread, beer, cyder, and commonly salmon, may be had ... and possibly a Welsh harper may be procured from Chepstow.'

Byng went on by river to Chepstow, where he stayed at the Three Cranes. He made the comment, tantalising in its absence of detail, that 'The Boatmen and steersman exerted themselves during the voyage in telling miraculous stories.' The 'voyage' was evidently a leisurely affair since the passengers 'often spoke to the salmon fishermen, who catch great numbers (some of 60 lbs weight) which are generally sold at 3 pence the pound.'

William Gilpin came in pursuit of the picturesque the following year. Duly impressed by the Wye Valley, he was nevertheless shocked by the 'poverty and wretchedness' of the people of Tintern, who, he reported 'occupy little huts raised among the ruins of the monastery and seem to have no employment but begging.' The 'coricles' he noticed on the river were the subject of frequent comment. Robert Bloomfield in his poem, *The Banks of Wye* (1811), mentions the 'whirling bowl' in which the fisherman displayed 'in his bow'ry station, / The infancy of navigation.'

THE FOLKLORE OF MONMOUTHSHIRE

Mr Thomas Rees with the last locally-made coracle on the River Usk, c.1904 (National Coracle Centre, Cenarth Falls)

Half a century earlier, Sir John Hawkins, the biographer and editor, provided a more careful description:

> Those of that country [Monmouthshire and Herefordshire] use a thing they call THORACLE, or TRUCCLE;—in some places it is called a COBLE, from the Latin CORBULA, a little basket. It is basket shaped like the half of a walnut shell, but shallower in proportion and covered on the outside with a horse's hide. It has a bench in the middle, and will just hold one person; and is so light, that the countrymen will hang it on their heads like a hood, and so travel with a small paddle (which serves for a stick) till they come to a river, and then they launch it, and step in.

Despite the craft's fragility it was very serviceable. A writer of 1863 claimed that passages from Chepstow to Bristol had been made in it, though its prime purpose was for fishing: 'Many a salmon of size has thus been taken and carried to shore; and in the season it is not unusual for a fisherman to fill his coracle with the smaller fish of the beautiful river [Wye].'

The Wye is tidal, exceptionally to Redbrook, normally to Llandogo. Salmon netting began at Bigsweir Bridge, between the two. The lave net—essentially a large landing net—was used at the bottom of the ebb to scoop up fish stranded in pools. The stopping net, which caught three out of four salmon netted, is described by H.A. Gilbert in *The Tale of a Wye Fisherman*:

> Imagine two long poles some 18 feet long fixed together like a pair of compasses with a net shaped like a purse fastened between them. The poles are tilted into the water over the side of the boat which is moored broadside to the flow of the stream ... The netsman catches hold of the string and waits for a fish to come into and strike the net. The feel of the strike is instantly communicated to the netsman by the string, and he immediately jumps on to the poles and levers the net out of the water with the salmon kicking and lashing in it. The netsman grabs the fish, hits it on the head, and after dropping his prize into the bottom of his boat, he merely pushes down the ends of his poles into the water and his net is at work again.

*Salmon fishermen using stopping nets on the Wye (John Summers).
The practice ended in the 1980s*

WATER

Similar methods were used on the Usk. In addition, Coxe described an elaborate and ingenious weir across the river by Trostrey Forge for catching salmon. The huge decline in the numbers of the fish in recent years has resulted in its now being caught largely with rod and line by individuals. Even so, the smallest catch ever by this method was recorded from the Wye in 1997. The following year, Wye fishermen, gillies and owners agreed on a voluntary 'catch and release' policy to try to restore dwindling salmon stocks. Conversely, elvering, at Llandogo, formerly a social and family event has become a commercial activity. 'Strange men in cars and refrigerated vans,' wrote a villager in 1994, 'come from as far away as Birmingham, stake their claim on the river bank and wait for the incoming tide. ... The greed for money has spoilt what was a happy annual village event. April and elvering were once synonymous, but sadly we no longer hear the happy voices of the village people.' The price of elvers in 1998 was £245 per kilo.

Llandogo, which proudly claims to have been a port before Chepstow, has a reminder of past river navigation in the Sloop Inn. The bell of the last commercial vessel to sail up the river, the *William and Sarah*, is kept in the church. (She was built at Llandogo in 1860, and broken up in 1925). The Llandoger Trow, a public house in Bristol, commemorates the sturdy little ships which came up the Wye on the tide, loaded cargoes such as hazel hoops and bark, and delivered them as far afield as Italy.

Trow at Tintern
(Chepstow Museum)

Incoming goods and passengers were usually transferred either at Llandogo or Brockweir to flat-bottomed barges, though trows did venture at times to Monmouth and beyond. Charles Heath of Monmouth had cause both to love and to hate the Wye. His son drowned in it when he was 12, but Heath made part of his living by writing and publishing books about the river. He tells us how 15 men would haul a barge laden with 25 tons to Monmouth, though five could pull it back empty to Llandogo. An extraordinary passage deals with the problem of shelves or reefs in the riverbed when water was low:

> In passing the weirs they fall with all their force flat on the ground, which is done by the chant of *yo, ho!* in which position they continue for a short space, when on another shout being given, they rise up, and securing their step, fall down a second time, and so on, till they gain a more peaceful and greater depth of water.

This was written in 1804, but H.A. Gilbert describes a conversation with a man called Parry, born in about 1878, who as a youth earned his living by hauling barges to Monmouth:

> He tells me that the crew of a barge used to be one man for every ton of coal, and that 20 men were needed to take a big coal barge upstream. When the barge got to a stream, tackle was got out, and every man harnessed to pull. It was hard work. He told me that very often 'we were pulling half an hour before the blankety-blank moved an inch. ... I earned my money in those days—every penny of it.'

St Tecla's Island, where the rivers Wye and Severn meet

WATER

Parry was later a champion netsman. In May 1913, during 17 hours of non-stop fishing just below Brockweir Bridge he caught 115 salmon. Some of his neighbours made less heroic efforts: they picked a rare spurge, *Euphorbia stricta*, which grew between Wyndcliff and Tintern, and threw it into the water; as a result, fish rose in a dazed state and could easily be caught.

Wooden bridge over the Wye at Chepstow, 1812 (Chepstow Museum)

Severn Sea

The exact place where the Wye and Severn meet is 'the Treacle', a patch of water immediately south of St Tecla's Island (see also chapter 1), which in turn is just off Beachley Point (once known as 'Treacle-land'). People travelling from Wales to England by this route crossed the Wye bridge at Chepstow, went down the Beachley peninsula to the Old Passage Ferry, then crossed the Severn to Aust. (For the relatively short-lived interlude of the New Passage, see chapter 2). The ferry took its last passengers in 1966, when it was superseded by the M4 motorway.

Various poetic tales purport to explain the courses followed by the Wye and the Severn, and also the Rheidol, which rises on the same mountain, Plynlimmon. This is one of them:

Aust Passage

A great landowner has three daughters. When they come of age he decides to share his estates among them. They are to leave home on a day appointed, and travel from dawn to dusk. Each will own the land she traverses, as long as she reaches the sea by nightfall; otherwise she shall have nothing.

The strongly-built Severn rises early on the due day and wanders 50 miles eastwards through hills, then turns south when a passing swallow tells her Wye has just wakened. Sweet-natured Wye, knowing Severn is long gone, rushes swiftly southwards through beautiful country. Lively Rheidol, having spent the night in celebrations, rises only at noon, and dashes westwards towards the nearest sea.

By sunset all three reach the coast, Severn muddy after her long journey, Wye pretty as ever, Rheidol breathless from haste. For his part, their father, Plynlimmon misses them so much that he turns into a mountain, his abundant tears having followed the ways taken by his three daughters.

The name, Severn (Hafren in Welsh), which may have been that of a pre-Celtic water spirit, is explained by Geoffrey of Monmouth. Locrinus, son of Brutus, and king of Loegria (England) defeats Humber, the invading king of the Huns, in battle. Humber drowns as he flees in the

WATER

Old Ferry Inn, with M4 bridge over the Severn beyond

Old Ferry in 1966, shortly before it gave way to the new M4

Beachley Passage and the Severn Ferry about 1807, from the billhead of Thomas Prichard, innkeeper

river now called after him. On a captured enemy ship Locrinus finds a very beautiful woman, Estrildis, daughter of the king of Germany. He is keen to make her his wife but must keep his word and marry Gwendolen, daughter of Corineus (Cornwall). Nevertheless, he has a secret dwelling made underground for Estrildis at Trinovantum, somewhere near the Severn, and visits her there over a period of seven years, explaining his absences to Gwendolen as times of private sacrifice to his gods.

When his father-in-law dies, Locrinus repudiates Gwendolen and takes as queen Estrildis, who now has a radiantly beautiful daughter, Habren. The furious Gwendolen raises an army in Cornwall and defeats Locrinus in a battle in which he loses his life. She then orders Estrildis and Habren to be thrown into the river which from then on is to bear the latter's name.

A later tradition added that Habren eternally battles against the Severn tide in a vain effort to reach land. Cries of distress heard from time to time by mariners, and the apparition of a swimming figure, have been identified with Locrinus's tragic daughter.

More prosaically, the fishing of salmon continues in the estuary. The drift or tuck net, eight feet deep and 400 yards wide, is stretched between two boats which then drift. A prime manoeuvre is to start south of St Tecla's Island and to drift down almost to the lighthouse on Charston sands.

Salmon are also caught in putchers, large, cone-shaped baskets of wickerwork (latterly, aluminium) set in ranks. Fish entering the wide end cannot back out, and so are trapped to be extracted at low tide. The practice at Goldcliff dates back at least to 1442. Currently, there are two rows, each four putchers high and amounting to 2,000 in all. Other fishermen stand on the sea wall with rod and line.

This wall, originally built by the Romans, has been reconstructed many times, the last in 1974. The 'musselpooled and heron-priested shore' at Goldcliff (as at Laugharne) can be a desolate place, with mist so dense that the engines of ships can be heard labouring past when the vessels themselves are unseen.

The creeks—or pills, as they are called—on this lonely coast were used by smugglers to bring in contraband, especially wine, spirits and tobacco. People in the area also ransacked wrecked ships. As early as 1334, the superior of Goldcliff Priory, Philip de Gopillarius, and a monk, some clergymen and 50 other persons from Newport, Nash and Goldcliff, Clevedon and Portishead, were charged with taking wine and other goods from a vessel wrecked off Goldcliff. A hole in the sea wall was thought to be the entrance to a tunnel leading to the priory.

Whitson Court reputedly possessed both buried silver and a smugglers' tunnel running to nearby Goldcliff. A passage from the banks of the Usk to a house at Kemeys Inferior is also said to have been used for moving contraband. Whether they were true or not, such stories could have served the turn of both smugglers and wreckers by causing people to steer clear of certain places.

Sea wall and shore at Goldcliff

THE FOLKLORE OF MONMOUTHSHIRE

Woodcut illustration of the Great Flood of 1607

The great sea wall has often been breached. In January 1606 (1607 by modern reckoning) Goldcliff Church floor was three feet deep in water. Among 25 more parishes flooded in the space of only five hours were, in the spelling of a contemporary account, Matherne, Portescuet, Caldicot, Undye, Roggiet, Llanihangiell, Ifton, Magor, Redwicke, Nashe, Saint Peire, Lanckstone, Wiston, Lanwerne, Christchurch, Milton, Bashallecke, Saint Brides, Romney, Marshfield and Wilfrick.

Some 2,000 people were drowned, but there were some amazing escapes. A man and a woman marooned in a tree saw a 'certain Tubbe of great largenesse' approaching. They got in, and were carried to safety. A self-sacrificing mother launched her four year-old daughter into the rising floodwater on a beam. The little girl survived, thanks partly to the warmth of a chicken which flew up and perched beside her.

Brass in Goldcliff Church

CHAPTER 6

Sickness & Health

Before the advent of modern medicine the precarious nature of health was keenly felt, particularly by the poor. Those anxious to avert evil influence or ill fortune tiptoed through a forest of taboos and obligations which we call superstitions.

To preserve health they relied on a great many traditional remedies, often drawn from wild flowers and herbs, and they also observed certain rituals. These procedures can be divided into four categories: medicinally beneficial, psychologically helpful (the placebo effect), totally neutral, and positively harmful. Such treatments were handed down in both families and communities.

Many were administered by 'wise' men or women, charmers and conjurors, who were felt to have extraordinary powers, though they also had practical skills. One of their roles was to seek out lost or stolen property another, to chastise wrong-doers. 'The charmer', wrote Richard Baker-Gabb in 1913, 'still largely takes the place of the doctor and veterinary surgeon. With his aid many ailments are cured; and bones, broken or dislocated are repaired and put in place.' For at least another decade, such practitioners operated in parts of Monmouthshire; and some of the floral and herbal lore of yesteryear is arousing new interest today.

With Luck
Miners in Monmouthshire, like their fellow-workers in the Forest of Dean, turned over the money in their pockets when they saw a new moon, in the belief that this would preserve good luck. In difficult times and in dangerous work the dividing line between disaster and prosperity could be

narrow, so it is not surprising that even the slim chance of favourably influencing the goddess of fortune should be taken.

'When my auntie and uncle has to do examinations,' an 11 year-old Blaenafon girl told Iona Opie in 1954, 'they always carry a piece of coal wrapped in paper.' In the same year Mrs Opie was informed at Usk that to keep a sprig of mistletoe from one Christmas until a new piece could replace it the next would preserve the luck of a household. As recently as 1985 a Tredegar woman, aged 48, said:

> We always throw the knives on the floor if we see them crossed. We've done this in our family ever since my grandmother saw crossed knives on the table and a telegram arrived soon after to say her son had been wounded. That was in the First World War.

Other signs of bad luck were (or are) when shoe laces snap (Pontnewydd), a calendar is turned forward before the due date (Abertillery), or a live bird enters a house (Newbridge). There are many others, including these from Chepstow, which may well be shared by other localities: to pick up one's own dropped glove, cut nails on a Sunday, point at a rainbow, talk underneath an arch, look into a mirror when someone else is doing so, see hay on the back of a lorry (formerly, a haywain), take bluebells, may blossom, lilac or snowdrops into a house, or open an umbrella there.

Plant Lore and Folk Remedies
In her study of the flowers of the Wye Valley, Alison Bielski has recorded many local names, including bee-in-a-bush (monkshood), black doctor (water figwort), butcher (early purple orchid), candlemas bells (snowdrops, which bloom on or near Candlemas, 2 February), come-and-kiss-me or two-faces-under-one-hat (pansy, a two-coloured flower), crazy (buttercup, to smell which was thought to cause madness), gardener's garters (variegated grass), Jack-in-the-hedge (treacle mustard), lady's laces (hedge parsley), laycock or prince's feather (lilac), love lockets (bleeding heart, which has heart-shaped flowers), old man's beard (southernwood), old woman (French lavender), Queen Mary's pin cushions (scabious), snappers (stitchwort) and Whitsun boss or queen's cushions (guelder rose).

Of these, several had medicinal properties. Black doctor was used for sores and wounds. The bitter seeds of Jack-in-the-hedge were eaten to produce a clear-out of worms. An infusion of the leaves of old man's beard also evacuated worms, and in addition acted as a tonic. Lungwort, known in Monmouthshire as Virgin Mary's milkdrops—from 'the common fancy throughout Europe,' as Geoffrey Grigson puts it, 'that drops of the Virgin's milk or the Virgin's tears had fallen on the leaves and spotted them'—was infused and drunk for a cough or catarrh.

During the First World War, people gathered quantities of sphagnum moss from the steep and winding valley of the Cleddon Brook, a tributary of the Wye, for use in dressing the wounds of both horses and men on the battlefields. This remedy, first recorded in 1014, is recognised by modern medicine.

Cleddon Falls

Self-heal (wood sanicle), according to a herbal of 1578, makes 'whole and sound all wounds and hurts, both inward and outward.' Its Welsh name is *craith unnos*, one-night scar. The plant was gathered in June because of the belief that its power would be lost if it were collected during the Dog Days, the period between 9 July and 14 August.

The house leek is not really a leek at all; its name derives from an Anglo-Saxon expression, meaning house plant, which parallels the Welsh, *llysiau pentai*, cottage herbs. At Chepstow, Rhymney and no doubt elsewhere, juice pressed from its fleshy leaves was used to cure ear ache by pouring it into the ear. At Devauden people used it to soothe sunburn and to remove warts. They also believed that the mere presence of the plant on a house warded off thunder and also witches.

Dwarf elder, known in Welsh as *dawle-gwad-gwyr-marw*, growing from human blood, was thought to sprout in places where blood had been shed such as Caerleon and Raglan. Its juice was considered excellent for swellings or bruises, 'and particularly in diseases peculiar to the female breast.'

The ivy-leafed cyclamen which grows in the steep woods of the Wye Valley was thought to be 'a good amorous medicine', causing anyone who ate small cakes made of its flowers to fall violently in love. However, the plant could induce a miscarriage in a pregnant woman who stepped over it. The tuberous rootstock, relished by pigs, whence the alternative name of sow bread, also had medicinal uses.

Vervain, which fastened friendship and achieved heart's desire, was gathered at the rising of the Dog Star by Welsh magicians with the left hand from ground where honey had been poured in libation, and then cast into a cauldron dedicated to the goddess, Ceridwen. Thanks to its supposed aphrodisiac powers it is known as *Herba veneris*, herb of love. On the other hand, a man who gathered the herb before dawn on the first day of a new moon and drank its juice would keep from love for seven years. One hopes that, while searching for his herb, he did not encounter the naked maiden who in turn went out on a moonlight night to find club moss, whose spores yielded a yellow dust which, according to the Druids, could confer the power of understanding the language of birds and beasts. The same powder is still used by herbalists in treating skin diseases though they do not use the same method of gathering it.

The Druids are also connected with *lili melyn y dwr*, the yellow water lily, which grows along parts of the River Trothy. Its flowers, which have a smell akin to that of brandy, rise above the water's surface at daybreak and sink beneath it at night. The Druids considered the movement as analogous with the death and re-birth of the sun.

In the west of Monmouthshire, miners' wives and daughters carefully collected herbs, wild flowers and berries for use as teas, cordials, medi-

The House Leek

cines and poultices. George Greeves (born in 1910) of Abertyswg provided a long list of infusions:

> nettle as a blood tonic and astringent raspberry, for migraine
> dandelion for nervous disorders and stomach trouble, and also as a tonic for the liver
> red sage as a throat gargle
> eye-bright leaf for sore eyes and styes
> camomile flower for feverish attacks and as a cure for boils
> narrow-leaved plantain [?ribwort] or mouse's ear [?hawkweed] for whooping cough
> rosemary for hair condition
> holly berries for asthma, rheumatism and gout
> holly leaves for stomach complaints, whooping cough and measles

Greeves adds that holly tea was thought to give additional strength and endurance, particularly during the hard months of winter. Older miners remembered that bunches of holly were sent to newly-weds as tokens of good wishes and congratulations. Some kept holly berries in the house to protect its occupants from 'the woodland spirits'.

Many of the treatments derived from herbs have been shown to be beneficial and after falling into disuse for many decades are increasingly favoured once more. Other curative methods owed more to desperation.

Bathing in salt water was thought to cure or prevent hydrophobia (rabies). In 1731, the hounds of the Monmouthshire pack were dipped in the sea near Newport to protect them from the disease. During a local scare at Chepstow in 1863, people dashed to bathe, and even a donkey believed to be infected was immersed 'till quite powerless'. A century later a local woman told Ivor Waters that 'A man suspected of possible infection ... was put into the salt water and towed about in the Severn at the stern of a boat.' If he were in fact suffering from rabies this must have been sheer torture. Dust ground from stones from the tump at Mynyddislwyn was also used to combat hydrophobia, though exactly how is unclear.

Less terrifying than the water treatment for rabies, but still bizarre, were attempts to cure a bleeding nose by tying one's left garter round a copy of the Bible, or to remove corns by immersing one's feet in the Mounton Brook, near Chepstow. Water does indeed have therapeutic powers (see chapter 5), though one doubts its efficacy in this instance noted in 1914:

> By the gate of St Woolos Church [Newport] there used to be a very old tree that was hollow inside. The water used to ooze through the bark and stand in the hollow parts and was then supposed to have healing properties. The little girls of the district used to bring their dolls and christen them in the water on Sunday mornings.

Thomas Jones (1870-1955) wrote of a doctor summoned to a small house in Rhymney where a child was ill with pneumonia. When he was shown in:

> The stench about the bed was such that he threw back the clothes and found the lungs of a sheep against the feet of the child, placed there, the grandmother explained, to draw into them the poison from the child's lungs.

A similar technique, using sheep's lights, was reported as successful in 1925 at Abergavenny, where another grandmother predicted that as inflammation went from the stricken child holes would appear in the lights—'And this is what happened.'

Still in Abergavenny, 100 years ago, a young girl was taken to a neighbouring parish to have warts cured on her neck by the nine times application of a dead man's hand. For a boy, a dead woman's hand would have been needed. The profusion of cures for warts reflects a widespread problem which can be intractable even for modern medicine. Warts could be sold, dipped in water previously used to quench a red-hot horse-shoe, or rubbed with the inside of a bean pod which was then buried. Alternatively, if the sufferer carved his or her initials on a tree the wart would disappear as the bark re-grew.

In 1937 the *South Wales Argus* published a list of cures which included the advice to rub on the wart a piece of raw beef, half an apple, or some hot bread, and then bury the item; or a piece of bacon and then hang it on the clothes line. Another expedient was to take a penny to a woman in a certain shop at Newbridge; she would rub it over the affected part, saying, 'Warts, warts on your hand, / I'll bury you in the sand,' and would then bury the coin in her garden. A remedy used at Pontypool consisted of rubbing on a mixture of lard and salt, for two or three nights before going to bed.

Fred Hando tells the story of a Newport boy taken by his mother to an old woman famed as a healer. The backs of his hands were disfigured by many warts. The healer said: 'Take the boy to the first cross-roads on Cardiff road. Let him pluck a twig from the hedge and, with his back towards his home, throw the twig over his right shoulder.' This was done. Next morning the warts had disappeared.

Healers and Charmers

Christchurch stands on a hill between Caerleon and Newport. Inside the building there is a tombstone, that of John Colmer and his wife, Isabella, both of whom died in 1376—though nothing further is known of them. Even so, for several centuries people were convinced that the Colmer Stone possessed near miraculous healing powers.

A revel or wake was held in the churchyard every Corpus Christi Day, a movable feast also called Trinity Thursday (since it followed Trinity Sunday, which in turn is the Sunday after Whitsuntide). At sunset the previous day sufferers went into the church and were locked in for the night, which they spent lying on the stone, or at least resting a limb on it if the press were too great. It was believed that the vigil would charm away the diseases of those present.

E. Donovan, 'author of the *British Zoology*, in twenty volumes, &c.', observed this 'visitation' in 1804 and described it as a 'religious farce', commenting:

Penance being made on the Colmer Stone

THE FOLKLORE OF MONMOUTHSHIRE

The Colmer Stone

We may conceive the number of poor deluded people, who formerly paid their devotions to this gravestone, was very great: of late years, even, so many as two and twenty persons, including both sexes, adults and children, have been known to lie either upon the stone, or the pavement round it, and in some manner touching it: a leg or an arm lying in contact with it, being thought sufficient to work the cure when the case is not very desperate.

Donovan also remarked that in the mid-18th century, Squire Van of Llanwern, who was presumably patron of the living at Christchurch, had ordered, in an attempt to suppress the ritual, that on the eve of Corpus Christi the church doors should be locked, and no one admitted:

> This was performed accordingly, when, marvellous to relate, at the hour of midnight the bells began ringing of themselves, and continued to alarm the whole country with their deep, incessant peals, till the dawn of morning, after which they ceased. The delinquent, fully convinced that he had acted against the will of Heaven, from this awful warning, could not possibly believe that any wicked rogue had secreted himself in the church to play the trick upon him, but expressing a due sense of contrition for the offence, protested he would never more be accessory, in any manner, to the abolition of this tolerated practice.

A rather less elaborate healing ritual, reported from Newbridge in 1954, consisted of passing a small boy through a horse's legs to cure him of whooping cough. Some 20 years earlier a 'forest man', presumably from Wentwood, said that for the same complaint children were passed nine times through the arch made by a bramble which had rooted at both ends. The source of this story is T.A. Davies, a remarkable man, the son of a miner, fluent in Welsh, keen on Sunday cricket, and vicar of Llanishen for 50 years from 1898.

Not far away, in the Trellech area, Mrs Briton told the young Beatrix Wherry in 1903 that one of her children suffered a rupture as a baby. Many remedies were tried—unsuccessfully, as one might have expected, since surgery could well have been needed. However, a cure was effected. On the advice of a charmer the mother took the infant at midnight on a Friday to a maiden ash ('one grown from its own seed and never touched with a knife'), which had been split and wedged open the previous night. In silence, the baby was passed nine times back and forth through the tree, which was then bound up. As the ash healed, so did the child.

Mountain ash was thought to repel witches, and some people carried a piece to ward off fairies. A kind of amulet known in Glamorgan and Monmouthshire as *maen magl*, stye stone, was employed to treat ailments

Memorial window in Llanishen Church to Rev. T.A. Davies

of the eye. The snakestone, as it was otherwise called—it was made of opaque glass, the colouring of which recalled that of a snake—was simply revolved across the eyelids; alternatively, the eye could be bathed with water in which the stone had been steeped.

A verbal formula written on a piece of paper might also bring about a cure. T.A. Davies's parishioners told him that the antidote to toothache could be sewn into her bodice by a woman or pocketed by a man. As long as the words were legible the charm would remain effective. A copy survived on the flyleaf of a Bible:

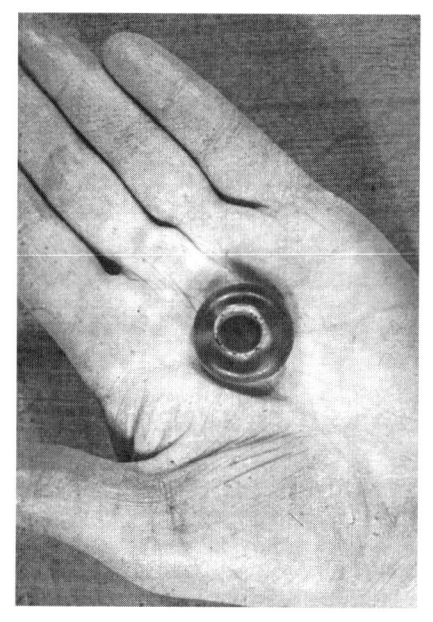

The Snakestone (Roger Davies)

> Jesus came to Peter as he stood at the gate of Jerusalem and said unto him: 'What doest thou here?' Peter answered and said unto Jesus, 'Lord, my teeth do ache.' Jesus answered and said unto Peter, 'That whosoever carry these words in memory with them, or near them, shall never have the teeth ache any more.'

A 19th century version now in the National Library of Wales headed 'A vers to ease the Tooth ake', is shown opposite. It reads:

> Petter lying by the gates of
> Jerusalem, serving greiff and
> Jesus came by and said why dost
> thou lye hear vexing greiff.
> Petter answered and said my teeth
> doth ake So that i can not take
> no rest nor Sleep. Jesus said
> thy health i will give thee
> and to all that carry these lines
> In the name of the Father
> and, Son and Holy Ghost

SICKNESS & HEALTH

> A vers to ease the Tooth ake
> Petter lying by the gates of
> Jerusalem, Jesus come by and
> Jesus came by and said why dost
> thou lye hear weeping grieff.
> Petter ansewred and said my teeth
> doth ake so that i can not take
> no rest nor sleep. Jesus said
> thy health i will giue thee
> and to all that carey these lines
> in the name of the Father
> and Son and Holy Ghost.

As early as the 12th century Geoffrey of Monmouth was writing of 'a certain Welshman who could explain the occult and foretell the future.' His name was Meilyr, and his skill derived from a painful experience which happened somewhere near Caerleon, where he lived:

> One evening, and, to be precise, it was Palm Sunday, he happened to meet a girl whom he had loved for a long time. She was very beautiful, the spot was attractive, and it seemed too good an opportunity to be missed. He was enjoying himself in her arms and tasting her delights, when suddenly, instead of the beautiful girl, he found in his embrace a hairy creature, rough and shaggy, and, indeed, repulsive beyond words.

The understandable shock drove Meilyr out of his wits for several years but when he recovered he was able to see 'unclean spirits'. It is not

WELSH Fortune-Teller,

THE

OR,

Sheffery Morgan's Observation of the Stars, as he sat upon a Mountain in *Wales*
To the Tune of, *Touch of the Times*.

> Since arrival, Proclaiming and Crowning is o're,
> And song upon song made, what wou'd you have more,
> Why yet after all, I a Prophesie bring.
> 'Tis writ here in Verses for Lasses to Sing;
> And therefore come buy this new Ditty, for why,
> The truth of this Story there's none can deny;
> We see by the Stars that promotion will be,
> Extended to persons of e'ery degree.
>
> When we are united all over the Land,
> Resolving against all the Romans to stand,
> Under the protection of William our King,
> And pay our Allegiance in every thing;
> And Protestant Boys, with a thund'ring noise,
> Has routed Tyrconnel, and all his Dear-Joys,
> Then all these three Kingdoms will flourish again,
> And we shall be blest with a prosperous Reign.

Part of an English ballad sheet, showing the commonly held view of the Welsh as wizards and necromancers

recorded whether he foresaw his own death, which occurred in 1174 during the capture of Usk Castle by Richard de Clare, earl of Pembroke.

It became a stereotype for the English that the Welsh were wizards and necromancers: one thinks of Shakespeare's view of Owain Glyn Dwr (see chapter 2). 'The Welsh Fortune Teller', a ballad published in London in the late 17th century, purports to give 'Sheffery Morgan's Observation of the Stars, as he sat upon a Mountain in Wales.' An illustrative woodcut shows goats, mountains, and a man (probably meant to be Cadwaladr) wearing a high, leek-crowned hat, and spitting a piece of toast with his dagger (to symbolise his incompetence as a soldier).

SICKNESS & HEALTH

Of course, there were charmers in Wales, as there were in England. Edmund Jones mentions several, including Rhisiart Cap Du (Richard of the Black Cap), who was well known in Aberystruth. Rhisiart gave advice to those who felt themselves to be suffering at the hands of fairies, though his neighbours believed that he himself was in the habit of leaving his house through a big hole in the thatch to join the fairies by night. One man who took to his bed, thinking that the fairies had caused him to ail, threw a stone weight at Rhisiart when he visited him, and said: 'Thou old villain wast one of the worst of them to hurt me.'

A contemporary of Rhisiart's, Charles Hugh of Coed y Paen in the parish of Llangybi, was famous for effecting cures and for discerning things which happened at a distance. An Aberystruth man, Henry John Thomas, worried about his sweetheart's health, took a sample of her urine to Charles Hugh, who greeted him with these words: 'Ha! you've come with your sweetheart's water to me.'

A Dr John Charles, active during the second half of the 19th century in Trosnant and Pontypool, was suspected of being in league with the devil

The Horse and Jockey at Llanfihangel Pont-y-moel

and also of being acquainted with 49 witches (an oddly precise number) between Pontypool and Blaenafon. One day in the Cross Keys Inn at Pontypool he asked for a pinch of snuff from Shonny Shon Isaacs of Cefn Crib and Hafodyrynys. When the old man got home and opened the box again hundreds of flies poured out and filled the whole house. Apparently this was a punishment inflicted by the doctor because of Shonny's inveterate cursing and swearing. In another public house, the Horse and Jockey at Llanfihangel Pont y Moel, Charles put a spell on the landlord, Tom Davies, because he felt that he had been overcharged for his bread, cheese, beer and tobacco.

A similar story is told of Jenkyns of Tregare, a well known conjuror who died in about 1900:

> One day old Jenkyns was going down town, an' 'e stopped at a public, the Cock and Feather [at Grosmont], to get some refreshment. 'E asked for bread an' cheese an' beer; when 'e'd finished 'e asked low much it was. 'Oh', says the landlady, 'let's see, six an' four's ten, that's tenpence, please.' Jenkyns said 'twas too much, but 'e paid 'is tenpence an' went off.
>
> Presently the 'ooman came back into the room an' went up to the place where Jenkyns had been sitting, an' calls out, 'Six an' four's ten, here's off agen.' An' she started runnin' round the table, an' when she came back to Jenkyns' place she called out again, 'Six an' four's ten, here's off agen.' An' started runnin' round agen. Presently 'er daughter came in an' seed 'er mother runnin' round the table an' callin' out, so she knowed she'd got a spell on 'er.

Tregare at dusk in winter

She went on like that for an hour and a half, then 'er son came back from work an' seed 'is mother runnin' round the tables callin' out, 'Six an' four's ten, here's off agen.' So he said, 'Why, mother, what's the matter?' An' she says, 'Oh, I don't know! Six an' four's ten, here's off agen.' So 'e said to 'is sister. ''As so-and-so been 'ere?' an' she said 'e 'ad, an' 'e said, ''Ow long's 'e been gone?' an' she said, 'Two hour.'

So 'e went an' caught old Jenkyns an' tells 'im what was wrong, 'an Jenkyns says, 'Serve 'er right for chargin' a poor man tenpence for a bit o' bread an' cheese. But,' 'e says, 'you go an' look under a candlestick on your mantelpiece; there you'll see a bit of paper. Don't you look at it or it'll be the worse for you, but throw it in the fire. An' I hope this'll be a lesson to yer mother.'

So the son went home, an' there was 'is mother, still runnin' round an' callin' out, ,'Six an' four's ten, here's off agen.' 'E ran to the chimney-piece, there was the paper, and 'e throwed it in the fire; 'is mother dropped into a chair, all exhausted like. An' it served 'er right.

In telling this to Beatrix Wherry Mrs Briton became so involved in the narrative that she rushed round the table, shouting 'Six an' four's ten, here's off agen', and was exhausted herself at the end. She later remembered another story of when Jenkyns 'was comin' up from Monmouth, and just on the pitch by the station [possibly Troy Station, near Mitchel Troy] was four horses strugglin' an' strainin' to drag a great piece of timber up the hill.' Despite the waggoners' best efforts the load was in danger of pulling the horses backwards. Jenkyns intervened:

He up an' shouts, 'Unhitch the fore horse!' So they unhitched 'im, 'cos nobody dared disobey anything that Jenkyns told them to do. 'Now hitch 'im on behind,' 'e said; an' so they hitched 'im on behind. Then Jenkyns took the whip, cracked it, an' shouted, 'Now, me lads, all together!' An' would you believe it, them 'orses that couldn't move a step before, galloped up the hill like a top spinnin', an' the leader dancin' behind!

Mrs Briton's friend, Mrs Pryce, remembered Jenkyns as an oldish man with a long dark beard, stooping, and walking with a stick. She greatly missed him when he died: 'Why, Jenkyns 'as been a comfort to me all my life. If I ever 'ad a pain of any sort, if I'd go to Jenkyns 'e'd always take it away. Anything that were lost, in all the countryside 'e'd always find it.' He could charm away toothache, and indeed other pain. Mrs Pryce provided an example of his skill in retrieving lost items. A young man on his way to Monmouth to see the races spots cattle intruding in one of his fields, and hangs his jacket on a gate while he drives them out. When he comes back he finds the jacket gone. He goes to Jenkyns and tells him that he suspects a certain woman. 'That 'ooman won't rest till she come an' put your coat back where she took'd it from,' says Jenkyns; and so it happens. Jenkyns insists on punishing the thief by causing a black mark shaped like a button-hole to appear on her cheek, near the eye. 'An' many a time have I seen that mark,' says Mrs Pryce. She adds that Jenkyns punished four men and women for stealing a farmer's cider by making them dance frenetically for two hours on the green, until he relented and took the spell off.

Writing some 30 years after Beatrix Wherry, T.A. Davies supplied many other stories of Jenkyns, which he obtained from a farmer at Llangeview, near Usk. A man nicknamed Toadskin manages to offend the conjuror while consulting him. As a result Jenkyns puts him into fits of fright and makes him believe that as he is on his way home to Gwernesey an evil spirit 'with open mouth and great claws' is after him. When a woodman loses a watch Jenkyns tells him to go back to the place where he was working and that he will find it there hanging by its chain on a bush. He does. A cottager at Llanbadoc loses a flitch of bacon. He is told to wait in his unlit kitchen on a certain night with some friends, to see the flitch returned. Two men and two women come, bringing the meat, which has been cut into two pieces, and hang it in its former place.

Despite his authority, and also suggestions that he had affiliations with the devil (see chapter 3), Jenkyns was tested by a sceptical young man, a shoemaker, who believed that he had fooled many people. The man took a wheel which Jenkyns had just made—he was a wheelright and cider seller—and hid it in a bush. Jenkyns searched for the wheel, but it only turned up when some passers-by came across it a fortnight later. Davies also writes of Nicholas Johnson, a Devauden charmer of the late 19th century, who could staunch bleeding and stop toothache by giving the sufferer a Bible text to read, or by reading it for him if he were illiterate. He could also 'make a small oak tree grow suddenly in his kitchen, and when the acorns fell would produce a sow and litter to come in and eat the acorns, much to the annoyance of his wife.' This was conjuring in the sense of sleight of hand; Jennifer Westwood observes: 'One can still watch this trick being performed in India, where it is done by means of a series of mango trees, at different stages of development, growing in identical earthenware pots, deftly substituted for one another.'

Like Jenkyns, Johnson was believed to have connections with the devil, as Davies records:

> On one occasion, when he was at an inn at Wentwood, he boasted to the half drunken men there that if they would come with him into Wentwood, at dusk, he would show them His Majesty. When they got to the wood the conjuror drew a ring, began to read from a book, and told his companions that when the Devil appeared, they were to join him in reading the book backwards or the Devil would get them. Presently there was the clink of chains, and the Evil One appeared with horns and hoof and tail—in the orthodox manner—and the half drunken men were so frightened that they could neither read nor run. But luckily for them the conjuror managed somehow to get through the words of the book backwards and the Devil had to go off without his victims.

The practice of doing things backwards seems to have excited a particular feeling. Church bells rung in reverse order signalled fire:

Llanishen Church

Newchurch

> When backwards rung we tell of fire;
> Think how the world shall thus expire.

A Caerwent charmer tried unsuccessfully to cure a Llanishen man of 'defective intellect' by making him walk downstairs backwards nine times for nine steps and anointing his forehead with oil at each step. A woman charmer, Mary Ann Locke, lived during the 1920s at Newchurch in a house called Cat's Cradle (previously known as Yew Tree Cottage). People in the locality thought it wise to avoid offending 'Mother' Locke. One farmer who declined to buy her remedy for his ailing pigs—rainwater at twopence a time—found that the animals died. Another complained that she was damaging his hedge as she gathered nuts. 'Ah, well', she said, 'this hedge will not trouble you long.' It died that winter. When Locke was serving at the Mason's Arms in Devauden a haulier she disliked happened to pass. She promptly put a spell on his horses, which then refused to carry on down the Trap Pitch. The man had to unhitch them and take them home, but the following morning they went down the hill with no trouble at all.

George Greeves relates that miners' wives visited fortune tellers not only to try to see the future but to protect themselves from bad luck,

SICKNESS & HEALTH

The Mason's Arms, Devauden, with Trap Pitch to its right

curses, malign spirits, and the evil eye. They would wear amulets, have their ears pierced and rings fitted (which sailors also did to avert ill-luck), fix horseshoes above doors and carry horseshoe nails in their pocket.

Such expedients had intangible power, but the work of bonesetters required skill and judgment. Some only treated animals. For example, Thomas Jones from Cardiganshire cured pigs of an apparently intractable disease while he was visiting Rhymney. His son, Thomas Rocyn Jones, settled in the area, and extended his ministrations to human beings. He was especially skilful in treating fractures, dislocations and muscular problems. One dark night as he walked home from Dowlais Top to Rhymney he was attacked by two men who probably meant to rob him. He fought them off. Next day one of them turned up at his surgery in Rhymney Bridge for treatment to an injured shoulder. He received the appropriate manipulation, though 'perhaps with a little more vigour than was actually necessary.' When T.R. Jones died in 1877 he enjoyed such esteem that a monument was erected over his grave by public subscription.

One of his sons, David Rocyn Jones, carried on the practice:

> He achieved as great a reputation as his father, and as far as one can judge was as skilful a bone-setter as his father and grandfather before him. From my own personal observation of him I can testify

that he was extraordinarily dexterous as a manipulator, with a sure instinct for the right type of case that was likely to benefit by manipulation. He had powerful arms and wrists, and was very quick both in his movements and in his thinking. In addition he was no mean musician, had a good tenor voice, and was secretary and choirmaster at Moriah chapel. His services for many years were in great request as a bone-setter, and he was frequently called professionally over the border to the English counties of Gloucester, Wiltshire and Shropshire.

So writes the (unrelated) Thomas Jones in his book, *Rhymney Memories*, to which I am indebted for details of the remarkable dynasty of bonesetters. D.R. Jones died in 1915. His three sons became respectively Medical Officer of Health for Monmouthshire, an orthopaedic surgeon in Harley Street, and a bonesetter in South Wales. Perhaps the fifth generation of this gifted family is still involved in medical care, either orthodox or complementary.

Curious relief on an outbuilding by the Mason's Arms, Devauden

CHAPTER 7

Life & Death

The two certainties in everyone's existence, birth and death, are landmarks which inevitably attract accretions of ritual and belief. Tangible reminders of birth are less obvious than those of death, with its wealth of monuments. Arthur Machen looked longingly back in his mind's eye from exile in London to 'the old graveyards of Gwent, solemn among the swelling hills, peaceful in the shadow of very ancient yews.' He particularly remembered Henllys, high on the mountainside, and its 'graves with flourished inscriptions, deeply cut, and queer Welsh rhymes.' He also reflected yearningly on 'the churchyard of Llanddewi [Fach], looking down the steep hillside into the chanting valley of the Soar, and Kemeys, between the Forest [of Wentwood] and the Usk, and Patrishw, in the heart of the wild mountains beyond Abergavenny.' One could list many, many more. The institution of marriage, not surprisingly, also attracted its share of stories and customs.

Marriage Guidance
Young Dick Jones of Dingestow Court had no hesitation in choosing a 60 year-old widow as his bride: she possessed a fortune. A friend of his commented in verse:

>Tho' odd to some it seems
>That one threescore you ventur'd;
>Yet in ten thousand pounds
>Ten thousand charms are centr'd.

THE FOLKLORE OF MONMOUTHSHIRE

Others looked for guidance to traditional signs. Two spoons on one saucer pointed to a marriage or a birth, believed one Newbridge family. A woman from Newport wrote in 1961:

> When I was at school I envied three classmates whose hair was so long they could sit on it, but my grandmother quoted: 'With hair below the knee / Ne'er a bride will she be.' That was 25 years ago and, although their hair is now short, those three girls are still spinsters.

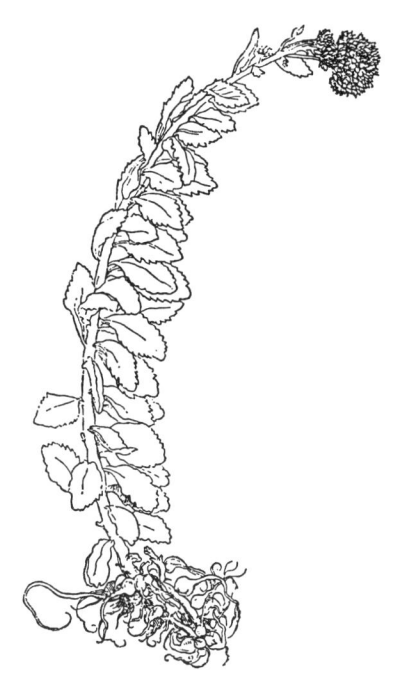

Orpine

At Llanthony and Cwmyoy they said that a girl who poked the fire too often would die an old maid, and that if she splashed too much when washing, her future husband would turn out to be a drunkard. To foretell the course of true love people took two of the flowers known as midsummer men (or orpine, *Sedum telephium*), and chose one to represent a young woman, one her suitor. The blooms were fixed in clay over the door lintel and left all night. In the morning, if both stood straight it showed that the man and woman did not care for one another; if one leaned while the other remained unmoved, one person cared but the other remained indifferent; whilst if they bent towards each other a wedding would follow within the year. John Aubrey noticed the same procedure with a final twist, in 17th century Wiltshire:

> I remember, the mayds (especially the Cooke mayds and Dayrymayds) would stick-up in some chinkes of the joists, etc., Midsommer-men, which are slips of Orpins. They placed them by paires, so: one for such a man, the other for such a mayd his sweetheart, and accordingly as the Orpin did incline to, or recline from the other, that there would be love or aversion; if either did wither, death.

In the area north of Blaenafon a divination ritual involved placing a large key on the first chapter of the Book of Ruth in the Bible, then closing the volume and binding it with the garter from the left leg of the girl making the enquiry. Two other girls then put their fingers into the key's loop and let the Bible hang down from it. If the Bible turned as they recited a special verse it meant that their friend would marry the man she had in mind. If the book fell there would be no marriage.

This account unfortunately omits the formula uttered. In Devon it was simply a reading from Ruth, chapter 1, beginning 'Intreat me not to leave thee, or to return from following after thee: for whither thou goest I will go', and so on. In Berkshire, 'If -- begins my true love's name, May the Bible turn round and do the same.'

One way or another, most people were anxious to be married. A cautionary tale explains why a handsome woman is married to an ugly little man. Her maid one day summons the resolve to ask why, but instead of answering the mistress gives her a sharp knife and tells her to go to the wood: 'Take the path through it and cut me the straightest stick you can find, but you must cut it as you go; you must not turn back, and the first stick you cut you must bring.' After a time the girl comes back with a gnarled and crooked stick. 'Is this the straightest you saw?' asks the mistress. 'No,' says the maid. 'Many a good straight stick I saw, but when I went to cut it I thought I'd see a better one further on. Suddenly I was at the end of the wood and this was the only stick left.' 'Now', says the mistress 'you have the answer to the question you asked me.' The story came from a Monmouthshire woman.

Weddings

During the 19th century, at Blaenau, Nant-y-glo, Rhymney, Tredegar and elsewhere, after the reading of marriage banns friends of the bride and groom-to-be were invited to a *pastai*—the word means pasty—at a local public house where cooked pies and beer were served at so much a head. The celebration could continue for two or three days or even a week, and the money raised helped the couple to set up house.

Sometimes the *pastai* carried on after the wedding. Families which considered themselves to be 'better class' would send out a printed invitation, known as a 'bid'. A contributor to the *Gentleman's Magazine*, who had spent the year 1783 living in Chepstow, explained:

There is an ancient custom in some parts of South Wales, which is, I believe, peculiar to that country, and still practised at the marriages of servants, trades-folks, and little farmers. It is called a *bidding*, and is of real use. For before the wedding an entertainment is provided to which all the friends of each party are *bid*, or invited, and to which none can fail to bring or send some contribution from a cow or a calf down to half a crown or a shilling. Nor can this be called absolutely a present, because an account of each is kept, and if the young couple do well, it is expected that they should give as much at any future bidding of their generous guests. I have frequently known of £50 being thus collected; and have heard of a bidding which produced even a hundred, to a couple who were much beloved by their neighbours; and therefore enabled to begin the world with comfort.

The wording of bidding letters varied little, save for details of time and place. This example was printed in 1937 in the *South Wales Argus*:

Cwmcelyn, Blaina.
As we have entered the matrimonial state we are encouraged by our friends to make a bidding at the ---- Inn, in the parish of

Old church, Penallt

LIFE & DEATH

Aberystruth, on Tuesday, where and when the favour of your good and agreeable company is humbly solicited.

Whatever donation you may be pleased to bestow on us, they will be thankfully received, warmly acknowledged, and cheerfully repaid whenever called for on a similar occasion.

By your most obedient servants.

Here the bidding took place after the wedding. On other occasions it took place on the day. 'Should the bride and bridegroom live some distance apart', says an article written in 1846, 'their respective retinues set out early in the morning, headed by a fiddler, whose native music enlivens the journey. They generally contrive to make a half-way meeting, where both parties amalgamate, and proceed directly to church.' It was customary for local young men to hide behind a hedge and, before the party reached the church, 'suddenly fire a salute, much to the consternation of the females in the joyous procession.' Similar gatherings, with up to 40 or 50 couples invited, continued at Tredegar, and possibly elsewhere in Monmouthshire, until the late 19th century.

At Itton, near Chepstow, a sort of mock ransom payable for the bride before she left the church after the ceremony was recorded in 1811. Later, a rope stretched across the road barred the way to the newly-weds until money changed hands; and later still, the best man came suitably furnished with small change which he scattered for bystanders to retrieve.

In the early years of this century at Penallt, four bouquets of flowers tied to the rope were detached after payment of 'toll', and given respectively to the bride, groom, best man and chief bridesmaid. Roping is reported from the same period at Newport and neighbouring villages. The custom is remembered at Trellech and St Arvans. It continued at Devauden until the 1970s and is still kept up at Penallt.

Arches of greenery, placarded with good wishes, were once

Trellech Church

erected at weddings in the Wye Valley. A woman who felt deserted or rejected in favour of another would protest by strewing bunches of rue (thought especially potent if picked in the churchyard) and a half-eaten slice of bread and butter in front of the bride and groom as they emerged from the church into the porch.

Births

According to a long-standing belief, the birth of a baby was always accompanied by the appearance of a shooting star. The choice of names for infants has fluctuated wildly over the years. In the 17th century at Grosmont on the evidence of church registers the favourites for girls were Maudlin (Magdalene), Honory, Betrex (?Beatrix) and Easter. At Rhymney, two centuries on, Thomas Jones recalled the Victorian preference for names drawn from the less familiar chapters of the Bible. 'I remember little Welsh boys and girls', he writes, 'whose parents were so lacking in patriotism as to christen their children Obadiah, Zechariah, Zephaniah, Azariah, Keziah, Keturah, Israel, and Lazarus.' One Baptist minister, he adds, turned instead to the world of science to call his sons Darwin, Huxley and Tyndall. Later generations sought names from the *Mabinogion*; and later still embraced the cosmopolitanism of Eira Nansi Rosemary, Morfudd Priscilla and Alexandrina Myrtle.

The sad story of a boy with no name was told in 1993 by a woman then aged 98. As a servant girl she was seduced by the son of her employers, who then dismissed her with no money and no reference. It took her a week of walking and begging lifts in carts to reach home in Pontypool.

> It was worse when I got home. I had brought shame on the family and I could not go outside the door at all. When I had my boy, no midwife would come, I was all by myself. I bit the cord, it was all by instinct I suppose. My boy was William and he was born with a hare lip. They said it was the mark of Cain for my shame—but I could not see how my shame could be visited on an innocent child. Anyway, babies were not registered in the valleys in those days. You had to take them to the chapel to be churched. Because of my shame, I could not go into the chapel, so officially my boy had no name. All his life he was known as Boy. He did not have an easy life, my boy, with his hare lip, my shame, and no name. He died when he was 32 in the Second World War—bullets did not see stigmas then.

Still referring to her employers' son as 'Mr Henry', she said 'That was my only love affair, but he wanted a *cwtch* you see.'(In Gwentian Welsh, *cwtch* means a cuddle.)

Stern treatment also attended certain misdemeanours within marriage. Until the early years of the 20th century those deemed to be guilty of adultery in Tredegar were tied to a plank and paraded through the streets, accompanied by a jeering crowd, then pelted with stones, mud, manure and rotten eggs. At Chepstow the payment of 10 shillings (50p.) could avoid the ritual; but in 1856 an offender could or would not pay, and so had to suffer. A decade later a punitive procession, headed by a drum and fife band, was halted by the police, and the custom brought to an end.

At least until the 1890s another expression of public disapprobation continued in Monmouthshire. When a husband was known to be beating his wife, straw would be tied round the gate of their house, with the tacit message that he should beat the straw rather than her. One hopes that the community's will proved effective.

Death Omens

A rhyme frequently engraved on church bells is to be found at Skenfrith:

> The living to the church I call,
> And to the grave will summon all.

The reference is to the passing bell formerly rung to announce a death.

A ringer at Monmouth is said to have been killed while adjusting the third bell in St Mary's Church; not knowing that he was working aloft, his brother attempted to ring the bell, with disastrous consequences. The bells at St Bartholomew's Church, Llanofer, also have lugubrious associations. Two maiden ladies at Capel Newydd, a hamlet then in Llanofer Uchaf and now in the parish of Blaenafon, kept their savings in a chest. Eventually they decided that their silver should be used for the benefit of the church, and they carried the coins in their aprons over the mountain, making several journeys to the foundry at Cwmafon where the coinage was cast into bells. When these were installed (and whether this was at Capel Newydd or at St Bartholomew's is unclear, especially as the latter still has five bells) they could be heard 20 miles off, and became known as one of the wonders of Monmouthshire. On Sunday mornings people would climb the Sugar Loaf, Skirrid Fawr, Mynydd Gadair Fawr and Hatterel Hill to hear 'the Llanofer chimes'. One day they rang no more: they had been stolen, and were not recovered. A farmer at Rhyd-y-Meirch commented that Sunday had become like any other day, without the music of the bells. The griefstricken benefactors did not live long afterwards.

The ladies of Llanofer died for lack of sound; but many people considered certain noises to be harbingers of death. Gwenllian Jenkin, some time in the 18th century, heard a mourning bell ring from Nash Church, for no good reason, whilst she was sewing buttons on her father's breeches. Next there came a loud rap at the door, but when she opened it no one was there. Then a tapping sound came from the table, and this caused her to faint. That same evening, Ewythyr Jenkin, her father, came home feeling unwell and died before the next morning.

Nash Church

The *tolaeth* is a name given to the mysterious sound which imitated 'some earthly noise or other, and [was] always heard before either a funeral or some dreadful catastrophe.' Then there was the *cyhyraeth*, which Edmund Jones described as 'a doleful dreadful noise in the night before a burying, and coming the same way as the corpse was to come to church.' At St Mellons,

> One time a boy sent to fetch a horse upon some occasion, heard it crying in the church: he heard it in one place, then in another, and then in the third place where it rested. Some time after a corpse was

brought to the church to be buried, but some person came and claimed the grave; they went to another place, and that was also claimed; they removed to a third place and there had quiet; just the same as the boy declared it.

Jones added that he knew a man who, having heard the sound of a voice rising and falling in pain behind him as he walked home from Abertillery, fell to his death from a tree shortly afterwards.

Signs of impending death included the fall of a picture from the wall and the unexplained breaking of glass. T.A. Davies mentions a sugar basin found split in two, followed next morning by news of a death; a glass is discovered unaccountably broken in a public house of which the landlord dies within a week. The sight of a *canwll corff* (corpse candle) also signified a death. This will o' the wisp-like flame showed by its size and colour the sex, age and even status of the person whose death it presaged. A red flame pointed to a son, grey to a daughter; big to an adult, small to a child; brilliant to someone in the prime of life, faintly glimmering to an aged person.

The sight of a phantom funeral, often associated with the fairies (see chapter 3), could also point to a death. Another doomful phenomenon was the pack of spectral dogs thought to hunt at night for souls destined for perdition as they left the bodies of the damned. Edmund Jones, inevitably has something to say on this subject:

> As Thomas Andrew was coming towards home one night, with some other persons with him, he heard, as he thought, the sound of hunting: he was afraid it was some person hunting the sheep, so he hastened on to meet and hinder them: he heard them coming towards him, though he saw them not: when they came near him, their voices were but small, but increasing as they went from him: they went down the steep towards the river Ebwy, dividing between this Parish [Aberystruth] and Mynyddislwyn, whereby he knew that they were what are called 'Cwn Wybir' (Sky Dogs) but in the inward parts of parts of Wales, 'Cwn Annwn' (Dogs of Hell). I have heard say that these spiritual Hunting Dogs have been heard to pass by the eaves of several houses before the death of someone in the family.

The dogs of Annwn—more properly, of Annwfn, lord of the underworld—go back to ancient Celtic mythology. They are associated with various early deities such as Nodens, god of the Severn Sea, who was worshipped at Lydney. Stories of the 'Hell Hounds' continued well within living memory in connection with Hygga Wood, between Trellech and Llanishen, where an old countryman told T.A. Davies that his parents could summon them by using their conjuror's book; and at Pen y Parc, near St Arvans, where they were seen singly and in packs, each dragging a chain.

There are also reports from Tregare and Penrhos, near Raglan. Thomas Phillips of Trellech heard the hounds, one of which seemed to be leading the others. He was surprised because the way they were travelling was not normally used for burials. However, a short time later a woman from a neighbouring parish died in Trellech, and when her body was taken home for burial the route followed was that traced for Thomas Phillips by the spectral sounds of *cwn annwn*.

Solitary black dogs could also foretell death. One tale records that as people searched for lost cattle at Penallt, when night fell, they came across 'a big, big, black dog, as large as a calf', with eyes shining in the gloom 'like lumps of fire'. One of the search party hit out with a stick, which passed straight through the beast. Realising what they has seen, they immediately drew the conclusion that the children of a woman in the group must have drowned in the Wye and rushed to her house. To their great relief, they found the children safe. However, next day, a telegram arrived with the news of a relative's death in a railway accident.

Birds, too, could be of ill omen. The Seven Whistlers were particularly feared by miners (see chapter 9). At Rhymney until the mid-19th century the *deryn corff* (corpse bird) was believed to signal impending death by metallic chirruping which could turn to dove-like cooing. At Cwmcarfan an old man's niece lay desperately ill for a long time until one night a beautiful white bird came and sang sweetly before tapping at the bedroom window. The girl died next day.

In the same village people positively sought news by divination of coming death. On Midsummer Eve (23 June) they moulded a piece of clay into the shape of a grave in which they stuck pieces of valerian (which locally may be another name for orpine), one for each member of the household. Next morning, those which had collapsed foretold death within the year; those droping, illness; those erect, good health.

Funerals

The churchwardens' accounts for April 1794 at Grosmont provide a good example of how seriously death was taken in Wales. The needy Martha

Williams received 4s. (20p.) during her last illness, of which half went to pay for hurds (the refuse of flax and hemp) for her children to spin. However, her funeral costs ran to 35s. 6d. (£1.72$^{1}/_{2}$p.), which included laying out, sugar (melted and poured on the eyelids to keep them closed), shroud, coffin, eight yards of black crepe, the parish clerk's fee, candles, bread, cheese and ale.

The candles would have been used for the customary purpose of keeping lit at night the room in which the body lay. The food and drink could well have been consumed during the night-watch before the funeral. Such a vigil or wake, *gwylnos* or *wylnos* in Welsh, once preceded every burial. The eating and drinking often led to reminiscence, practical jokes, and games such as blind man's buff (*bwbach dallan*). Edmund Jones complained that night-watches were 'very profanely kept in some parts of Wales', and 'turned the house of mourning into a house of mirth.' He tells of a wake for Meredith Thomas's four year-old son at Bedwellty during which two men ceased to play cards and swear only when they became terrified by ghostly groans outside the house which even the dogs dare not investigate.

The Methodist Revival transformed such disorderly events into earnest prayer-sessions which showed respect for the dead, of whatever status. T.A. Davies, describing such a service as 'an insanitary custom', wrote: 'the kitchen or parlour would be packed with religious neighbours, who stewed for an hour or two in their own juice while one or another of them prayed for the mourners, or they sang sad hymns suitable for such an occasion.'

On the day of the funeral, food would be provided for mourners before the ceremony. 'There was always a buxom, buoyant and managing aunt who took charge and pressed the cold boiled ham on the visitors', wrote Thomas Jones of Rhymney. In the east of the county it was the same for, according to Baker-Gabb in his book, *Hills and Vales of the Black Mountain District*:

> Before leaving the house a meal is provided, of which a homecured ham is usually the staple dish, and care is taken in many farm houses to have a ham always in readiness for such an occasion. After the meal the company are invited to take a last look at the deceased before the coffin lid is fastened down, then the body is carried by the special bearers out of the house and placed upon the bier, around which the company stand. Cake and wine, both of

which have been especially reserved for this part of the ceremony, are then produced, and care is taken to hand them round from east to west, 'the way of the sun', as this is considered to be of the greatest importance. Everyone present is expected to partake, and this is called 'The Last Sacrament'.

In earlier times, as is confirmed by the illustration from *Cambrian Popular Antiquities* (1815), by P. Roberts, food and drink were handed to the poor over the coffin, a custom which may have been a relic of sin-eating. Until the mid-19th century at least, certain people, usually marginal figures, in return for small payments assumed the sins of the deceased by taking bread and salt from a plate on the coffin. 'In a parish near Chepstow,' it was stated in 1852, 'it was usual to make the figure of a cross on the salt, and cutting an orange into quarters, to put one at each termination of the lines.'

Until the Reformation, and in many places long afterwards, the parish sexton led funeral processions with a handbell. A bell of this kind, inscribed '1648 Memento Mori' was formerly preserved in Tregare vicarage. There are references in the churchwardens' accounts at Skenfrith to corse-, herse- and lick-bells (corpse-, hearse- and death-bells), which may be different names for the same thing.

Coffins were sometimes carried over considerable distances by mourners. Once, every able-bodied man had to turn out to take turns in bearing a coffin over Twyn Pentre, the 1,350 foot mountain

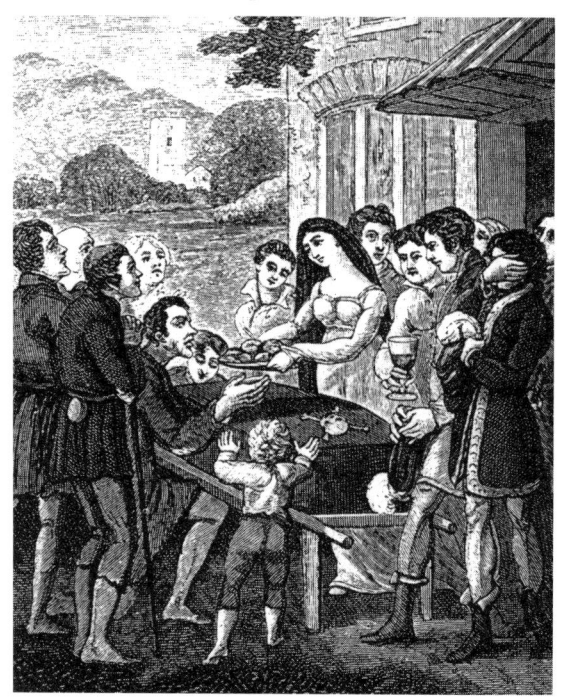

Giving food over the coffin, 1815

which divides Cwmtillery from Abersychan. During times when the chapel at Capel-y-Ffin (described by Kilvert as 'squatting like a stout grey owl among its seven great black yews') was in a state of disrepair, the dead had to be carried some four miles to Llanigon, near Hay-on-Wye. In winter, severe weather could force families to keep bodies for weeks at a time until conditions improved sufficiently to permit the journey.

When the occasion demanded, neighbours appeared, wrote Baker-Gabb, 'in considerable numbers, without any invitation being necessary or expected.' He continued:

> A few of the more intimate friends are invited to act as 'special bearers', their duty being to carry the body from the house to the bier; from the churchyard gate to the church and from the church to the grave. Over the remaining distance the body is carried by those not so specially invited, who are told off by the undertaker from time to time for the purpose, in parties of four, so that every one present may, if possible, bear his share.

Such practices were still remembered by people living in the 1990s:

> In those days when somebody died, it was the neighbours that laid them out. Everyone had to have everything new for a funeral, down to their collar studs. There were no hearses at that time, not even the horse-drawn ones. The undertaker would walk in front of the funeral procession and the men would carry the coffin on a bier. As they walked along, the undertaker would shout 'change' and the four men in front would drop out and the next four would take their place until it was their turn to take it up again.

With walking funerals like this, it is not surprising that from time to time bearers should need to rest. The base of a wayside cross near Trellech (see illustration on page 100) was just such a place. Until a century ago, and possibly later, all funerals which went that way used it as 'a resting cross': 'the bearers carry the corpse from north to south and, resting the coffin on the step on the west side, change bearers and proceed to the church, which is about half a mile distant.' When a funeral approached the other way, from the north, it was the custom until the 1930s for the bier to be rested as soon as the parish church came into view.

At Penallt the bearers and followers paused to sing a hymn or psalm while the coffin rested on 'the base of a cross which was thrown down [in the 17th century] by men crying "No Popery".' The adjacent 'Corpse Tree' is now a horse chestnut.

There was a long-standing belief that to carry a dead body over any land created a right of way. As late as the 1950s, when Newport Council promised to make up a road and charge the residents under the Private Street Works Act, people cudgelled their memories as to whether a corpse had passed that way and so created a 'highway repairable by the public.' Legally speaking, it would have made no difference, but the old belief persisted.

An aversion to burial on the north side of churches also dates back many years. T.A. Davies wrote that people in his area shared it, 'perhaps originally because the devil was supposed to come from the north, and for that reason the gospel used to be always read at the communion or mass with the face of the reader turned north.' In addition, the associations of the south are so much more pleasant. In February 1998, I found two jovial gravediggers at work to the south of the church at Newchurch with the pneumatic drill they needed to cut through the rock which lay so near to the surface of the ground. They told me that a woman from Swansea had just been buried in the next plot, brought back to the peaceful parish of her childhood.

Others sleep less well. The Norman church at Sudbrook is now gone, swallowed by the sea. One of the last interments there, which took place in the mid-18th century, was of a sea captain called Bleddyn Smith. His wish was to be committed to the waters of the Severn where it rushes past Black Rock, but he was dissuaded from this by friends, six of whom attended his burial in the east end of the chancel. However, the Severn claimed him in the end.

The miller at Penarth Mill on the Olway Brook near Llanishen died in the 1840s and was buried at Trellech, perhaps because there was no church at Llanishen at the time—the present building dates only from 1854. His relatives knew that he would have dearly loved to be buried at Llanishen, so in due course they arranged for him to be exhumed and re-interred there. Local tradition maintained that the Llanishen men who carried the body back paused for a drink at the Carpenters Arms. The landlord, himself a carpenter, had the idea of giving the corpse a drink; he proceeded to unscrew the coffin lid and to do so, and hence the rhyme:

LIFE & DEATH

> Who lies here? Old Will
> Of Penarth Mill.
> Let's give him a drink.
> What? Give a dead man a drink?
> 'Cos why?
> When he was alive he was never dry.

At one time, only male mourners were allowed in St Woolos's Churchyard at Newport during an interment. They threw sprigs of rosemary—for remembrance—into the grave, and scattered soil from the Holy Mountain on the coffin. The people who took part in walking funerals all carried flowers with which to deck the deceased's grave, and on it some would plant rose trees. The graves of unmarried men and women were, however, allowed to grow weeds—a sort of protest or prejudice against their failure to marry.

Miss Ann Pritchard: the photograph sent to Queen Victoria (see opposite)

On Sul y Blodau, Flowering Sunday (Palm Sunday), relatives, having carefully tended the graves of their loved ones the previous day, brought wreaths and remembered their dead. During Easter Week and again at Whitsuntide graves received special attention. Relatives made a special point of doing the necessary work with their own hands as an act of piety and remembrance.

The custom of Flowering Sunday seems to have been widespread in the border counties. As recently as 1994, a woman recalled that when she was a child at Oakdale 'Palm Sunday meant chapel and always in our best clothes we trooped to Cwrt-y-bella churchyard to place flowers on family graves.'

Monuments

In the churchyard at Bedwellty is the tombstone of Catherine Dillin, who died in 1859 at the age of 110. Skenfrith boasted several centenarians including Elizabeth Charles, aged 106, who died in 1887. She had only once travelled as far as Hereford, and had never seen a train. 'Granny' Powell died in 1919, her hundredth year. Miss Ann Pritchard, born in 1799. at first declined to be photographed when she reached her century, on the grounds that making 'the likeness of anything that is in heaven above or in the earth beneath' was contrary to scripture, 'and the devil would be sure to have you if there was a likeness to go by.' In the end she relented, and a signed copy of her photograph was sent to Queen Victoria. Miss Pritchard was 'the village poet, and had a rhyme for every occasion.'

Many long-serving parsons are commemorated in Monmouthshire churches. The appropriately-named Theophilus Morgan (died 1886) ministered for 56 years at Oldcastle. Another Morgan, William (died 1827), served as curate and vicar at Llanfihangel Crucorney for 59 years. Archdeacon William Crawley had officiated in the parish of Bryngwyn for 62 years when he died in 1896. This keen cricketer is commemorated by a stone on the tiny green near the little 13th century church. Another cricket lover, Reverend Thomas Arthur Davies, was incumbent at Llanishen from 1898 until 1948 (see above).

Reverend David Powell

LIFE & DEATH

At Llandegfeth, two parsons covered over a century between them: Gibbon Williams from 1740 to 1790, and Thomas Addams-Williams from 1790 until 1842. James Hughes, rector of Llanhiledd, had been in place for 52 years when he died in 1895. The curiously named Francis Chambré Steel (died 1875) is commemorated near the chancel arch in Llanvetherine Church, where he served as curate and rector for 50 years. In the same church there are striking monuments to Reverend David and Mrs Mary Powell. He died in 1621. She sports a high-crowned Welsh hat and wears her wedding ring on the second finger of her right hand, which is worthy of remark because, until 1549, it would have been worn on the fourth finger. Her feet on the flat slab are curiously represented at right-angles to the legs. Dorothy, the wife of Thomas Lewis, another rector here, died in 1734 at the age of 156, says a gravestone now fastened outside the east wall of the church. However, close scrutiny reveals that the first digit has been added by a careful but irreverent hand.

Of all the ancient items preserved in Monmouthshire churches the oldest is perhaps the early second century stone at Tredunnock Church which was originally erected by a loving Roman widow to her late husband, who died at the age of 40 after serving for 18 years in the Second Legion. It addresses in abbreviated Latin not the Christian God but the infernal deities:

Mary Powell

THE FOLKLORE OF MONMOUTHSHIRE

D.M.
Julius Julianus
Mil. Leg. II Aug: Stip. XVIII. anno:
XL., hic situs est cura
agente amanda coniuge

Lower Machen was once a centre for Roman lead mining, brick making and iron forging. In the church vestry is a stone slab found in 1901 on which is carved a face with great staring eyes and a voracious mouth. This has been identified as the Romano-Celtic representation of a gorgon.

Rather later effigies are to be seen in St Mary's Church at Abergavenny. Eva de Braose (died 1246) is shown with a squirrel in her hand, which has given rise to the story that she fell into a well and drowned while trying to catch the animal. Her husband, the last William de Braose, was summarily hanged in 1230 on the orders of Llewelyn the Great whose wife he had seduced. In the same church a recumbent figure with a bull at its feet is thought to be that of the first Sir Edward Neville, lord of Abergavenny in 1450, who was reputed to be so strong that he took a bull by the horns and tore them out of its head.

A cross-legged knight of the 14th century with a dog at its feet was long claimed to be Llewelyn and his dog, Gelert, but the sculpture pre-dates the (fictional) story of the faithful hound by several hundred years. Some effigies of this kind, particularly those made of wood, were carried at the head of the funeral procession of the person depicted. Such was the case with that of another lord of Abergavenny, George de Cantelupe, who died in 1273.

The wooden carving of Jesse, father of King David, in St Mary's Church, Abergavenny

Green Man, Llantilio Crosseny

The greatest of the church's treasures, though, is the magnificent 15th century carved wood representation of Jesse, father of King David.

Another David, ap Hywel, a 15th century prince and warrior, may have been buried beneath the great stone marked with a cross of battle axes in low relief which is kept in the church at Llangattock-nigh-Usk. A mutilated stone figure at Magor in the church known as the Cathedral of the Moors—the moors hereabouts being the coastal plain—is supposed to be that of the original founder, but is familiarly called 'Old George'.

The same church has a green man carving. Another example in the north chapel at Llantilio Crosseny looks slightly drunk, with tongue lolling from half-open mouth and dark nose looking as though it would be red in colour if it were not made of stone. There are three more at Llangwm Uchaf on the imposts of the chancel arch just behind the extravagantly-carved rood screen. Lady Raglan wrote in 1939 of one of these specimens:

It is now about eight years ago since my attention was first drawn by the Revd J. Griffith, then vicar of Llangwm, in Monmouthshire, to a curious carving. It is a man's face, with oak leaves growing from the mouth and ears, and completely encircling the head. Mr Griffith suggested that it was intended to symbolise the spirit of inspiration but it seemed to me certain that it was a man and not a spirit, and moreover that it was a 'Green Man'. So I named it ...

Green Man, Llangwm

For Lady Raglan the Green Man was a figure from May Day celebrations. In a recent book Eric Wood suggests that it 'symbolised the unity of human beings with the natural world, and also spring and resurrection; it may also be an echo of the Celtic cult of the head, a symbol of power.' The anonymous author of the current guide to Llangwm Church, hinting at fertility rites and paganism, suggests that 'the good Christian men' who built St Jerome's were 'hedging their bets just in case there was something valuable in the Old Ways that should not be neglected and thereby bring disaster.'

In fact foliate heads, as they are called, go back to Roman times, but when St Bernard castigated them he complained not that they were pagan, but grotesque, silly and expensive. Whatever the truth of their origin and significance, they continue to exercise a mysterious attraction and to

LIFE & DEATH

arouse widely different responses, including this, from the guide to St Jerome's church.

> What do you Green Men have to tell,
> Whose sightless eyes our spirits quell?
> 'From our dead lips the oak branch grows,
> And to you who fear, this green branch shows
> That even from death a new life flows.
> And for that promise give thanks to God
> In this lonely *cwm* where the Romans trod.'

If the Green Men remain ambiguous there is no doubting the message of frescoes in some Monmouthshire churches. At Skenfrith there are traces of a doom painting over the chancel arch; round the window in the east wall of the south aisle, the lower part of a demon, a cask and a wheel may be vestiges of a depiction of the torments of the damned. Equally menacing is the gaunt skeleton of time, with scythe, spade and hour glass at Partricio. Worshippers once believed that the red pigment used to paint it was human blood, and hence indelible.

In the church at Llangybi the walls must once have blazed with colours showing Christ as patron of tradesmen. There is also a pictorial warning against sabbath breaking. On the north wall of the nave is St Christopher, patron of travellers. A person making a journey would have gone to the church to ask for a safe

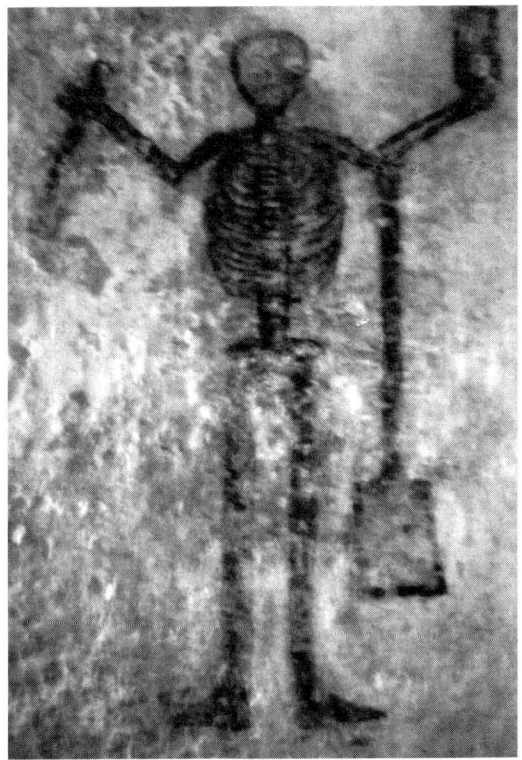

Wall painting of Time at Partricio

167

return, and as he left by the south door would have cast a final backward glance to see the reassuring figure of St Christopher.

Epitaphs

Outside the north wall of the same church is the grave of William Watkins of Cefn Llech Cottage, his wife and their three young children, who were stabbed to death one July evening in 1878. Joseph Garcia, a Spanish sailor aged 21, was released that day from Usk Prison after serving a sentence for burglary, and on his way to Newport to find a homeward-bound ship he stopped to ask for a drink of water at a cottage. When this was refused he murdered the whole family, stole some clothes, and set the place on fire. Garcia, when he was arrested, fiercely denied involvement in the crime, yet he had some of William Watkins's clothes in his possession. After being found guilty he was hanged at Usk. The case featured in printed ballads in English ('Trial and Sentence of Garcia for the Terrible Murder of a Family in Wales'), Welsh ('Cân Llofruddiaeth Llangybi', Llangybi Murder Song) and in both languages in a single booklet:

COFFADWRIAETH GALARUS

> Am y gyflafan ofnadwy a gyflawnwyd ar deulu yn Llangibby, Sir Fynwy, Nos Fawrth, yr 16eg o Gorphenaf, 1878, yn cynwys Tad a Mam a Thri o blant sef William Watkins ac Elizabeth ei wraig, y ddau tua 44 oed, a'u plant, sef Charlotte, wyth mlwydd oed; Frederick, yn bump; ac Alice, yn bedair blwydd oed. Cafwd y gwr a'r wraig yn gorwedd yn yr ardd, tua phedair llath y naill oddiwrth y'llall, a'u gyddfau wedi ei tori, ac amryw archollion eraill ar ei cyrph; a'r plant i fynu y grisiau, un tan y gwelu, a dau ar y gwelu, y tri wedi cael yr un driniaeth a'u rhieni. Ymddengys fod y ty wedi ei osod ar dân, mewn tri o fanau, ac yr oedd y plant wedi llosgi yn druenus.

> 1 Y Cymry hoff o rinwedd,
> Rwyf yn eich galw mlaen,
> Dewch a byddwch astyd
> I wrandaw geiriau'r gân,
> S'yn traethu am y camwedd
> Ar deulu a fu'n byw,
> Mewn anedd yn Llangibby;
> O fewn i fynwy wyw.

LIFE & DEATH

2 Ond ar nos fawrth mae'n galed
   I draethu hyn i chwi:
Rhyw spaniard a ddaeth heibo,
   Sef llofrudd, creulon cry,
   A hyrddio William Watkins
     A wnaeth ef yno'n awr,
   Pan oedd yn bwyta'i swper
    I'r tragwynddoldeb mawr.

3 Ar ol Llofruddio William,
   Ei daflu wnaeth i'r ardd:
Y wraig oedd yno'n gwaeddi
   Fy mhriod hawddgar hardd;
   A chyn pen fawr fynydau
     Y llofrudd ddaeth i'r lle,
   A hyrddio Eliza Watkins
    I wyddfod Brenin Ne'.

4 Y plant oedd yn eu gwely
   Yn llefain heb wellhad,
A'u hanwyl hoff rieni
   Yn gorwedd yn eu gwaed;
   Ty allan i'r aneddle,
     Yn feirwon yno'u dau;
Archollion dwfn dychrynllyd
   Heb obaith eu gwellhau.

5 Pan glywodd gwas y gelyn
   Fod lleisiau yn y llo,
I'r llofft yr aeth y llofrudd
   A'r gyllell gydag e';
   A llad rhai bach diniwaid
     Oedd yn eu gwely clyd,
   Peth sobr, torcalonus,
Pum' bywyd 'n myn'd o'r byd.

6 Ond ar ol llofruddio'r teulu,
   Fe roes y ty ar dan,
   Y weithred drist, ysgeler,
   Na fu ei bath o'r blaen,
   A llosgwyd yr adeilad
     O'r gwaelod hyd y nen;
   Mae'r llofrudd wedi ddala
    Diolchwn byth Amen.

               Hugh Roberts, *Pererin Mon.*

AN APPALLING TRAGEDY

At Llangibby, Monmouthshire, on a Family, consisting of a Father, Mother, and Three Children, on Tuesday, the 16th of July, 1878. The Father and Mother, William and Elizabeth Watkins, were about 44 years of age, and the children; Charlotte, Eight years of age; Frederick, Five, and Alice, the youngest, Four years of age. The Father and Mother were found dead in the garden, about four yards from each other, having been stabbed in several places; and the children upstairs, having suffered the same treatment. It seems that the house was set on fire in three different places; and the children were severely burnt.

    1 Attention give kind people,
       And listen one and all,
     While I relate these verses,
       Draw near great and small,
   In Monmouthshire, remember
       A crime so very great,
     Has been committed lately
       I am sorry now to state.

    2 It was within Llangibby,
       The truth to you I tell,
     The father and the mother
       Through brutal hands has fell,
   And the three harmless children
       Were murdered in the place,
  When thinking of what happened,
       Who now can be at ease.

    3 The father and the mother,
       When found were in their gore,
    Those that were gay and lively,
       Will never meet no more,
    It was outside their dwelling
       There lives were took away
     In a most brutal manner,
       As many now do say.

LIFE & DEATH

> 4 Upstairs, in bed the children
>   When found, oh! what a sight,
>   And burnt and charred most shoking,
>   And stabbed both left and right,
>   They little thought when going
>   To rest within their bed,
>   To meet their deaths so sudden;
>   And numbered with the dead.
>
> 5 Who ever done those murders,
>   And shed their blood so free,
>   While on this earth remaining,
>   How can he happy be,
>   Five lives that were so precious,
>   Were took so very soon,
>   Those that were seen quite lively
>   On Tuesday afternoon.
>
> 6 After he had killed them,
>   And take their lives away,
>   He thought to burn the dwelling,
>   And that without delay,
>   Oh! may it be a warning
>   To people, great, and small,
>   From wicked deeds and murders,
>   Pray God protect us all.
>   Hugh Roberts, *Pererin Mon.*

Another murder, at Llangwm, is recorded in an epitaph:

> Here lies the body that lost its life
> By bloody Villian [sic] full of strife
> Who coveted boath gold and land
> As anybody may understand
> Wo be to those infernall foes
> Who dipt their hands in blood
> The king of Kings who knows all things
> One day on them will vengeance bring

This marks the grave of Elizabeth Gwyn, a member of the well-to-do family which owned Pwll Farm. In June 1743, at the age of 82 she made

Llangwm Church

her will and a few days later was found stabbed to death on the stone stairs of her own house. No trace of her murderer or murderers ever came to light. One still feels a sense of shock, 250 years later, that so violent a deed was committed in such a peaceful place.

Even without murder, lives end suddenly, and epitaphs often give warning to the living. From the north wall of the chancel at Bryngwyn, William Taylor (died 1695) calls for our attention:

> Behould the place where I do lye:
> as thou art now so was I:
> but as I am so shalt thou be:
> Com life com deth com follow me.

In the porch at Newchurch is the tombstone of Walter Prichard, who died in 1803 at the age of 72:

> Behold and see what death has done,
> This is the race that all may run,
> Repent in time make no delay,
> For death will take us all away
> Youth age nor virtue can Prevail
> Death gives no quorters takes no bail.

At Llansoy, a gravestone near the church porch with the carving of a beautiful woman and a coiled snake marks the resting place of Ann Morgan, who died of snakebite in 1835 at the age of 20. In the same churchyard another stone has the laconic message:

> Remember me as you pass by
> As you are now so once was I
> And as I am so shall you be
> Therefore prepare to follow me.

LIFE & DEATH

The simple statement made on behalf of Philip Stead, once churchwarden at Mitchel Troy, whose stone is now preserved inside the church

Nicholas Williams died at Cwmyoy in 1732, aged 85. His wife, Joan, who was then 44, lived for 20 more years before joining him beneath this verse:

> Death like an overflowing stream
> Sweeps us away; and Lifes a Dream
> An emty Tale; a morning Flow'r:
> Cut down & withered in a hour.

IN
Memory of phiLip
Stead Who died des.
ember The 13th
1736 Aged 67

Life is Unsartain
And deth is so shuer
Sin is The wound
& Christ is the Cuer

Spans of 85 and 64 years seem rather longer than that of a morning flower, which might, however, have been appropriate (still at Cwmyoy) for two more Williamses, Mary, who died in 1788 at the age of eight, and her sister, also Mary, who died two years later, aged 14 weeks. Instead, they have these lines:

Cymyoy Church

> I was but young and Death came soon
> My sun was set before 'twas noon
> My glass my run'd god thought it best
> To take me to Eternal rest.

An awesome record of infant mortality can be read in epitaphs. On the chancel wall at Caerwent are commemorated four 18th century babes who each in turn 'Just peeped out and uttered infant cries / Disliked the scene, and shut their eyes.' From the south-west corner of the nave at Llangattock Lingoed, Samuel Prichard's son, James, who died in 1796 at the age of 10 months, says:

> Weep not for me my parents dear
> I am not dead but sleeping here
> Here I am free from all pain
> Hopeing in heaven to meet again.

At Capel-y-Ffin's Baptist chapel, Noah Watkins, who died at the age of eight in 1738, tells us that he 'would. not take a hundred pounds in money for Breaking the Sabbath but keep it holy.'

As parents lay dying, their thoughts turned to the children they were leaving behind. Again at Llangattock Lingoed, the epitaph of Ann Watkins (died 1816, aged 28) appeals to her husband, John:

> Farewel dear friend my life is past.
> My love to you so long did last.
> But love our Infant for my sake.
> And ever on her pity take.

Mary, wife of William Jones of Newport, makes a similar request. She died in 1740, aged 42, and is buried by the chancel steps in St Woolos's Cathedral:

> Since Husband dear my life is past
> my love to you so long did last
> but now for me no sorrow take
> Yet love my Children for my sake.

Llanfihangel Gobion Church

A headstone by the south porch at Dixton Church commemorates William Harris, who died in 1745 at the age of 101. He, too, thinks of his children, though by then they could have been anything up to 80 years old themselves:

> Death took me off this earthly stage
> When I had lived to a good age.
> I left behind me children seven;
> I hope to meet them all in Heaven.

Traditional epitaphs recur in different places. Moses Williams (died 1778, aged 40) is remembered in the chancel at Partricio with these lines:

> Great sickness sore,
> Long time before,
> Physicians was in vain;
> Till God was pleas, to give me ease
> And took me from my pain.

Almost the same verse at Llanfihangel Gobion is applied to Mary Jennings, who died over 60 years later (in 1844, aged 72):

> Sick and sore long time I bore
> Physicians strove in vain
> Until God alone did hear my moan
> And eased me of my pain.

Intriguingly, the same stone marks the resting place of David Harris, who died seven months later, aged 70:

> A sudden change by death was gave
> That I now longer time could have
> Believe in Christ make no delay
> For sudden death do call away.

James Hughes, a blacksmith at Llanfihangel Crucorney who died in 1766, shares an epitaph with many others of his trade:

> My sledge and hammer lie reclined,
> My bellows too has lost his wind,
> My fire's extinct, my forge decayed,
> And in the dust my vice is laid.
> My coal is spent, my iron is gone,
> My nails are drove, my work is done.

John Lee lived at Mathern in a cottage by the pound, facing Trelenny Lane. He died in 1825 at the age of 103 and lies beneath a flat stone close to the south door of the church with the verse of a song (sometimes called 'Old Abram Brown') as an epitaph:

> John Lee is dead, that good old man,
> We ne'er shall see him more;
> He used to wear an old drab coat
> All buttoned down before.

Reverend Chest, the Chepstow parson who had the body of Henry Marten moved (see chapter 2), was the subject of a punning epitaph written by his son-in-law, a Mr Downton:

LIFE & DEATH

Here lies at rest, I do protest,
One *Chest* within another;
This *Chest* of wood was very good;
Who says so of the other?

John Rennie, or Renie, who died in 1832 at the age of 33, worked out his own quirky epitaph in 285 letters which read to the north, south, east or west, 'Here lies John Renie'. The secret is to start from the centre. The joke is on him, though, because his stone was moved from elsewhere in the churchyard to its present position by the east end of St Mary's, Monmouth, so he does not lie there at all

Llangattock Vibon Avel, not far from Monmouth, currently has just 36 people on its electoral roll. During the First World War 13 men of the parish died, three more in the Second. The present small numbers, though, owe more to the general reduction in manpower working the land. An interesting collection of gravestones in the church includes that of John Powell (died 1816, aged 73):

> Praiseis on tombs are rare
> Trifles vainly spent
> A mans good name is
> His own monument.

CHAPTER 8

Words

Welsh, 'the language of heaven', is no longer the predominant tongue in Monmouthshire as it was some 200 years ago. John Byng, driven by rain into a public house at Trellech in 1781, was told by the landlord, with whom he conversed 'about goats and the Welsh language', that 'in his village they spoke English, but at the distance of six miles, understood it no more than a dog.'

The actions of two clergymen neatly illustrate the fortunes of Welsh. Robert Frampton arrived at Bryngwyn, near Raglan, in 1694 and set about learning Welsh so as to be able to minister to his flock. Almost two centuries later, in 1870 to be precise, James Oakley, deeming it to be of no further use, removed the Welsh Bible from his church at Llanishen and buried it in his garden. This was the fine translation made in 1588 by William Morgan, and revised in 1620.

The decline of Welsh was not unopposed. In their book, *Tours in South Wales* (1809), Reverend J. Evans and John Britton complain that despite 'continual attempts' to eradicate Welsh manners, customs and the language in Monmouthshire, 'antipathy to the introduction of English is still great and inveterate.' They add: 'the natives of ... the parts which are sequestered and mountainous retain their ancient prejudices and still brand everything assimilating to English with the opprobrious appellation of Saxon.'

Nevertheless, even 'the natives' of such a 'sequestered and mountainous' place as Blaenafon numbered only 21 monoglot Welsh speakers in 1841 out of 5.000 inhabitants, though 61 per cent of them could speak Welsh as well as English. The census of 60 years later showed, in the whole of Monmouthshire, only 3,500 Welsh speakers, or 13 per cent of the population. Only in a single town, Rhymney, were they in a majority; and by the mid-20th century this was 'one of the few places in Monmouthshire where Welsh is still spoken.'

Ironically, the Welsh national anthem, 'Land of My Fathers', with its fervent desire for the perpetuation of the ancient language ('O bydded i'r hen iaith barhau'), has a connection with Monmouthshire. The father and son, James and Evan James, who were inspired to write it while walking by the River Rhondda in 1856, previously lived at the Ancient Druid Inn, Argoed, and Ewan was born there.

Though the Welsh language has receded in Monmouthshire it has left an enduring legacy in place and field names, albeit mingled with English.

Places

Many simple Welsh words for features of the landscape recur in names of settlements. *Cwm* (valley), *pont* (bridge), *porth* (port or gate), *aber* (confluence or estuary) and *ynys* (water meadow or island) are among those which appear in Monmouthshire, some of them frequently.

Cwm standing alone serves for a village between Ebbw Vale and Aberbeeg. The name of a river is added to form Cwmbrân. Cwmyoy—or Cwm-iou in the correct Welsh spelling—means ox-yoke valley, a name it takes from the shape of the hill overlooking it. Cwmynyscoy, near Pontypool, means valley with water meadow in the hollow.

Streams and rivers result in many bridges, which in turn give such names as Pont-hir (Longbridge), Pontrhydyrun (Bridge at ash-tree ford) and Pontllanfraith (seems to be Bridge of St Bridget's Church, but was originally Pontllynfraid: bridge where river widens and stones show above the surface). Pontypool itself—Pont-y-pwl—has an elaborate traditional etymology (see chapter 3) involving a contest of strength with the devil, but in fact simply means bridge over a pool—in the River Sirhowy. The derivation of Sirhowy is in turn unknown, though the meaning of 'pleasant or cheerful water' has been suggested.

Croes-y-ceiliog (Cock's cross) on the A4042 between Newport and Pontypool is one of a number of places which grew up round a public house, the Upper Cross Inn, in this case. However, a story long told in the area suggested that on a hillock in a neighbouring field there once existed a big sculpted figure of a cock in the act of crowing, a mediaeval reminder of Peter's denial of Christ. The monument is said to have been smashed in 1646 by a band of Roundheads travelling to Raglan Castle. In 1839 the Chartists' eastern valley contingent, led by William Jones, stopped here for refreshment on its way to Newport (see chapter 2), and dried gunpowder in the oven.

Trefil is a small village three miles north of Tredegar and, incidentally, 2,000 feet above sea level. Idris Williams has ingeniously suggested two possible origins for its name: from local landowners, called Mills; or from the mules which were used as a means of transport during the early years of the industrial revolution (*mul* in Welsh, pronounced mill, mutates to *ful*, pronounced vill). Unfortunately, in a way, the argument is settled by reference to the Llandaff Charters of about 910, in which the village appears as Tre Il, meaning Il's estate.

Personal names are frequently preserved in placenames. Skenfrith appears in early written records as Kenefrid (1190), Skynefrith (1291) and ynys Gynwreid (*c*.1400). Interpreted as Ynysgynwraidd, it would mean Cynwraidd's river meadow. Some have suggested that it should be Ynyscynfraeth, after Cynfraeth, a 6th century chieftain, son of Cyndrwyn, prince of Powys. A third possibility links the place with Fraith, better known as St Bridget (see chapter 1).

The names of saints, combined with the familiar *llan*, are widely remembered in Monmouthshire, as elsewhere in Wales. A clutch of places called Llangattock (Llangatwg), Cadoc's church, includes Llangattock Lingoed (lake-wood), Llangattock Vibon Avel (an anglicised form of Feibion Afel, the sons of Afel) and Llangattock nigh (or juxta) Usk (Dyffryn Wysg, in the Usk valley).

There is also a Llanfihangel-nigh-Usk (Dyffryn Wysg), one of a total of 23 Monmouthshire villages with the same first element, St Michael's Church. As Ivor Waters memorably put it:

Llangattock Vibon Avel Church

THE FOLKLORE OF MONMOUTHSHIRE

> When asked how to reach Llanvihangel,
> Said the native, 'I don't want to wrangle.
> Do you want Crucorney,
> Tor-y-mynydd, or journey
> To one of the rest? It's a tangle.

Llanfihangel Crucorney (Crucornau) takes its name from the rounded hills nearby. Gobion (y gofion, the smiths) is close to the River Usk at a point where a forge might have existed in Roman times. The Roman name for Usk Town, Gobannium, has a similar derivation. The second element of Llanfihangel Llantarnam may come from Nant Teyron, the valley of Teyron, an early ruler of Gwent; or from Torfaen (breaker of stones), an early name for the Afon Llwyd. Llanfihangel Rogiet means St Michael's Church by the roe (deer) gate; Torymynydd, by the fold of a hill. Ystern Llewern, a corruption of ystum llywern, stands at a river's bend shaped like the leg of a fox. A different interpretation has 'burning will o' the wisp', a name given by Ynyr, king of Gwent, who was benighted and lost hereabouts in a bog, then founded the church in thanks for reaching safety.

Another of these names, Llanfihangel-y-fedw (of the birch tree) has half gone into English as Michaelstone-y-Vedw. Llanfihangel Troddi (by the River Trothy) has been transformed into Mitchel Troy. The series also includes Llanfihangel Pont-y-moel (Bridge of the Bare Hill) and y Traethau (the Beaches)—and the list is still not exhausted.

As well as saints, giants have contributed to Monmouthshire place-names. Bwch, which in Welsh normally means buck (in the sense of male animal), is said to have been the name of a giant who lived at Castell Bwch, between Caerleon and Llantarnam, or at a hamlet of the same name near Henllys. Little more is known of him, save that he had several sons as big as himself who built their own fortresses. Ernallt or Arnallt lived at Castell Arnallt (Castle Arnold). three miles south of Abergavenny, near Penpergwm, which was burned down by William de Braose in 1176. Buga held Castell Bryn Buga, which may refer to the town of Usk (Bryn Buga in Welsh) or the hillfort on Gwehelog Fawr nearby. Clidda's stronghold, Cloddeu Caer Clidda, could be Coed y Bwnydd, a hillfort on Clytha Hill. A fourth giant son, Trogi, gave his name to Cas Troggy in the forest of Wentwood. His castle may have been a forerunner of the structure raised on the site in the 13th century for Roger Bigod, lord of Chepstow. Troggy Brook, which rises close to the ruins, reaches the sea at Caldicot Pill after

Cas Troggy

changing its name to Nedern Brook. There are vague stories of an earl of Trogi, unfortunate in love, and almost as shadowy a figure as his giant namesake.

Edmund Jones firmly believed that a giant as tall and powerful as Goliath lived near Aberbeeg. He had six fingers on each hand, says another source. When he died his relatives decided for some reason to bury him at Llanwenarth, near Abergavenny. They were struggling over the mountains with the body when, on Twyn Wenallt, just over the Breconshire border, they were overtaken by a great storm. They decided to bury the giant there at a place which since Elizabethan times has been known as Bedd y gwr hir or Bedd y dyn hir (Long Man's Grave). Sightings of the giant's ghost have been reported from time to time near his resting place.

Successive incomers to Wales brought new names or changed the old. Caerleon appears in Roman sources as early as *c.*150 AD as *Iskalis*, from Isca, the Old British word for the River Usk. Later the Romans called the place *Castra Legionis*, Camp of the legion, in this case the second. In Welsh this became Caerllion, to which ar Wysg (on Usk) was added to distinguish it from the other Caerllion (Chester), though in modern Welsh this is just Caer.

Chepstow, from *ceap*, market, and *stow*, place, is a classic Anglo-Saxon coinage. However, the Normans called the place Striguil: in the Latin of the Domesday Book, 'Castellum de Estrighoiel'. This in turn was perhaps their attempt to pronounce Ystraigyl (bend), or, even more intriguingly, Ystrad Iwl, which could be a Welsh rendering of Strata Julia, the Roman road which passed through the town.

As early as 1188, Gerald of Wales wrote of a feature of the landscape with a decidedly un-Welsh name:

> High above the water, and not far from Caerleon, there stands a rocky eminence which dominates the River Severn. In the English language it is called Goldcliff, the Golden Rock. When the sun's rays strike it, the stone shines very bright and takes on a golden sheen.

The same place fascinated a rather bad poet, some 700 years later:

> There is a hill near fam'd Caerleon,
> Which if the sun but dart a ray on,
> It shines like gold; hence Goldcliff hight [called];
> But if there's gold, 'tis out of sight.

People ignorant of Welsh inevitably garbled names. Mynyddislwyn has been recorded as Mynydwssllwyd, Montythusloin, Monethuslin, Munithuslan, Mjunith Islloyne and Monithisloyn. Ffawydden (beech tree) became Devauden; Porth Iscoed (port of the lower wood), Portskewett (also Portascyth and Portscwit). The spelling of some names was changed to represent Welsh pronunciation more or less phonetically: Crymlyn to Crumlin, Llanffwyst to Llanfoist, Llangyfiw to Langeview. Other Welsh names were simply translated into English, as from Hengastel to Oldcastle, Castell Newydd to Newcastle. Yr Eglwys Newydd ar y Cefn (the new church on the ridge) became just Newchurch.

In many cases the Welsh word was simply abandoned in favour of a new coinage. Dingestow, replacing Llandingat; and Wonastow, Llanwarrw, must have been the work of Anglo-Saxons. Rogerstone, after the Norman landowner, Roger de Berkerolles, replaced Tre Gwilym, in the 11th century, though according to Olive Phillips the

Welsh name continued in use at least until the 1950s, a remarkable length of time.

Bryn buga, meaning pointed hill, which can now again be seen on road signs, was dropped in favour of Usk, the Celtic river name. A poetic formula such as Tre newydd gelli fach (New town in little grove) became the prosaic Shirenewton. Tre newydd dan y gaer (New town under the fort, this being Y Gaer Fawr) was transmuted into Wolvesnewton, the first element of which derives not from a wild animal but a family called Wolf which was the chief landowner in the area until the 16th century.

Llanddeiniol, Llangoronwy and Llangadwaladr lost their connection with early saints, and turned into Itton, Rockfield and Bishton respectively. Llangadwaladr, like Magor, was founded by Cadwaladr, king of Britain and last native prince of Wales.

During the industrial revolution, new English names appeared as fresh settlements were established in the valleys in the west of Monmouthshire. Both Beaufort and Dukestown were called after the absentee aristocrat on whose land they were built. Markham, Wattsville and Wylie commemorate directors of coal companies, the last dating from only 1925. Griffithstown enshrines the name of Henry Griffiths, the first stationmaster at Pontypool. Cross Keys, Hollybush and Six Bells grew up round public houses.

Nevertheless, the majority of places in Monmouthshire continue to bear the ancient names used by so many generations. From his youth in Newport, W.H. Davies remembered a litany of Welsh names—and one Norman:

> Can I forget the sweet days that have been,
> The villages so green I have been in;
> Llantarnam, Magor, Malpas, and Llanwern,
> Liswery, old Caerleon, and Alteryn?

Field and Thoroughfare

Names for features of the landscape, houses, and even the streets of towns and villages can provide intriguing reflections of past events. Sometimes the background stories have been forgotten. One can only speculate when presented with Ogof Lladron (Thief's Cave) on Twyn Gwrhyd (Giant's Hill) in the former parish of Aberystruth, or Black Morgan's Wood, Hangman's Oak, Nun's Walk, Big Monday and Lower Mad Owls (all fields near Chepstow).

THE FOLKLORE OF MONMOUTHSHIRE

Alteryn, near Newport

Trefil village is flanked by twin mountains, Trefil Ddu to the west and Trefil Las to the east. They are said to be called after two armies, clad respectively in black and green, and each 3,000 strong, which assembled locally before joining battle. At Hirgân (Long Song) Farm the Greens chanted prayers before fighting. Purgad (Pure Battle), the name of another farm, may have been the Blacks' war-cry.

Hummocky ground north of the village, called Maes y Beddau (Field of Graves), marks where casualties were buried. A short distance to the south-west are Traed y Milwyr and Rhyd y Milwyr (Soldiers' Path and Ford). Pwll y Duon (Blacks' Pool) in the River Sirhowy nearby is thought to have indentations in its rocky bed made by the Blacks' horses' hooves.

These names may be distant echoes of battles between Welsh and Normans. Folk etymology jokingly claims that the Sirhowy itself derives its name from the reply which Welsh soldiers gave when their general asked whether they were ready to fight: 'Syr wy i - Sir, I am.' In 1850 Dr William Price of Llantrisant in Glamorgan called an open air assembly of bards at Trefil (perhaps in part due to the folk tale) to honour the Welsh struggle. Price, a Chartist who took part in the Newport rising and afterwards escaped to Paris dressed as a woman, is better known for his pioneering struggle to legalise cremation. Fighting continued at Trefil in the 19th century in the form of bare-knuckle contests which took place on

Hirgân Farm in a field known as Duke's Table. One would be tempted to think that this derives from 'dukes', for fists, but this slang word was first recorded only in 1874.

Another Welsh-Norman clash is commemorated in the name of Coed Dial (Revenge Wood), where in 1136 Richard de Clare, who had been entrusted by William the Conqueror with the task of subjugating Wales, was killed. Just over 50 years afterwards the story was related by Gerald of Wales, who passed that way with Baldwin, archbishop of Canterbury. Pont yr Escob (Bishop's Bridge), sometimes garbled to Pont yspig, is called after Baldwin, by one account because it was specially built for him, by another that he merely passed over it. It is on the River Grwyne Fawr near the hamlet of Fforest, a short way downstream from Coed Dial.

This is Gerald's account of a classic ambush:

> It happened that Richard de Clare, a nobleman of high birth who, in addition to the Clare estates, held Cardiganshire in South Wales, passed this way on a journey from England to Wales. He was accompanied by a large force of men-at-arms led by Brian de Wallingford, then overlord of this area, who was acting as his guide through the pass. When they reached the entrance to the wood, Richard de Clare sent back Brian and his men, and rode unarmed into the forest ... Ahead of him went a singer to announce his coming and a fiddler who accompanied the singer on his instrument. From then onwards things happened very quickly. The Welsh had prepared an ambush for Richard. All of a sudden Iorwerth, the brother of Morgan of Caerleon, and others of their family, rushed out from where they were hidden in the thickets, cut down Richard and most of his men, and made off with their baggage which they had seized in this savage way.

The site of the attack, which Baker-Gabb attributes to private revenge, is marked by a stone, Dial Cerrig.

A few miles away, near Capel-y-Ffin, once stood Ty Dial (Revenge House), which owed its name to a completely different case of vengeance. The spot, in a dingle on the mountainside, lay under a curse because of some crime committed there. Workmen starting to build the house heard a disembodied voice telling them to move because the curse had nine generations to run. Nevertheless, they persisted, but only at the third attempt did they succeed in building a house which stood. One winter's night a young man went to court his sweetheart there, but despite every effort at persuasion, his greyhound would not go inside. The man took this as a bad omen, and went back home. Later that night a landslip swept away the whole house, killing everyone in it.

At Llantilio Crossenny, Maes y Groes (Cross Field) is said to be the place where St Teilo's cross was planted before a battle with the Saxons (see chapter 1). Trellech has its Bloody Field where, in protest at some past massacre, nothing will grow but gorse. Other fields have more peaceful histories. At Skenfrith, Ynys yr Eglwys and Ynys y Gloch (Church and Bell Meadow) were respectively dedicated to the maintenance of the church and its bells. The Poor's Six Acres at Nash (which itself derives from 'an ash') is a field with a cottage bequeathed in the time of Charles II so that the rental might benefit the indigent of the parish. Not far away, Dancing Hill at Undy is where fairies were thought to besport themselves on Midsummer Eve (23 June); and Cobblers' Pitch at Langstone is so called because the shoemakers of Newport traditionally walked there with their wives and camped over night on the same occasion.

Many field names are self-explanatory. Whitson (which comes from the white stone of the locality) has a Greenmeadow and a Pye (magpie) Corner. Spytty must be *ysbyty* (hospital), land once owned by a hospital. At St Pierre there are fields called Wharf, Hays (land enclosed by hedges), Colts Hay, Baker's Close, Peter's Slade (valley), Tump Ground, the Warren, Brannels (site of burning), Maes Fawr and Maes Fach (Big and Little field). Coalpit Hill above Fforest points to charcoal burning.

The Wye Bridge and The Kymin

WORDS

Cae is another word for field in Welsh. Across the Wye from Monmouth is Cae Maen (stony field), which has become Kymin. Llanfrechfa has (or had) a whole series of such names, including Cae bont (bridge field), bras (luxuriant), ffynnon (spring or well), gross (possibly from *garw*, coarse), glas (green), Mair (Mary's), vellyn (*felin*, mill). *Wain*, another word for meadow, which can also mean moor, is represented at Llanfrechfa by Wain dan y tye (sic) (Meadow below the house) and Main llandy (Church house meadow).

Among derogatory names are Starve Crow Farm and Hell's Wood (Skenfrith), Coldharbour (Whitson), Botany Bay, implying remoteness, and Bargain Wood, originally bare gain (near Tintern). Barbadoes Hill in the same parish takes its name from the place of exile in the West Indies chosen at the Restoration by Lewis Morris, who had fought for Parliament during the Civil War, and owned an estate at Tintern. He went on to make his fortune in America. Paradise (Skenfrith) and Truelove Farm (Whitson) must reflect approval though such names were at times employed ironically.

Maesgwenith (wheat field) was beside the Troggy Brook just above Llanfair Discoed. The name has now gone but the ancient story remains. A swineherd called Coll had charge of a wilful, wandering sow, Dallwaran. Wherever she went he followed, clinging to her bristles. Eventually she swam up the Troggy Brook from the sea and dropped on its banks three grains of wheat and three bees. Both flourished, and Maesgwenith became famous throughout Wales.

Some names are destined to remain mysterious. Squabbles at St Arvans may have been disputed land, or perhaps a boggy place (from 'quabbs'). Gloryhole Valley at Skenfrith may imply a higgledy-piggledy sort of place, but what of Cupid's Pitch at Grosmont? At St Pierre, is Nosbun the Welsh for night maid, and if so, how did the name arise?

Artie Bella, a farmhouse at Llangeview, is merely a corruption of Allt-y-Bela, wolf's cliff. Another farmhouse near Caerleon, Bulmore, comes from *pwll mawr* (big pool) in the adjacent River Usk. Many years ago a woman at Skenfrith lived at a cottage called Toad's Hole until her daughter who had gone to service in London, refused to write home until the address was changed.

Many parishes have a Ty Mawr (great house), a Lower House and a Church Farm. Scattered farmsteads, sometimes established on land awarded under successive enclosure acts, where previously they would have been within villages, are often Pentre (village end) and Pentwyn (hill end), not to mention Pant (hollow, valley), Nant (valley), Cwm, (valley) Lan or Glan (bank). The tower overlooking Pontypool is not a house at all but a folly, erected in 1712, and called Kemeys Folly. Its builder, George, turned out to be the last male heir in the distinguished family whose name is perpetuated in the villages of Kemeys Commander and Kemeys Inferior, north and south of Usk respectively. When he boasted one day to his uncle that he could see 11 counties from his folly he received the reply, 'I am sorry, nephew, that 11 counties can see *thy* folly.'

Kemeys Folly

The streets of villages and towns also have their stories. Jingle Street at Dingestow is said to take its name from the sound of bells on the harness of passing horses. Heol-y-glo (Coal Lane) at Michaelston-y-Fedw was a route used for transporting coal. Some roads and fords called after soldiers are mentioned in chapter 2.

Writing in 1906. Lewis Browning described some of the old street names at Blaenafon:

> King Street was formerly Heol-ust-tewi (Hush-silence-road): Broad Street bore the name Heol-y-nant (Brook Street), [after] a brook running down from the Bridgend underneath the buildings all the way to Avon Lwyd ... Hill Street was a very stony, crooked, and narrow road, called by the Welsh people Heol Garegog [Stony Street], which was a most suitable name. Let us walk to the top of Broad Street, and we shall find a path below Davies Bros's top shop turning to the left and nearly up to the back of the Jolly Colliers Inn, on through a meadow behind the Old Duke, and crossing Hill Street into Mr Francis James's wood, and Shams o'r Coed (James Edwards) wood. This path was called Llwybr 'Rhyd-y-nos (Along-by-night-path), and that is why we have also 'Rhyd-y-nos Street.

Similar details could be supplied for many other towns and villages in Monmouthshire.

Nicknames
Rivalry, and sometimes animosity, between different communities led to exchanges of derogatory epithets. In a friendly spirit, the people of Monmouthshire in general were called 'blacklegs' by their Herefordshire neighbours, and responded with 'white faces'. The former indicated, not strike breakers, but colliers; the latter derives from the appearance of Hereford cattle.

Gloucestershire dwellers flung a taunt across the Wye to those living in Tintern, which was once a by-word for poverty:

> Abbey cowats [jackdaws], thin an' small;
> Half a loaf 'd feed 'em all.

The rejoinder would have been unhesitatingly delivered:

> Brockweir toads, big an' small,
> One abbey cowat 'd beat 'em all.

When the stocks were removed to Chepstow from Portskewett, local people sagely commented: 'They needed 'em more than us.' Chepstow tradesmen, wary of the Bristolians' reputation for sharp practice, used the expression, 'Bristolman's sleep', to mean a state of cunning alertness. A saying in Trellech, 'I've been to Coleford—got both eyes open', reflected the belief that a visit beyond the Wye sharpened the wits. On the other hand, Trellech people's opinion of their neighbours down-river was not high:

> Chepstow born and Chepstow bred,
> Strong in the arm and weak in the head.

Within Monmouthshire several places enjoyed (if that is the right word) generic nicknames, some obvious, others more mysterious. There were Abergavenny bulldogs, Goytre dandies and Monmouth knives. Usk or Pontypool butterflies were so called because these towns produced japanned trays, vases and screens on which butterfly motifs prominently featured. Perhaps the same activity contributed at least partly to this saying: 'Pontypool is paved with gold, Trosnant is lined with silver, and Pontymoil [Llanfihangel Pontymoel] doth stink with oil.' In the village of Penhow, from where until about 1960 children had to go to school either at Llandevaud or St Brides Netherwent (the Pike School), they used to say:

> Llandevaud bulldogs,
> Pike School cats;
> If you see a Penhow child,
> Please raise your hats.

In common with others up and down Britain, the people of Risca acquired their nickname of cuckoos (Cogau Rhisga) by allegedly building a high hedge to pen the bird and so retain the good weather it brought. 'Dear bird of good omen', they said, 'sing here always and you shall lack neither meat nor drink nor comfort, all through the year and for the years to come.' When the bird unaccountably flew away, crying, 'Cuckoo, cuckoo', they sighed: 'Alas, if only we'd made the hedge higher.'

Other traditional examples of suggested gullibility included stories 'of the wonders of Trelleck treacle and the Treacle Pits there, of submarines in Mounton Brook, and of Callythumpians who worked themselves into a frenzy and hugged hot stoves in Shirenewton.' Ivor Waters, who reports this, adds: 'There were Llandogo Ducks (an allusion to flooding which could have been applied just as aptly to Tintern); Earlswood and Shirenewton Gorsehoppers, because of their large tracts of bracken or gorse; Chepstow Knowers, because pundits used to stand at street corners on market days informing the rustics, "Oi do know"; as well as a few others rather more offensive.'

Personal nicknames have a long history. One thinks of Dafydd Gam ('crooked'), who died at Agincourt in 1415 (see chapter 2). As two examples from the early 17th century show, nicknames can be found even in church registers: at Grosmont, 'Elizabeth Vytha, alias vz William Tho. David Parry' (*fyddar* means deaf, and *vz* is a contraction of *ferch*, daughter of); and at Llantilio Crossenny, 'Morice David alias Gwyddil' (Irishman). At Caldicot the church records mention Thomas stop-and-drink and Thomas Shone Cattey.

Early in the 19th century the low-life Newport district of Friars' Fields had 'certain nymphs of the pavement' known as the Duchess, Nancy

View of Newport Dock, 1842. Lithograph by J.F. Mullock (1818-92)
(Newport Museum and Art Gallery)

Bwlch, Mary the Cripple, Ann the Doctor, Julia the Slattern, Amelia the Smut, and Mary the Pickaxe. Among the men of the area who 'plundered hen-roosts, broke into warehouses and waylaid honest travellers' were Dick Cochin, Bill the Fighter, Bill the Drummer and Evan the Milkman.

The relatively small stock of surnames in Wales undoubtedly encouraged the use of nicknames as a means of identification. In his *Reminiscences of Monmouthshire* (1908) J.H. Clark recalled from the Usk of the 1830s over 60 nicknames from 300 households. They include Jemmy the Nailer, Jack the Harper, Tom the Ostler, Jack the Post, Old Curious, the Old Fancy, the Young Fancy, Tom the Dragon, the Little Rock, Jack Bat, Jack the Giant, Tom Thumb, Will Ellick, the Cricket, the Lark, the Boar Pig, the Woodcock, Tom the Tiger, the Duck, the Bull, the Buck, the Flat Fish, the Robin, the Forester, the Merlin, the Duke of York, Lord Berkeley, Wacky, the Griper, the Baron, Scoggins, Bottle Green and Will the Gardener.

The Welsh language is conspicuous by its absence from the list but from Blaenafon Lewis Browning gives Dai Ty Bwlch (House in the gap), Dai Mawr (Big), Dai sydd fwy (is bigger), Dai sydd fwy na hynny (is bigger than that), Emwnt o'r byd (from the world), Ianto i bara brith (presumably from his predilection for 'speckled bread', a sort of fruit loaf), Shoni Sgubor Fawr (Big barn—the name of a hamlet), Richard and Rees Bach o'r Fferm (of the farm), Twm Cerrig Calch (Tom Limestone), Shoni Tafarn (Johnny Tavern), and Peggi Pysun (? poison).

When Thomas Jones started school at Rhymney in the 1870s eight boys shared his name. He was allotted Number Five, which had been vacated by a boy who had left; as a consequence to his schoolboy contemporaries he was for the rest of his life Tom Jones Five. Nicknames in Welsh which he remembered include Mari'r Ochor Draw (Mary from the far side), Evan Bolgi (Glutton) and Enoch Brynbrith (Speckled Hill); in English, Johnny Fresh Air, John One Suit, John Every Bit, Dai Goose, Mary Jane Quavers (pronounced *quavvers*) and the intriguing Mrs Williams More About.

Preachers with common names added their village as a form of identification, such as John Jones Talysarn or John Williams Brynsiencyn. At Trefil three men called Williams, all ardent leaders in the Horeb Congregational Church, were differentiated as Pentwyn, John Liza and Will Nanny. A Llanishen midwife called Betsy Williams was known as Betsy the Bleeder.

The use of often inventive and humorous nicknames was particularly strong among miners (see chapter 9). It remains in the community at large. At the village of Fleur-de-Lis, which itself is nicknamed the Flower, a chemist who readily offered an alternative when an item was not in stock was dubbed Willie-something-similar. At Undy a man who went round with a van selling paraffin became Johnny Oily. Itinerant Bretons who came hawking onions received the generic name of Shoni Onion. Lynn Davies from Marshfield, who enjoyed spectacular success as a long jumper in the Tokyo Olympics of 1964, acquired the local name of Lynn the Leap. In 1987, Edmund J. Mason wrote of a young friend of his from Devauden who could not make up her mind whether to marry Dai the Milk or Dai the Bread. He knew another woman called Elsie the Bull, 'a strange combination of the sexes, but the truth was that her father kept "The Bull".'

CHAPTER 9

Work

'Black forges smoke, and noisy hammers beat, / Where sooty cyclops, puffing, drink and sweat': so wrote Edward Davies in 1786 of workers at a foundry by the River Angidy originally established by the monks of Tintern. Between 1801 and 1845 Monmouthshire's position at the forefront of the industrial revolution led to a 245 per cent increase in population. It is scarcely surprising that ironworkers, quarrymen and miners evolved their own sub-cultures and bodies of lore.

The list of occupations may seem heavily masculine, though women did at one stage work in Welsh mines. They were also employed in many other capacities—as teachers, nurses, factory operatives, domestic servants—but unfortunately their attitudes and practices have been less well documented than those of men.

Both sexes are represented in another of Monmouthshire's essential industries, that of agriculture. Here, too, changes have consigned many traditional ways and methods to the past.

Quarrymen and Metalworkers
Trefil (see previous chapter) is famous for its limestone. Many thousands of tons of it were used in steel production and before that in lime burning. Transport was provided by mules which plodded over mountain tracks. Later, horses pulled trams on wagonways with gutter-like rails which led to the ironworks of Sirhowy, Beaufort and Ebbw Vale. When they were first introduced, locomotives used the same primitive rails. The stone was painstakingly loaded by the quarrymen, eight tons to a tram. Trefil villagers rode back home with their shopping in the empty trams. Drivers

The abbey furnace on the River Angidy above Tintern

of both horses and locomotives were renowned for their partiality to drink. In his essay on Trefil, published in the late 1940s, Idris Williams wrote:

> Many are the tales of the haulier returning at night drunk at the bottom of the empty tram, and appearing again in the morning to take Silver or Boxer out of his stable for the trek to the Iron Works at Beaufort, Ebbw Vale, or Sirhowy in order to keep the economic wheels turning. Only men of very tough calibre could work as they did, and drink as they did as well.

Williams describes a tightly-knit community in which 'everybody calls everybody by Christian name; each neighbour knows the troubles and tribulations of the others, and runs to the rescue.' He attributes much of the closeness to 'a quarry institution, the cabin where the men take their meals, and where they congregate during bad weather.' This, he says, is a 'forum of discussion about literature poetry, religion, and politics. Many of the current problems of the day are discussed in these cabins, and it seems, always have been discussed since limestone quarrying has been the chief means of livelihood in the district.' Trade union meetings were held there, too. The Chartists also gathered secretly in a cave within a few hundred yards of the quarry.

Williams emphasises the Trefil people's love of music, and it seems fitting that in the copy of his book kept in the National Library of Wales the words of a song have been written by hand:

> We had a supper fine in Trefil
> Who the hell will pay the big bill
> Did you ever see
>
> There is Ted Prosser in the chair
> Fit for any maiden fair
> Did you ever see
>
> William Paynter is chief guest
> In this meeting he gets zest
>
> William Bevan tried to sing
> He thinks he's another Bing
>
> Tom Jones is fair & fat
> None the worse although for that

The iron works at Blaenafon, from an engraving of 1800

THE FOLKLORE OF MONMOUTHSHIRE

Walter Price is on the brink
Of a marriage sweet I think

Well that is all for now this night
I do hope the song is right

Ted (Edwin) Prosser was a Labour Party and trade union stalwart in Trefil, William Paynter a leading figure in the National Union of Mineworkers in South Wales. The tune intended for the song must have been the traditional Welsh 'Lili Lon', better known as 'Y Mochyn Du' (The Black Pig), which was also used for an earlier composition on the ironmaster, Crawshay Bailey (1789-1872).

Bailey and his brother, Joseph, with the help of their uncle, Richard Crawshay, became powerful figures in South Wales and MPs at Westminster. They jointly owned ironworks at Beaufort and Nant-y-glo,

Bailey's Tower, Nant-y-glo (Chris Barber)

the latter one of the biggest in the world. Both amassed fortunes. Crawshay Bailey also promoted the sinking of coal mines and the construction, first of wagonways, such as that from Nant-y-glo via Clydach Valley to the canal wharf at Gofilon; then of railways, such as the line from the Forest of Dean to Pontypool, via Monmouth and Usk.

Various monuments to Crawshay Bailey, intended or otherwise, can still be seen. Near Blaenau, for example, one of the two round houses built for the family in 1816 remains. The Baileys commissioned these fortress-like structures with walls four feet thick and doors of plate iron because they feared their own workers. Indeed, the first large-scale strike in South Wales began in October 1816 when Tredegar ironworkers came out in protest at wage cuts. They marched across the mountains to invite widespread support, and the planned reductions were duly rescinded. At the time trade unions were illegal, but even after their legalisation with the repeal of the Combination Acts in 1824, they were still fiercely resisted by employers. A decade later ironmasters and coal owners in South Wales announced that they would sack anyone failing to sign a document dissociating himself from Robert Owen's Grand National Consolidated Trade Union.

Workers adopted clandestine tactics. This anonymous notice was posted in 1830:

> This is to Certify that whosoever Will Work on the Varteg will not only have is Goods all the Pecises, but will have his Life Lost the first that will go into any of the Levells to cut 1 oz. of coal he shall certainly Looss his Life from the 22nd of February.

Men known as Scotch Cattle, disguised in animal hides and with faces blackened, 'scotched' men prepared to take pay below union rates by beating them up or smashing their furniture—though they carefully refrained from spoiling any food or damaging anything which contained it, possibly out of a deeply-ingrained reluctance to destroy victuals. Under their symbol of a red bull's head, they were particularly active early in 1832 at Nant-y-glo and Pontypool. A backslider from one locality would be punished by a 'herd' from another to avoid identification. Meetings for co-ordinating activity took place at Croes Penmaen, near Blackwood, which was 'noted through Wales, as the rendezvous for ... the disaffected, and no more strategical ground for the purpose could the most experienced general have selected; easily approachable in a day on foot from all parts, by five small roads—in the centre of the different works, yet near no town sufficiently inland—easily made inaccessible in those days to cavalry.' So wrote 'Ignotus' in 1867.

In the summer of 1834, a shop at Blackwood was destroyed because the owner, Thomas Rees, had denounced workmen for trying to combine against their employers. The Blackwood herd was particularly active until its leader, a Staffordshire man, saw fit to disappear after being involved in the murder of a constable.

Despite—or more likely, because of—his strong resistance to workers' demands for reasonable rates of pay, Bailey, like many other Victorian entrepreneurs, had money to spend on 'good works' such as the imposing clock he donated for the town hall at Abergavenny and the spacious park for the townspeople's use. With his brother he paid for a church at Beaufort. His grave at Llanfoist is marked by an imposing obelisk and the church there was restored in his memory at the expense of his son (also called Crawshay).

Many stories were told about him. He decided to sell the ironworks at Ebbw Vale, which was not doing well, but became enraged when his former manager, Thomas Brown—not known to be well off—began bidding in the auction. 'Let him have it, lads', shouted Bailey. 'Knock it down to him, Mr Auctioneer. Let's see if Tom Brown has enough money even to pay for the transfer.' The other bidders obediently dropped out, and the works was knocked down to Brown at a low figure. When the auctioneer asked for sureties binding the sale Brown left the room amid laughter and sallies such as 'That's the last we'll see of him', only to return moments later with his principals, the Darby brothers of

Coalbrookdale in Shropshire. Furious at being made a fool of, and at having parted with the works at a low price, Bailey rushed at Brown and gave him a black eye.

At least he saw the joke on another occasion when at Winches Pit he happened to hear an argument between the banksman, who controlled the movements of the cage, and one of the tippers on the screens. He immediately intervened, told them to stop arguing and get on with their work, ending by saying: 'I am the gaffer here.' The story, as told by L. Twiston Davies, continues:

> The pit was of the old water balance type, and the speed was regulated by a hand-brake manipulated by the banksman. Mr Bailey was a man who believed in seeing for himself how everything was proceeding at his works and with that object would descend into the mines, as well as scour every nook and cranny of his iron works on top, to see that the work was carried out efficiently. Having restored peace at the top, he took his stand on the bond (or pit cage) preparatory to going down into the bowels of the earth. The fangs being released, the wheel slowly revolved, and the cage disappeared in the darkness, when suddenly in No Man's Land, i.e. halfway between the top and the bottom, it stopped, hanging in space. Mr Bailey was perplexed, but presently he heard a hoary voice travelling down the shaft, asking the question, 'Mr Bailey, who is the gaffer now?' The feeble response came from the depths, 'O Lewis, you are the gaffer now.' With that admission, Lewis released the brake and lowered Mr Bailey gently to the bottom. He chuckled many a time afterwards when relating how he had placed Crawshay Bailey in such a quandary, that he (Mr Bailey) had to admit that 'Lewis of Twyncynghoody was his gaffer.'

It has been suggested that boys from Cowbridge School in Glamorgan made up the song about Bailey, which must have been in existence by 1851 because one of its many verses runs:

> Crawshay Bailey went to London
> By a very cheap excursion;
> He was to see the Exhibition
> And the Patagonian Mission.

Whatever its origin, the song circulated widely, with variations. In Rhymney the first verse was:

> Crawshay Bailey had an engine,
> She was puffing and a-blowing;
> She could go ten miles an hour,
> And faster if you shoved her.

A different singer, possibly from Newport, preferred:

> Crawshay Bailey had an engine
> And he found it wouldn't go,
> So he pulled it by a string
> All the way to Nantyglo.

Well over 40 verses in all have been noted, some of them ribald. The song is still often sung, with Bailey's first name corrupted to 'Cosher'.

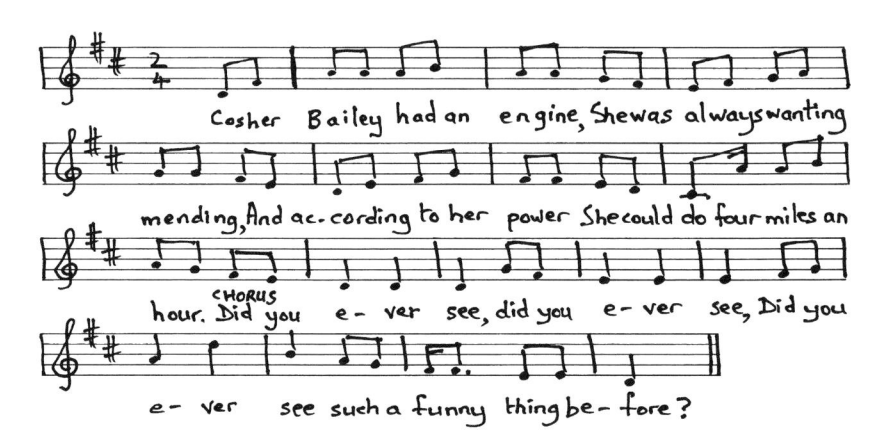

Cosher Bailey had an engine, She was always wanting mending, And according to her power She could do four miles an hour. Did you ever see, did you ever see, Did you ever see such a funny thing before?

> Cosher Bailey had an engine,
> She was always wanting mending,
> And according to her power
> She could do four miles an hour.
> (Chorus)
> Did you ever see, did you ever see,
> Did you ever see such a funny thing before?

WORK

When she come into the station
She did frighten all the nation;
She was wiggle, waggle, wiggle,
She was shiggle, shaggle, shiggle.

Cosher bought her secondhand
And he paint her up so grand;
When the driver he did oil her
She went and bust her boiler.

Cosher Bailey's sister Lena,
She was living up in Blaenau;
She could knit or darn our stockings
But her cooking it was shocking.

Oh the sight it was heart-rending,
Cosher drove his little engine
And he got stuck in a tunnel
And went up the blooming funnel.

Cosher Bailey he did die
And they put him in a coffin;
But alas they heard some knocking:
Cosher Bailey only joking.

Well, the devil wouldn't have him
But he gave him sticks and matches
For to set up on his own
On the top of Beaufort patches.

Patches were small open-cast workings not normally in production. The devil's refusal to accept a person as being too great a sinner or nuisance for hell is a well-loved motif in industrial lore.

Miners

In Monmouthshire, 'where toil the Cwmry deep in sunless pits', (to quote a line by W.H. Davies), coal was dug at Abercarn, Abertillery, Bedwellty, Blaenafon, Blaenau, Cwmbrân, Ebbw Vale, Nant-y-glo, Pontypool, Rhymney, Tredegar, and many smaller places. As recently as the 1970s production ran to 15 million tons a year. Now there is none. Of all the Monmouthshire mines, only Bit Pit, Blaenafon, remains—as a museum.

Ty Trist Colliery

In 1910, at the age of 13, Aneurin Bevan started work at the Tredegar Iron and Coal Company's Ty Trist mine. His daily wage was 1s. 4½d. (just over 6p.). Like other youngsters before and since, he joined a tightly-knit fraternity with its own codes of conduct, customs, and fierce loyalties.

The typical miner set off from a terraced house, 'two rooms up, two down; / Flung there by sullen pit-owners / In a spasm of petulance, discovering / That colliers could not live / On the bare Welsh mountain', as John Ormond put it in his poem, 'The Key'. The way to work could be arduous, as this memory, quoted by Sue Pickavance, shows:

> You would often see the lights from the miners' lamps all over the mountainside as they made their way to and from work in the dark. It was a harsh journey and heaven only knows how they managed when the rain lashed across the mountain or the cloud would come down to blanket everything.

Clothing was normally a dark cloth cap, flannel shirt with red muffler, moleskin trousers tied ('yorked') below the knees (some say to keep rats from running up one's legs) and supported by a leather belt, and hobnailed boots. A tommy (food) box and water jack (bottle or tin) were essential items of equipment.

A raw newcomer might be initiated by being sent on fool's errands in search of such things as glass wedges or buckets of blast. He might also be required to pay his footing—a sort of entry fee—in the shape of a chew of tobacco or a pint of beer for each of his butties (fellow workers). In the Rhymney area a lad refusing to pay would be promised exemption if he could make a notch with an axe at a chalk mark on a post after being blindfolded. The task seemed easy, but as soon as the blindfold was on, his cap would be hung over the mark. Again and again he would swing the axe, to be told each time that he had missed. Only when his cap was suitably tattered would the blindfold be removed, for him to rue his decision not to pay the footing.

Young miners would listen 'in silent awe to [stories of] feats of strength, butties rescued from roof falls, inrushes of water and gas, runaway journeys.' They also acquired the complex vocabulary of mining, some of it peculiar to certain areas. Characteristic terms used in South Wales included fireman (deputy), post (prop: see previous paragraph), pinching (noise made by roof as it adjusted under excessive weight), sounding (assessing the safety of the roof by tapping it with the handle of a pick), and hocking (removing dirt, dust and worthless coal from the floor to provide additional height). The last of these recalls the classic tale of two miners, Twm and Ifor, each of whom has charge of a pit pony. A mines inspector praises Ifor for his glossy beast but threatens to sack Twm if he cannot cure the sores on his pony's back. Twm asks: 'How do you stop your pony rubbing his back against the roof, Ifor bach?' 'Well, now, I'll tell you, Twm. I take out my shovel and clean out the small coal from

Woman and young miner of Pontypool, c.1868

between the sleepers.' '*Duw catwon pawb*' (God save us all), shouts Twm. 'The pony's sores are on his back, not his feet, mun.'

A broader education in mining lore was supplied through endless conversations between pitmen. Idris Davies (1905-53), who from the age of 14 spent seven years as a miner, wrote in his poem, 'Young Man from Rhymney':

> We used to gather together back at the heading
> To eat our grub, and argue about politics
> And football and gambling and religion. ...
> Sometimes we talked sense, and sometimes nonsense,
> And were often very merry in the gloom,
> Sometimes singing old Welsh hymns in chorus
> Or very unholy songs from Tiger Bay.

In *Gwalia Deserta* (1938) Davies told how a young miner might:

> ... call to your side some veteran, grey and scarred,
> And listen to the anecdotes of Chartism
> That the veteran's father told,
> And listen, listen to the frantic footsteps of the past
> When the red-coats rode to Gwalia to beat the toilers down.

A poem from the same volume was set to music in 1959 by the American singer, Pete Seeger, under the title of 'The Bells of Rhymney':

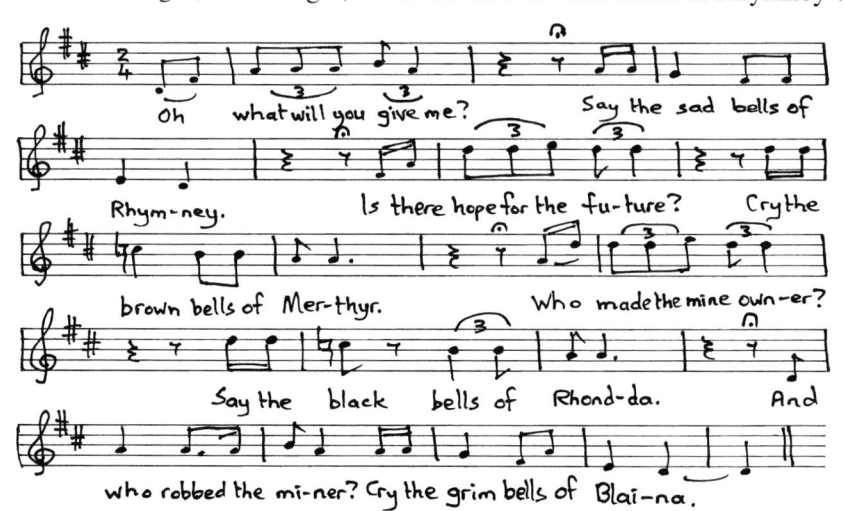

WORK

Oh what will you give me?
Say the sad bells of Rhymney.
Is there hope for the future?
Cry the brown bells of Merthyr.
Who made the mineowner?
Say the black bells of Rhondda.
And who robbed the miner?
Cry the grim bells of Blaina.

They will plunder willy-nilly,
Cry the bells of Caerphilly.
They have fangs, they have teeth,
Shout the loud bells of Neath.
Even God is uneasy,
Say the moist bells of Swansea.
And what will you give me,

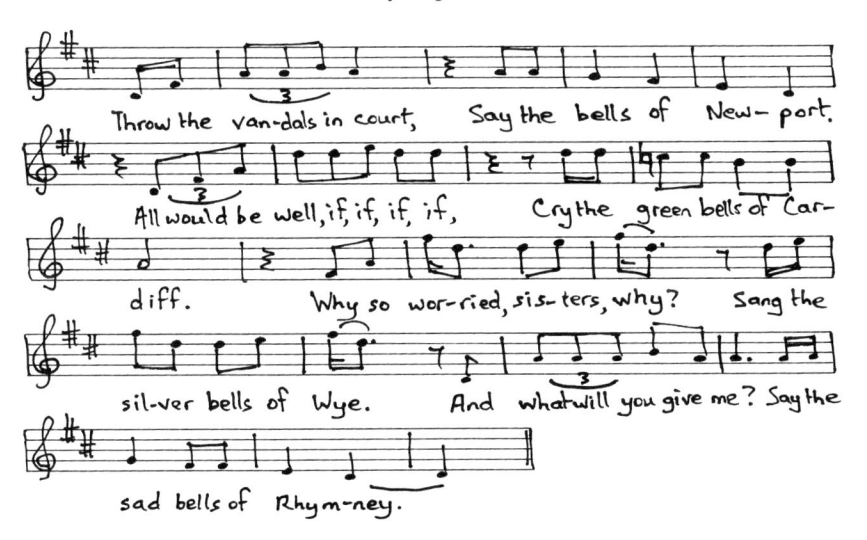

[musical notation: Throw the vandals in court, Say the bells of Newport. All would be well, if, if, if, if, Cry the green bells of Cardiff. Why so worried, sisters, why? Sang the silver bells of Wye. And what will you give me? Say the sad bells of Rhymney.]

Say the sad bells of Rhymney.
Throw the vandals in court,
Say the bells of Newport.
All would be well if, if, if, if,
Cry the green bells of Cardiff.
Why so worried, sisters, why?
Sang the silver bells of Wye.
And what will you give me?
Say the sad bells of Rhymney.

Verses on the AWFUL
EXPLOSION BY FIRE DAMP,
At the Black Vein Pit, Risca,
WESTERN VALLEYS, DEC. 1st, 1860,
LOSS OF NEARLY 136 LIVES.

Subscriptions have been opened and nobly responded to from all parts of the country especially among working men and goods rounds sums are daily reaching the committee in aid of the sufferers.

Come christian people pray attend,
Unto these humble lines here penn'd,
What awful loss of life we hear,
In the western valleys in Monmouthshire.

At the black vein pit at early morn,
Some time before the day did dawn,
On Saturday morning void of fear,
They left their wives and children dear

At Risca in the Western vale,
How sad and dismal is my tale,
Sorrow and grief has fill'd each home
Poor widows grieve & children mourn

But God who hears the widows prayer
Will make them now his anxious care
He'll bless and guide the tender youth
And lead them on to paths of truth.

The workmen in the Western vale,
Rendered assistance without fail,
And from the distant works around,
Brave hearts that labour under ground

That day will long remembered be,
Poor weeping mothers you may see,
Their cries did seem to rend the air,
And all was woe and dark despair.

How nobly did these men behave,
They came to rescue from the grave,
Amid the ruins nobly strives,
But near two hundred lost their lives.

The stoutest heart that e'er was known
Their cries would melt a heart of stone
With uplifted hands to God on high.
The orphan children to hear their cry

Kind heaven bless each noble heart,
That in the trouble took a part,
To risk their lives without regard,
In heaven they'll meet a rich reward.

Come all ye noble of the land,
And help them with a christian hand,
A small subscription far and near,
Will dry the widows and orphans tear

Thank heaven still there's english hearts,
In the time of need play well their parts,
To the orphan children they are kind,
And mourning widows left behind

In the north and all throug staffordshire,
The working men their spirits cheer,
In Bristol City and country round,
The willing hearts were quickly found

Help! help! each husband and each wife,
What a dreadful loss of life.
You'll have the weeping widows prayer
In the western valleys Monmouthshire

John Chapman, Printer, Lamb Street. Bristol.

Broadside (Bristol Library)

WORK

The sorrow and bitterness expressed in 'The Bells of Rhymney' are not surprising in view of the miners' history of struggle. Their work was difficult, dangerous and often poorly paid. In the early 1920s, for example, in a working week of 54 hours (six days of nine hours each) a full collier earned 48s. (£2.40) and a 14 year-old boy, 14s. 3d. (just over 71p.). This at a time when one shilling (5p.) would have bought 3½lb. of bread, or 5¼oz. of tea or 13oz. of sugar, or 4½oz. of butter, or 3 pints of fresh milk. At the same time compensation for a man killed in the mine was £25 if he were married, £18 if single. The value of a pit pony was £40.

Many lives were indeed lost. Apart from the army of miners slowly killed by stone or coal dust in their lungs (silicosis or pneumoconiosis), others suffered in accidents. The constant attrition runs through every miner's memories. Lewis Browning remarks that cases of single deaths in accidents at Blaenafon were 'too numerous to mention'; he gives details of two young men killed in the Old Coal Pit by a roof-fall, eight men burned (one fatally) by explosions of gas in the Coity Pit, John Ellis crushed by a fall of stone in Dick Shon's Level, five mangled after being spilled from the cage at Milfraen Colliery, 14 young men and women drowned in a flood at the Cinder Pit. Such incidents could be multiplied many times over by reference to other localities.

In addition, there were disasters in which large numbers of men and sometimes also boys lost their lives. A single explosion in the Prince of Wales Mine at Abercarn in September 1878, caused 268 fatalities. The Primitive Methodist Chapel lost half its members at a stroke, and its choir was reduced to one. In successive explosions of fire damp (gas) at Risca 35 were killed in January 1816, 142 in December 1860 and 120 in July 1880. A sheet printed in Bristol (see illustration) pleaded in 1860 for financial help for widows and fatherless children. Pit disaster ballads typically describe an incident, often in melodramatic and moralistic fashion, then make an anguished request for relief, addressed to a wide audience.

The east window at Trefethin Church commemorates the 176 men and boys killed at Llanerch Colliery in 1890. This disaster brought the number of fatal casualties in Monmouthshire pits between 1837 and 1927 to over 3,500. The slaughter did not stop then. At Six Bells Colliery, near Abertillery, 45 men died as recently as 1960. 'There's blood on the coal' is an expression with ample justification.

The spectacle of an accident victim being carried home on a stretcher was routine, but none the less dreaded for that. Thomas Jones (born 1870) wrote:

THE FOLKLORE OF MONMOUTHSHIRE

COPY OF VERSES ON THE
EXPLOSIONS
AT
PENTRE YSTRAD
AND
EBBE VALE COLLIERIES,
February 24th & March 3rd, 1871.

The following is a list of the names of the persons who lost their lives at Ebbe Vale

John Price, aged 18, single	G. Turk, aged 18, single
James George, 24, married	J. Chapman, 23, married
Thomas James, 21, single	John Gallop, 30, married
George Gallop, 25, married	Charles Ford, 20, single
David Philips, 21, single	Thomas Mitchell, 39, married
Samuel Cook, 18, single	John Evans, 31, married
William Plumber 24, widower	Philip Philips, 59, married
Joseph Harries, 12, boy	George Williams, 23, single
Francis Adams, 21, single	Jonathan Price, 50, married
James Turner, 50, married	

Fathers, mothers, sisters, brothers,
Listen to this mournful tale,
Of the fate of those poor Colliers,
At Pentre Ystrad and Ebbe Vale;
More than 60 fellow-creatures,
Men who felt no care or woe,
In the evening left their dwelling,
And in death were soon laid low.
Farewell friends and dear relations,
These poor Colliers may have cried,
Where at Ebbe Vale and Pentre Ystrad
Scarcely a week has gone aside.

More than 70 hardy Colliers,
On them fatal afternoons,
Went below the earth's bright surface,
To labour in the pit's deep gloom;
The fiery damp soon came upon them,
And carried death both far and wide,
Till scorched or stifled by the vapour,
Sixty of their number died.

The frightful sound of the explosions,
Cast a gloom on all around,
And many a prayer went up to Heaven
For those poor Colliers underground.

The fatal pits were soon surrounded,
Hundreds stood in blank despair,
With trembling hearts and anxious faces,
Watching for the dear ones there.

The fiery damp had come upon them,
In manly strength and youthful pride,
And some poor fathers and their children,
In death's embrace lay side by side,
Some were stifled at their labour,
Others as they turned to fly,
Some so burnt that no one knew them,
What a fearful death to die.

The air was rent with cries of sorrow,
As the bodies did appear,
Wives lamenting for their husbands,
Children for their fathers dear.
Aged mothers for their offspring,
Perhaps their best support and stay,
Many more with grief were trembling,
For some dear one passed away.

H. Disley, Printer, No. 57, High Street,
St. Giles, London.

Explosion broadside (British Library)

WORK

No child in the Rhymney of that time can forget the silent procession of miners through the street after a colliery explosion when those hurt or killed were carried home on stretchers and then the anxiety as to which house in the row was destined to receive the still living or the dead father or son.

Yet he went on to reflect that miners were far from being passive sufferers, instancing one Rhymney man mortally injured in the pit, who

Gathering shindles (small lumps of coal) for fuel during the strike of 1873

was being carried home on a stretcher. 'Realising that he had not long to live he raised himself on one elbow, shook a fist in the direction of the hated workhouse at Tredegar, and shouted: "Ffarwel i ti, bwci"—"Farewell to you, devil".'

Miners struck in 1822 before strikes were legal, and during the course of violent attempts to stop coal reaching Harford and Company's ironworks at Ebbw Vale, fought a series of running battles with soldiers of the Scots Greys who fixed bayonets and opened fire. When, a decade later, the South Wales miners started a union, its ruthless repression by the employers helped to swell the ranks of the Scotch Cattle. After a lull in the 1840s, militancy increased and led to the formation in the early 1860s of the Amalgamated Association of Miners. A series of desperate strikes and bitter lockouts followed until, in 1875, after a five month struggle, the miners had to accept defeat.

Thomas Jones, who saw men near Rhymney Churchyard breaking stones for road metal to qualify for relief during the lock-out of 1875, later heard the story of how some starving men went to a pit manager's house and demanded to see him:

> He professed to be suffering from a cold and unable to come outside, but he agreed to receive a deputation of three. When they returned their leader reported as follows: 'The manager says that times are very bad and there is little or no work and it is impossible to pay the wages demanded. His advice is that Englishmen should go back to England, the Scotch to Scotland, the Irish to Ireland.' A voice from the crowd: 'Where are the Welsh to go?' 'They can go to hell.'

The union broke up, unable to sustain the struggle. Wages fell by $12^1/_2$ per cent, and were from then on linked to the price of coal in a sliding scale which put dividends for shareholders before wages for miners. Resentment helped to motivate various small, new unions in Monmouthshire which began to campaign for a working day of eight hours 'from bank to bank'—that is, including travelling time within the pit:

> Wyth awr i weithio, wyth awr o rhyddid;
> Wyth awr i gysgu, a wyth swllt y dydd.
> (Eight hours work, eight hours play;
> Eight hours sleep, and eight bob [shillings] a day).

WORK

Not until 1908, with the Coal Mines Regulation Act, did the eight hour day become law, and even then a loophole allowed an extra hour 'not more than 60 days in a year.'

During a strike in 1893, matters were deemed serious enough by the authorities for a state of siege to be declared and soldiers to be sent in. Six years later the military was called out again when some 120,000 South Wales miners, many of whom were earning under £1 a week, came out for a 2s. (10p.) increase. The strike lasted for five months, and severe hardship led to ballads appealing for support. 'A Bitter Cry for Help' begins:

> Dear friends, will you listen a moment,
> A tale of distress we now bring,
> Our wives and our children are starving;
> The thought checks our breath while we sing;
> But forced from our homes by starvation,
> Your sympathy now we implore,
> Oppressed as we are in the coal mines,
> We feel we can bear it no more.

The sheet, with supporting Bible text ('The labourer is worthy of his hire') at the foot, would have been hawked in the streets for a penny. Another, entitled simply 'A SONG', is also biblical in tenor:

> All fellowmen and Colliers,
> And workmen everywhere;
> Come listen to our story,
> A tale full of despair:
> It tells you of depression,
> We've suffered many years;
> Thro' Monmouth and Glamorgan,
> Which fills our eyes with tears.
>
> Cast down in pits of slavery,
> Amidst dangers manifold,
> Beneath the lash of tyranny,
> Too shameful to be told:
> We are working for low wages,
> But food and rent being high;
> Our children and all ages,
> From pangs of hunger cry. ...

> They saw the military might,
> To coal owners is sent;
> To terrify by fear and fright,
> Glamorganshire and Gwent;
> By firearms and gun-powder,
> The innocent they'll smite;
> While many a praying mother
> Prays God defend the right.

Walter Haydn Davies (born in 1903 at Bedlinog, just a few miles outside Monmouthshire) remembered that his Bopa (Aunt) Sarah sang about the issues of the strike, to the tune of the Welsh national anthem:

> Mae'r glowyr Morgannwg, Sir Fynwy a'r Fro
> Yn ymladd yn brysur a'm bris ar y glo
> Ond gwrthod mae'r meistr i wneud sylw o'm Bil
> Gwell ganddynt rhyw gynllun Syr Wil
> Syr Wil sy'n gwrthod wneud cymorth 'm Bil
> O Gymru wen, cwd fyny'th ben i helpu'r glowyr. Amen.
> (The miners of Glamorgan, Monmouthshire, and elsewhere
> Are seriously fighting for a price on the coal
> But the masters take no notice of our Bill
> They prefer some scheme of Sir Will
> It is Sir Will who ignores our Bill
> Oh beloved Wales, raise your head to help the miners. Amen.)

'Our Bill' was William Brace (1865-1947), miners' leader, powerful orator, and fierce opponent of the sliding scale which when the market price of coal dropped led automatically to a reduction in miners' wages. He was born in Risca, and started work in the pit at the age of 12. Sir William T. Lewis (1837-1914), was chairman of the Colliery Owners' Association of South Wales and Monmouthshire and, according to Sidney and Beatrice Webb, 'the most hated man in the Principality.' The self-styled 'Billy Fair Play', known to the miners as 'Billy Foul Play', presided over the sliding scale joint committee from 1880 until 1899.

Several major strikes after the struggles of 1893, the miners reached 1926, and 'the angry summer', to borrow a phrase from Idris Davies. When the TUC called off its general strike after 10 days in May, the miners held out alone until between July and December they were forced

Men digging for coal at Sirhowy patches in 1926

to return to work for longer hours at lower pay—the dreaded 'Double Blow' they had resisted so hard. To survive for up to seven months on strike required steely determination and intense solidarity.

Tim Greeney of Rhymney, interviewed in 1970 by Tony Conran and others, recalled:

> With the coalowners we were practically living in the age of tyranny, see. It was bad at that time. And the wages underground were practically nothing, two pound odd, minimum wage. Just a few months after the '26 strike the Cwm explosion was just over the mountain here in Ebbw Vale. 52 went there. It was a battle of the coalowners then, see. The PDs [Powell Duffryns]—they owned South Wales practically.

Striking miners went digging in the 'patches' for coal to sell and to burn. Strikers received no welfare payments, so to raise funds for the soup kitchens which offered one free meal a day they formed touring minstrel

THE FOLKLORE OF MONMOUTHSHIRE

The Newbridge Miners' Choir, 1926

troupes and jazz bands. Music, as the earlier ballad makers knew, raised morale as well as money. In addition it could attract sympathy for the miners' cause. It played a part at Cwmfelinfach's Nine Mile Point Colliery where, after the general return to work, miners began a stay-down strike which eventually lasted for seven and a half days. Other pits at Risca, Cross Keys and Pontllanfraith came out in sympathy, with either stay-down or stay-out strikes.

Montagu Slater, who described this protest, said that the Nine Mile Point men passed the time in 'singing and yarning and going after rats' in the pit bottom. From the depths below the police at the top could hear the singing, a measure of its intensity. 'The solo passages were sung by a miner with a fine tenor voice and the rest of the men joined in chorus. "Cwm Rhondda" was sung over and over again. "Hold the Fort" was another favourite.'

The sustaining power of music persisted during the miners' last great battle, the strike of 1984-5. Many songs emerged, some written by professional singers such as Ewan MacColl, who sympathised with the miners; others by local people seeking an outlet for the passionate feelings they experienced. Music played its part at the end when the miners, defeated but unbowed, marched back to their doomed pits with bands and banners to the fore in a ceremony of moving and memorable dignity.

The mining community, renowned particularly in South Wales for its solidarity and militancy, had great depths of resource in terms of humour and lore. Nicknames were so adhesive that the use of a real name in an enquiry might be met with genuine incomprehension, even by the person in question. All must have had a story behind them. These examples could be multiplied many times over: Dai Niffy and Jurgen Jug of Beer (from Abertyswg); Sam Half a Mo', Johnny Pull Hard, Ianto Shwm Mae (Ianto How do you do), Dynamo Dan, Tom Dead Slow, Dan Deialog (Dialogue), Ned Fine Talk, Davies Whiff, Cough and Spit, Tom 'Falau (Apples), and Billy Welsh Cake (from Rhymney and the Tredegar Valley).

Like others, such as fishermen, engaged in dangerous work, miners were superstitious. With the possibility of accident or even disaster often at the back of their minds, they were not always keen to work, especially on Mondays, when dangers might have developed unnoticed during their absence from the pit on Sunday. In Glamorgan as well as Monmouthshire a group of men would nominate one of its number to throw his cap into a tree near the pithead. If it stuck in the branches they would go to work; if it fell they would go home. Unless for some reason the nominee were particularly keen to work, the cap usually fell. At Rhymney as it was thrown these words were said: 'Un, dau, tri. Cap lawr i mi' (One, two, three. Cap down for me).

Miners and their families had a sixth sense about disaster. One morning a man called Evans simply refused to get out of bed to go to work. That day an explosion caused casualties in his pit. Of course, it is highly likely that he and others stayed in bed on days when no accidents occurred, but the unusual sticks in the memory. In the same lucky family, Mrs Evans's father was driving a pony in the pit when a roof fall buried him and between seven and 10 other men. Workmates tried to dig them out, but failed. A small group of men went to tell the pony driver's wife the bad news, but she responded with complete confidence: 'Don't you worry. My Davie's all right. He'll come back.' A rescue party which worked all night to free the bodies found one man alive the next morning—Davie: the fall had knocked him down beneath a tram, which had taken the weight and saved his life.

There was a widespread belief that to meet a cross-eyed person on the way to work was an evil omen, and many miners would turn back home. Eugene Cross (born 1896) of Ebbw Vale recalled that a cross-eyed girl who lived in the same street as several miners was inadvertently responsible for a good deal of absenteeism in the local pit. He also said that some would turn back if they met a rag and bone man. His mother stopped him going to work one morning when a solitary bird sang at the top of the garden. Tom Hopkins (born 1906) of Tredegar told how a collier returning from morning shift met a cross-eyed postman, the adverse consequence being only that his least favourite meal, stew, was for dinner when he got home.

At Garndiffaith, north of Pontypool, miners believed that a black dog, benevolent unless it were derided or scorned, would appear in front of them if they were to be involved in a pit accident that day. If they took its warning and went home, all would be well. In contradiction to the usual belief, miners at Risca thought that for a black cat to cross their path boded ill, and they too would turn back, as would the men of Abertyswg if a lone blackbird flew across in front of them. The cries of curlews or swifts—the latter known as the Seven Whistlers—also presaged disaster; T.A. Davies wrote: 'One good elderly lady of Narth [near Tintern] told the writer that, years ago, she heard them about the Narth Wood and next morning the sad news came that her brother was killed in the pit.' Actions which could bring bad luck included whistling underground, riding in the 13th train carriage on the way to the pit, and starting to drive a new heading on a Friday, especially Friday 13th.

Unexplained tappings, whistling noises, shadows, shapes and lights in the pit also warned of impending doom. Some Monmouthshire miners complained on a day when nothing went well that they had on their shoulders 'the old black dog' which brought bad luck, illness or accident. George Greeves of Abertyswg (born 1910), a miner like his father and grandfather, visualised the creature in many forms: half man, half goat; or alternatively, dark hangman, dirty knacker's man, devil, black gypsy, wicked Argus (dog), evil echo, Headman-Bacchus, devil's advocate, black intolerance, and human monster. In short, not at all friendly; and as a protection against ill-hap George's grandfather (who lived from 1841 until 1924) said people would hurry home to touch the wooden cross which hung on the wall of most kitchens.

George Greeves himself recalled:

> We knew of cases of pit horses giving due warning of impending disaster by running away from a place which a little later caved in, or prior to run-away trams, saving many lives. It has been said that many pet dogs gave due warning of impending trouble in the mine before a shift commenced and during a working shift.

He also mentions coal miners who refused to wash their backs for fear of weakening them, and omitted to shave their necks because doing so was supposed to cause 'bad eyes'. He goes on to list a wide variety of homely remedies. Cobwebs were used to stop bleeding, and a chew of tobacco to cauterise an open wound. Miners applied urine to their hands to harden them, to feet to prevent corns, and to knees and elbows to avoid housemaids knees and elbows. When corns and callouses appeared they were rubbed with a black slug, the slime from which was thought to provide a cure.

For heartburn a piece of marking chalk or coal was chewed or sucked. Miners quenched their thirst from a four-pint jack filled with water to which a pinch of salt had been added; alternatively, barley water replaced moisture lost as sweat, though the expedient preferred by some was 8 to 10 pints of beer at the end of the shift. Miners' wives and daughters collected many herbs and berries for medicinal use; details of these are given in chapter 6.

The beginning of mining is evoked in a story told in the Rhymney Valley until the early years of the 20th century. At Gilfach Fargoed, just over the border in Glamorgan, the fairies kill a giant and steal his treasure. They dig a great hole in which to bury the body, but only succeed in part. As the corpse smells so strong, they light a fire round it, but become terrified when the pit itself begins to burn. After dousing the flames, one of them picks up a piece of black rock and takes it to the wisest among the *tylwyth teg*, who says: 'If this pit burned, doubtless it was the black rock which set it alight.' Some is put on the hearth, and indeed makes an excellent fire. Other fairies collect more of the black rock, and they use it to keep warm in winter. They call it coal, which was thus first known in the Rhymney Valley as a result of a giant's death.

But the end of mining had no such flight of fancy. Tom Edwards, a friend of George Greeves, wrote this disenchanted but prophetic poem many years before mining in fact ceased in Monmouthshire:

McLaren Colliery Rubbish Tip

Great slag heap, monument of toil,
Black sore upon the earth's sweet soil,
Thrown up from darkest depths below,
The very opposite of snow.

Tower of toil and aches and fears,
A gathering cloud for seventy years,
Crouching like some headless hound,
Forever to the village bound.

This huge black monster without legs,
The biggest of all cuckoo's eggs,
The hill made by human moles,
This aftermath of getting coal,
Like scum it sticks around the pot,
It's ours now, the bloody lot.

Farm Workers

In the time of the Mabinogi a legendary sow deposited three grains of wheat and three bees by the Troggy Brook (see chapter 8). Ever since then the best wheat and the best honey have been said to come from Gwent. The Lower Wye Valley certainly continues to produce excellent honey because of its profusion of wild flowers.

Agricultural attitudes and techniques have radically changed here during the past half-century, as they have elsewhere in Britain. An hour's visit to the Gwent Rural Life Museum at Usk will demonstrate the great gulf between old and new which is nevertheless bridged by the memories of many people. D.L. Driscoll, who was brought up in Machen, recalls butter churned by hand, bread baked by residual heat in an old-fashioned oven, and hay cut by scythe-swinging men:

> We were forbidden in the field when this was in progress, but once the grass was spread out to dry, we played there all through the lovely long summer evenings until our mothers appeared to order us home for bed. We watched the men with pitchforks toss the hay on to the horse-drawn haywain, and what delight it was to be given a lift on this on its way back to the field from the farm. This [method of working] of course took far longer to harvest the hay, but the farmers seldom lacked helpers then for wages were so low, men were glad to earn a little extra to supplement them. Supper was always provided for the men before they went home; the scrubbed table in the farm kitchen was spread with wedges of fresh Caerphilly cheese, butter, thick slices of home baked bread, salads from the garden, cider and herb beer to drink.

Haymaking in the Wye Valley (Chepstow Museum)

The corn harvest followed a broadly similar pattern. James Davies, the Devauden schoolmaster, noted in 1841 how people from his area went off to 'distant parishes' as soon as the corn was ripe: 'They often go out in companies on the Monday and return home on the Saturday nights; during their absence they sleep in barns or stables, or wherever they can get shelter.'

More recently, a reaper-binder cut the corn after men with scythes had cleared a way for it round the edge of the field. Sheaves were then propped up in small groups—usually of six or eight, though some preferred seven—to dry thoroughly before being loaded on wagons and taken to the stockyard.

In the days of hand reaping, a small clump of corn was left uncut in the middle of a farmer's last field and plaited to form a sort of mare's tail, called *caseg fedi* or *caseg ben fedi* (harvest mare or end of harvest mare). The reapers, standing 10 yards off, would in turn throw their sickles in an attempt to cut off the tail, the successful man taking it into the farmhouse, where it stayed until the following year. By custom, the womenfolk of the house tried to drench man and 'mare' with water 'or any other available liquid' as he tried to get in. A dry mare was a good omen and its bearer obtained a place of honour at the harvest home feast. A wet mare boded ill, and sometimes was not given house room at all. Its unfortunate carrier either paid a forfeit to the women or sat at the foot of the table as a butt for jokes during the meal.

In some eastern parts of Wales ornaments of corn straw, called babies or dollies, were made. In 1952, Fred Hando saw a corn dolly fixed to a pew-end in Cwmyoy Church for the harvest festival which superseded the boisterous old harvest home, a banquet provided by the farmer for his workmen.

In the late autumn or during the winter the 'drum', as the mobile threshing machine was called, travelled from farm to farm. William John Duffield (born 1906) of Trellech Grange described the event:

> We used to go to Great House to help with the threshing and it was always my job to cut the bands of the sheaves. The dust got in my eyes and it took a couple of months to get the thistles out of my fingers. When they stacked the sheaves they used to build a sort of platform out of logs and broust [brushwood] to keep the sheaves off the bare ground. The rats used to get under the sheaves and make tunnels inside. When we got to the bottom of the stack, the rats would run out in their hundreds. Men and dogs would chase them and have a lot of fun.

Until the late 19th century people turned out on Easter Sunday to 'walk the wheat'. The occasion was partly a commemoration of the battle of Toulouse, fought on 10 April 1814, in which local men had taken part; those with war medals sported them. Cider and cake were distributed at the four corners of the field. Toasts to the crop were drunk in the cider, whilst the cake was eaten, scattered, and also buried. These words were said:

> A bit for God, a bit for man
> And a bit for the fowls of the air.

Double helpings of plum cake were given to anyone who found a corn cockle in the wheat. This attractive purple flower, once common, made bread bitter-tasting, and possibly even poisonous, if its seeds got into the wheat and were milled in the flour.

The farm workers of those days are evoked in a poem written in 1879 by Richard Crawley (1840-93), the oldest son of the rector at Bryngwyn (for whom, see page 162). Crawley was a classical scholar whose translation of Thucydides is still used. He travelled widely, and once visited the

WORK

Richard Crawley

elderly Garibaldi on the Italian island of Caprera: 'I spent two or three hours with him under an almond tree, already laden with fruit, whither he ordered two seats to be brought. I was much struck with the kindness and simplicity of his character; he ordered his gardeners to pick some oranges, and made them stop working for a minute or so to eat some, nor was my boatman forgotten. He discoursed for some time generally on politics, showing a good sense and moderation that I do not remember to have met with before in a continental republican: he told me that England was his ideal of a republic, as his definition of the word was a state of things where the people really governed themselves.' Richard Crawley lived mainly in Oxford and London, but throughout his life continued to visit his father at Bryngwyn.

Poem of Bryngwyn People

We're nobody particular we're just the men you meet
At harvest with sickle, or at seedtime dropping wheat
From Mondays until Saturdays we work from morn till night
And only in these latter days we've learned to read and write.

Our little place is poor enough though clean as any pin
Who e'er you are, you're sure enough of welcome when you're in
The rich man has his valets, and his locks to guard his store;
But we have empty wallets, and we only latch the door.

Besides, perhaps, a pair or two of blankets and a bed,
An oaken chest, a chair or two—all bought when we were wed—
There's little you would lend upon we've neither house or lands
We only depend upon the labour of our hands.

When these begin to fail you, and you're thrown upon yourself,
Or anything should ail you, and there's nothing on the shelf,
Though anxious looks the mother, and our own is almost bare
We feel for one another, and we find a bit to spare.

You ask me what we think about in raining weather, when
We sit and pass the drink about and speak but now and then,
Sure all may spend their leisure in the manner that they will
And poor men find a pleasure just simply sitting still.

We're up to tend the cattle, when the Londoner's in bed;
We hear the thunder rattle; when there's nothing overhead
To shield us in the racket, and when down doth pour the rain
We only shake our jacket, and we go to work again.

Our daughters serve for wages, and our boys go on the farm
According to their ages, and the power that keeps from harm.
The sparrows and the likes with their glory doth array
Our hearts doth know, and still is with our little ones away.

To every man his station, and his work is set I ween:
The queen doth rule the nation, and the soldier guards the queen
From the men that would harm her, and their number is not small
We labour for the farmer, and the farmer keep them all.

Then, do not judge us blindly, as you'll hear some people do;
Think only of us kindly, as you'd have us think of you;
To other folk than we belong the pulpit and the pew,
But England were not England without her common men.

The message of the penultimate verse is expressed in words and pictures on the sign of the Five Alls Inn at Chepstow. 'I fight for all', says the soldier; 'I pray for all', the priest. 'I rule all', says the king; 'I plead for all', the lawyer. Finally, the farmer, complete with Union Jack coat and bulldog, says: 'I pay for all'.

Farm workers, male and female, could seek engagements at annual hiring fairs. A ploughman would display a piece of whipcord as an emblem of his calling; a shepherd sported a tuft of wool and a servant maid, a strand from a mop. In Monmouthshire hiring fairs were held, mostly in May, at Caerleon (on the 1st), Monmouth (second Monday),

WORK

Abergavenny (14th), Raglan (31st) and Usk (Friday after Whitsun). Few if any of these survived the First World War. A farmer's wife wrote to E.J. Dunnill in 1913:

> There is a fair in Abergavenny on May 14th, and one the first Monday in May in Monmouth. They are the hiring fairs, but there are very few girls to go to them now. The custom seems to be dying out. There used to be one in Caerleon, May 1st, but there are no servants go there for hire now. The farm servants about here change [employment] very much the same as a town girl would. They don't mind when they leave, as they think they can always get a place.

The Five Alls Inn, Chepstow

Nevertheless, some of the old ways persisted. Farmers travelled to the Holy Mountain, Skirrid Fawr, to gather a small amount of its sacred earth to scatter round their houses and outbuildings to avert evil, and in their fields to promote fertility. Especially in the Llanthony and Cwmyoy area, pigs were slaughtered only under a waxing moon, lest the bacon should waste away in the curing. On the other hand, peas and beans were sown only when the moon waned.

If a cow had an infection in the cleave of the hoof a cure could be effected by digging up the print it made in the soil and throwing it into the hedge. Charmers attempted to heal such things as lameness in animals, not always successfully, by verbal formula or simply looking. One such practitioner dealt with a sick and allegedly bewitched calf by burying it in a dunghill up to its neck to break the spell. He had probably spotted that the animal was undersized and suffering from hypothermia, and that the warmth of the manure would be sufficient to revive it.

Traditional weather lore included rhymes such as this, from Usk:

> Dry May and dripping June brings all things in tune,
> But if May takes to dripping, June flood never did good.

A verse in Welsh was translated by Iolo Morgannwg:

> When the hoarse waves of Severn are screaming aloud,
> And Penllyne's lofty castle's involved in a cloud,
> If true the old proverb, a shower of rain
> Is brooding above, and will soon drench the plain.

Walter Powell of Llantilio Crossenny noted in his diary in 1612: 'this was the Greatest Yeare of ffruite that eu' [ever] I saw. I made 50 hogsheades of sider of the tieth [tithe] of both p'ishes.' A poem on the respective products of the 13 Welsh counties written in 1720 said of Monmouthshire:

> Gwaith y merched hyn yn union
> Nyddu rhai gwlanenni meinion
> Trin seidr o'r perllanau tewfrith
> A gweithi hetiau gwellt y gwenith.
> (The women here are employed
> In spinning some fine flannels
> In making cider from bounteous orchards
> And in making hats from wheat straw).

Towards the end of the same century, Edward Davies concentrated on just one of these items:

WORK

No better cider does the world supply
Than grows along thy borders, gentle Wye:
Delicious, strong, and exquisitely fine,
With all the friendly properties of wine.
A vast extent of country owns the Sway
Of sweet Pomona, blooming queen of May,
Who guards from blights thy apple-planted vales
From Chepstow upwards to the alps of Wales.

By the 1880s cider orchards in Monmouthshire, mainly in the Usk Valley, covered 3,000 acres. Varieties grown included Green Apples and Perthyr, the latter called after a hamlet in the north of the county. Many farmers had their own mills. Charles Harper, visiting Tintern in the 1890s, wrote:

> Cider making is now the occupation of all this neighbourhood. We saw them making it by hand-mill at Coedithel Farm, near here, and the farmer gave us each a glass of the newly pressed juice. There was a large admixture of pears with the apples and the drink was delicious. We told the farmer it was nectar fit for the gods, and suggested what a pity it was that it could not be kept in that condition. He seemed rather inclined to think us somewhat blasphemous,

Old cider mill, Anchor Hotel, Tintern. The mill is still there, on display

but said that to the countryman's idea fresh cider was not drinkable. Now, this time next year it would be in prime condition, and if we were in the neighbourhood then, we should have a glass. Do you know, I was so charmed with Tintern that methinks I shall be here at this time next year, to take him at his word.

It is not known whether Harper did return. If so, one hopes that he was careful. There is a local word, 'stunnem', which Ivor Waters defines as 'a mixture of perry and cider in the proportion of two to one', for a particularly powerful brew.

The cider mill and press by the church at Redwick are among several which survive. A press used by the Watkins Brothers at Wern y Cwm, Llanddewi Skirrid, is preserved in the museum at Usk. A portable cider mill from Dingestow can be seen in the Museum of Welsh Life at St Fagans. Such devices continued in regular use until the 1950s. Mr C.T. Morris of Raglan worked as a travelling cider maker for over 30 years. When he began, in 1928, 'he went to 40 farms, a number which increased to 67 after the Second World War. On average, he made 400 gallons for each farmer at a price which rose from 7s. (35p.) per 100 gallons in 1928 to 33s. (£1.15) in 1959. On the other hand, over the same period the

Mr C.T. Morris (Welsh National Folk Museum)

volume of cider he made annually fell from over 18,000 gallons in all to only 180.

Perhaps the last of the old travelling cider makers worked from Llanfihangel Torymynydd until 1990. This account comes from Llewelyn Richards (born *c*.1915) of the same village:

> A big event was the cider mill round. Every farmer made cider, it was the only way he could get help at harvest time. A two-gallon jar of it was always by the rick in the field. The outfit was a mill to crush apples, a small petrol engine to drive it and a press to squeeze the juice out of the *muss* [pomace], as the crushed apples were called. The press had a flat circular bed, five or six feet across, with a groove all round leading to a sort of spout to collect the juice. A large coconut fibre mat was placed on this and covered with a layer of muss. The ends were folded inwards, another laid on top and the process repeated until the press was full. A wooden cover was placed on top and screwed down to press out the juice. This was left overnight to get as much juice, as possible, then the process was repeated the next day if necessary. Gathering apples was an unpleasant, laborious job, especially on cold winter mornings when the grass in the orchard was long.

The decline in production of cider apples has been reversed in recent years. Bulmers of Hereford have planted 100,000 trees on 420 acres at Penrhos Farm which will be in production by the year 2000. Appropriately enough, most of the real cider sold in local public houses is Bulmers Traditional. The Ship Inn at Raglan formerly sold a local Seidr y Berllan (Orchard Cider). Andrew Canning, landlord of the Clytha Arms at the village of Clytha makes a small quantity of perry each year from the fruit of old trees at the back of his pub. Ben Jones of Grove Farm, Llanfoist, also makes perry, but is better known for his Black Mountain Cyder. Another farmer, at Tredunnock, still makes cider for himself and neighbours, in time-honoured fashion.

Arthur Machen, who observed that when apples were short people were happy to add a few pears or even a barrow load or two of parsnips to the cider-making, wrote appreciatively of the local product:

> It was a greenish yellow in colour, with a glint of gold in it if held up to the light, as it were a remembrance of the August and

September suns that had shone mellow on the deep orchards of Gwent. It was of full body and flavour and strength, smooth on the palate, neither sweet not sharp; and I do not think there was anyone in Llanddewi [Fach] parish so poor as not to have a barrel or two in his cellar against Christmastide and snowy nights.

CHAPTER 10

Play

A passion for sports and pastimes of all kinds seems to be one of humankind's essential characteristics. It is no surprise that the complete gamut of modern sports is found in Monmouthshire, from sedate boules (for which there is a special *piste* at Redwick, by the village hall), to boisterous rugby. Hunting, somewhat controversially now, remains from the blood sports of old. The proverbial Welsh love for taking drink and making music continues to be a significant feature of local life.

Blood Sports
Few reminders are left of the cruel sports of the past. In front of the Market House at Newport bulls were once fastened to a ring to be baited by dogs. The same ritual took place in the Bull Ring at Monmouth with both bulls and badgers. Cockfighting took place in a pit behind the Three Cranes at Chepstow. A possible explanation for the origin of Croes-y-Ceiliog (Cock's Cross) has to do with fighting cocks.

At least otters were wild creatures with a chance of escaping, though hunting them has now been illegal for many years. The Wye Valley Otter Hunt formally acquired its name in 1917, though the organisation dates back to 1879. Its 'country' consisted of Herefordshire and Gloucestershire in England, Glamorgan and Monmouthshire in Wales. Meets were regularly held at Dingestow, Llangenny, Monnow Mill, Mitchel Troy, Newbridge-on-Usk, Pant-y-goitre, Rockfield, Sor Bridge at Caerleon, Tintern and Usk. As well as the Wye, the Monnow, Trothy and Usk rivers were hunted.

To a later eye, some of the triumphant records of killing otters make sad reading:

The Bridge Inn at Chainbridge

One of the longest hunts on record took place in his time [that of P.J. Pryce-Jenkin, Master from 1917-22] on the Usk at Bryderwyn [Bryn-derwen] above Chain Bridge. This otter was found in the large pool below Trostrey Court above the old weir. The pool runs deep and is well over half a mile in length and in those days held plenty of thick cover on both banks and several strong holts. Scent was good and hounds hunted well and on several occasions swam long distances with plenty of cry. Finding at 11 a.m., hounds bustled their otter all day and several times he was evicted by terrier and spade from strong holts. Eventually, the pressure being too great, he left the pool and tried to cross the weir to the next pool below, when the hounds caught him, a 25 pound dog, at 7 p.m., an eight-hour hunt without a dull moment.

The huntsmen, with their distinctive bright blue coats, knee-breeches and red socks, were still to be seen in the 1950s, by which time the otter had more or less disappeared. Some 50 years later there are signs that, now protected, it is beginning to re-colonise stretches of the Wye.

Attempts in the late 1990s to make the hunting of foxes by dogs illegal have aroused strong feelings on both sides of the argument. On Boxing Day in 1997 seven hounds from the Tredegar Farmers' Pack lay critically ill from poison allegedly administered by renegade hunt saboteurs.

For generations Boxing Day has been a high point in the hunting calendar. The Llangybi Hunt, one of the oldest in Wales, meets at the White Hart in Llangybi. Its hounds contributed a strain to Lady Curre's famous rough-coated white pack, based at Itton Court.

PLAY

Past and present officials of the Wye Valley Otter Hunt at the Beaufort Arms, Tintern, in 1936

In 1786, during the early years of foxhunting, Edward Davies, vicar of Mathern and rector of Portskewett, devoted a sequence of his poem, *Chepstow*, to the sport. A century later, very much on traditional lines, an anonymous writer produced his own song on the subject:

Hark Forward

On the first of No-vember bright Phoebus shone clear, and we had not been hun-ting for quite half a year Squire mounted Black Sloe — that horse of great fame Oh to hear his horn blow and to shout "Tal-ly ho! Tally ho-o-o-o! Hark for-ward huz-za tally ho!"

THE FOLKLORE OF MONMOUTHSHIRE

On the first of November bright Phoebus shone clear
And we had not been hunting for nearly a year
Squire mounted old Dick that horse you all know
And away down through Mounton like blazes we go
(Chorus)
Tally ho-o-o-o!
Hark forward huzza, tally ho.

We had not been hunting ten minutes or more
Before Dr King he d---d and he swore
For up rode his man and Come home Sir did say
To young Mrs Jones for her time's up today

Then up came Lord Beauclerk he cared not a pin
And he crasumed [?crashed] at the Brook and the horse tumbled in
And as he crawled out we all laughed at the fun
Hung him up on a hurdle to dry in the sun

There are three jolly sportsmen in Brecon did dwell
So fond of foxhunting we all know them well
Colonel Lloyd and Rees Williams and Penry Lloyd third
And each rides zealous and straight as a bird

Our hounds and our horses are all very good
To crawl through a cover and rattle a wood
Then fill up your glasses and now let us drink
To the true hearted Sportsman who never will shrink

Now of Ladies a couple or perhaps three or four
We have got in our Hunt and we wish there were more
For when the wind reaches their skirts upon high
Their boots and their breeches are plain to the eye

This version of the song, by 'composer unknown', was arranged in 1888 by Julian Waugh of Monmouth, who was possibly part of Robert Waugh & Sons., 'fancy and general stationers, booksellers, pianoforte, harmonium and American organ dealers & tuners & music sellers &c. 2 Church street & 25 Agincourt square', listed in 1891 as having been established for half a century. The Dr King mentioned may have been Thomas (died 1890) of Chepstow or his son, Edward (died 1899), to whom 'it was

PLAY

largely due ... that cruelty to animals became far less prevalent in the district.' Lord Beauclerk, who became Duke of St Albans in 1898, would have been 18 years of age a decade earlier. He lived in Lincolnshire and Nottinghamshire, and his connection with Monmouthshire is not known. The Colonel Lloyd may have been Thomas, of the Cardigan Artillery and Militia (born 1853); Rees Williams and Penry Lloyd could have been visiting from Brecon.

But not all antagonism was against animals, for men pitted themselves against other men in bare-knuckle fights, illegal though these became. One well known pugilist was John Jones, nicknamed Sioni Sguborfawr (Big Barn) after the hamlet of his birth in the Sirhowy Valley. With his friend, the poet, Dai'r Cantwr, he fled west after the Chartist rising of 1839 (in which they were involved), only to be transported for life to Van Diemen's Land four years later for his part in the Rebecca Riots.

Prize-fighting had very few rules. Rounds lasted until one of the combatants was knocked down, whilst the contest only ended when one of the fighters failed to come up to the scratch (a line scratched on the ground) for a fresh round. Lewis Browning wrote in 1906 of the savagery of encounters in Blaenafon:

> A fight took place on one occasion near the south corner of Victoria Road, between two men named Bowen and Dai Lewis, in which Dai Lewis met his death, receiving a fatal blow from Bowen. The latter was committed for trial at the assizes, but was discharged. Dai Andro and Will Keare fought many times on our mountains and in our meadows. Will James y Coed and Jim Plummer from Blaina fought above the Whistle Inn, and Tom Morgan, Llanelly, fought with Jim Morris, shoemaker, on Waunavon ground. The wild animals from the woods never brutalized each other any worse than these brutes, who, I suppose, would expect to be called human beings.

Rather more wholesome were the foot races in which men (and sometimes women) ran either against the clock or other runners. A traditional anecdote illustrates the fleetness of foot of at least one lad. A shepherd reproves his son for taking two minutes longer than usual to round up a flock of sheep on the mountain. 'I should have been here in time, father', says the lad, 'but for this red sheep'; and he pulls from inside his jacket a hare which he has chased and caught.

For 200 years after the event, people talked of an epic contest between Gutto Nyth Brân (Griffith of the Crow's Nest), a noted runner, and a man called Prince, who challenged him to race the 12 miles from Newport to Bedwas Church. In the early stages Gutto showed a touch of arrogance by pausing to chat to old friends in the crowd while his opponent forged ahead. When he began to take the race seriously he was handicapped by broken glass scattered on the road after Price had gone past. Taking great leaps to overcome the hazard he caught Price and passed him on the slope just before Bedwas Church. His time for the 12 miles was 53 minutes. The story may or may not be true that he died when his sweetheart, Siân o'r Siop, clapped him on the back in congratulation; but his death did take place when he was only 37, in 1737.

Even Gutto's athleticism was surpassed a century later by a celebrated pedestrian, J. Townsend. In 1825 he not only walked 66 miles in one day—from the White Horse at Abergavenny to the Robin Hood at Monmouth and back, then the same again, and after that to the Lamb and Flag at Llanwenarth and back—but he performed the same feat six days in a row.

Fair Play
The original purpose of fairs was the buying and selling of goods and animals. The element of entertainment which grew up alongside in most cases came to overshadow and then supersede the commercial side. Abergavenny's two annual fairs, in May and September, are devoted to pleasure, except that the latter holds special sales of ponies, sheep and cattle. In addition to Abergavenny, almost a score of places in Monmouthshire had a fair, some several. They were: Chepstow, Christchurch, Grosmont, Maesycwmer, Magor, Monmouth, Newport, Peterstone, Pontypool, Raglan, Redwick, Risca, Tredegar and Usk.

To these one could add the wakes, originally celebrating the patron saint of a particular church, and held on the first Sunday after his or her day. These, too, became largely pleasure fairs, much to the ire of the clergy. Rev. Miller of Skenfrith put a stop to his in 1841, 'for which he had to defend himself against the attacks of indignant villagers; but he was a big, strong man, and paid them in their own coin, with an amount of determination that carried his point', said a contemporary account. The event was sorely missed, wrote M.N. Jackson:

PLAY

Skenfrith on this great holiday of the year was gay with booths and coloured streamers. There was wrestling in the churchyard when I the farmers of the parish settled their differences of the year past in a free fight. ... The custom in Skenfrith was to put a big bun on a stake, and the rush and struggle to get a bite were sufficient to rouse the temper and start the fight, in which many were disabled 'and knocked about a bit'.

There were at this time five public houses in the village, and, during the wake, dances at most of them. Fifty couples could 'take the floor' at one house, and fiddlers were never tired: 'for them, the drinks were free'. One old woman of 89 spoke of her friend of 80 as 'a rare dancer she were, not one as could touch her. Eh! but them *were* times, seems folk has lost all their spirit now', and the old face flushed with excitement at the memory.

At neighbouring Grosmont, too, when villagers had occasion to disagree they deferred settlement until fair day, then 'fought it out'. They had several opportunities since the village had three fairs and a wake. On the latter occasion, after a service in the church in honour of St Nicholas (to be precise, his translation, on 9 May), sports and wrestling matches were held on the castle green. A ring was formed, in which two men fought for cakes displayed on sharpened sticks. The victor of one combat took on all comers in turn until either he remained alone undefeated, or, if he lost, the new victor took on his role; and so on. Any spectator overstepping the ring had his toes rapped by men with cudgels who policed the events and their actions could lead to subsidiary fights. The cakes and also gingerbread were traditionally supplied by old Mrs Whitehorn of Orcop.

Fairs in the bigger settlements also received censure from moralists. The 'annual saturnalia' is how a local schoolmaster categorised Chepstow's autumn fair, held on the Friday before 29 October, when there were boxing booths, cheapjacks, waxworks, fortune tellers, ballad singers, photographers, acrobats, roundabouts and a shooting gallery. Notorious throughout the county was the fair held an Ascension Day (40 days after Easter) on Stow Hill in Newport. Though its main *raison d'être* disappeared in 1844 with the opening of a stock market in the town, the fair became if anything even more popular. A mock mayor who presided over the occasion sentenced 'obnoxious persons' to be put in the stocks or dipped in a muddy pool unless they opted to pay a small fine. Local people exercised a customary right to sell beer, which they advertised by hanging out the traditional bush. Eventually, though, Stow Fair fell victim to its own success:

> Special trains from the Eastern, Western and Rhymney Valleys brought thousands of colliers, miners, and ironworkers from the hills; the rural population flocked into the borough, whilst the children released from attendance at school, with townsfolk, increased the multitudinous assembly. In the fair fields a few itinerant gingerbread and toy vendors set up their stalls, the calculating pig and pony were exhibited in their wondrous performances, the penny peepshow amused the juveniles. The space (once probably the village green) in front of the old Six Bells Inn was filled with seats and casks of ale. At the entrances to the churchyard [of St Woolos], and at a score of cottage doors by the side of the road leading from the town to the fair, casks were visible, the owners having invested in a supply of ale for the occasion, and now busily sought to make a harvest by plying thirsty souls with drink as they unceasingly wended their way up the hill towards the fair field. The fair commenced early in the day, and its uproar continued far into the night, scores of persons being the next morning found in the field helplessly sleeping off the effects of their debauch.

So wrote W.H. Johns in the late 19th century, by when the Victorian city fathers of Newport had already suppressed Stow Fair (in 1860).

Echoes of such events persisted within living memory. D.L. Driscoll remembered the visits to Machen, before the First World War, of the cheapjack, a hawker whose ploy was to begin with high prices and then dramatically reduce them:

> 'Who'll give me two bob for these handsome Jugs?' he would roar —no bid —'One and a tanner then?'—no bid and down would come the price, until 'Well, I'll smash 'em before I bring 'em down any further', and we held our breath as he did so.
>
> The travelling fair, with its swings, roundabouts and stalls, stayed for several weeks; the circus made a one night stand. The cockle man came with his wares piled high on a cart in sacks, and the chip man, his horse standing perfectly still as he cooked the chips on an oilstove on his cart. Then there was a barrel organ man with his monkey, and another with a bear which danced to the music of an accordion.

Ball Play

Much of the opposition to a variety of popular pastimes came from puritanical and sabbatarian clerics. Men like Reverend T.A. Davies of Llanishen were exceptions to the rule: he was quite happy with Sunday cricket as long as the players attended church before or after, and there is a story that once, when a game was unfinished by the time of evensong, all the players trooped into church in their whites, then went back after the service to finish the match.

Edmund Jones of Aberystruth would have had none of that. The liberal declarations issued by James I in 1617 and Charles I in 1633, later known as 'The Book of Sports', which specifically endorsed church ales and encouraged customary celebrations, still enraged Jones almost 150 years later when he claimed that people obeyed these 'wicked orders' by 'crying all manner of sports in churchyards, bringing music there to animate them in their evil exercises.' He was particularly incensed that in some parishes the parson himself acted as musician. He went on:

> All Hell rejoiced at it, for there was a dreadful harvest of souls prepared for it. Now did the fairies frisk and dance and sing their hellish music, for the darkness of ignorance and vice had returned once more and the feasts of sin were made for them.

Clerical anger became intense when ball games spilled on to the sabbath. At Llanfair Discoed a 17th century stone slab, once used as a stile into the churchyard but now preserved in the porch, provided this stern warning

As well as the wakes, to which Jones seems to be referring here, churchyards hosted many village recreations. The north side of churches was felt to be undesirable for burials, and the empty ground thus left provided useful space for games. Examples can be seen at Llangattock Lingoed and Llanvetherine. At Skenfrith fives was played against the north wall of the church on summer evenings while spectators sat on adjacent walls or tombstones and drank cider.

Ball games of all kinds seem to have been very popular. Fives, and also quoits, was played in the ruins of Tintern Abbey in the 18th century. In 1838 W.H. Thomas saw a 'picturesque group of peasants playing ball' on Devauden Green, and not far away, above Brockweir, he noticed a 'dreary parched plain', called Stobbal Green, 'where ancient games were formerly celebrated.' Stoolball involved knocking a ball from point to point marked by a stool or even a convenient stone. The 'peasants' could have been playing some sort of football, which would have been more akin to today's rugby than to soccer.

Olive Phillips witnessed a curious game called knobblers, played by families until the late 1930s 'down on the marshes', the area along the coast between Newport and Cardiff. The chief exponents, though, were members of Newport Rugby Club:

> The basis of the game was the throwing of a stone at an eighteen inch 'tower' of stones. The rules seemed to be a variation of bowls, as the stones had to hit the target or fall closely to it. Simple enough, but popular while it lasted.

It was in the 1870s that rugby came to the fore in South Wales, partly thanks to the Anglican Church, which in 1919 became the disestablished Church in Wales, whose curates, largely products of the English public schools, were apostles of muscular christianity. Industrial workers took to the game, whereas their counterparts in England favoured soccer.

The black and amber shirts of Newport became justly famous, and teams from Monmouthshire built a reputation for passionate play. In the 1970s, Pontypool's front row men were celebrated in song by Max Boyce. With Cardiff, Llanelli and Swansea, Newport was one of the big four clubs in Wales.

In the late 1990s, after the advent of professional rugby union, the future of clubs in the area looked less than rosy. Even so, they were still well represented in the upper levels of the Welsh game, with Newport and Ebbw Vale in the premier division (the former relegated in 1998, then reinstated after the defection of Cardiff and Swansea), Abertillery, Blackwood, Cross Keys, Newbridge and Pontypool in the first, and Tredegar in the second. In addition, more lowly sides such as Garndiffaith were capable of beating superior opposition on their day.

Cwrw Da

During the course of his walks in 'Wild Wales' George Borrow made a habit of marching into public houses and demanding 'cwrw da' (good beer). Archdeacon Coxe in 1801 described beer as the Welsh 'national liquor', which is probably still true. In earlier times the church was remarkably well disposed towards the beverage and summoned the faithful on occasions to drink it in a good cause. Those who organised village sports were rewarded at parish expense with what was called Parson's Gift Ale; those who took part in the events received free beer on Whit Sunday and Monday—Whitsun Ale.

A man in debt could organise a Bid Ale, which meant that he made a brew and 'bid' parishioners to come and buy it at modest rates and take part in sports. The proceeds, if all went well, cleared his debts. Bid Ales also featured in weddings (see chapter 7).

In many Monmouthshire parishes the clerk received no fee but in lieu was allowed to sell beer outside the church on Easter Sunday. This was called Clerk's Ale; Lamb Ales, in which women took part, are described in chapter 11. Bride's Ale, by courtesy of the lady's parents, was given away on the Sunday after a wedding. Leet Ale came in a punchbowl passed round at the Court Leet after the annual beating of a parish's bounds. As late as the 1930s old people at Pontllanfraith and in the mountains between the eastern and western valleys of Monmouthshire remembered such occasions with great pleasure.

Even payment for work done on the church roof, boundary walls or parsonage might be given in beer, as the Panteg churchwardens' accounts show. In Victorian times itinerant nonconformist preachers might receive free beer. The records of the Calvinistic Methodist Church at Newport include sums of 3s. (15p.) paid as a fee for taking a service, as well as sixpence for drink, 7d. for tobacco and 6d. for oats for the horse.

Not surprisingly, drinking by parishioners at times of service was not tolerated. At Skenfrith churchwardens visited the public house, arrested offenders and confined them in the stocks, which conveniently stood under the yew tree by the churchyard gate.

Among strong supporters of teetotalism was Lady Llanover, who suppressed three public houses (the Oak, the Nightingale and the Grey Goat) on her estate, turned one into a post office (the Nag's Head, or Penceffyl—see also chapter 11), one (Y Seren Gobaith, the Star of Hope) into a temperance house, and one (the Old Duke) into a tea shop called Y

Gwesty Dirwestol, the Temperance Hotel. Only one in the immediate area survived—the Goose and Cuckoo, as it does to this day—because it was separately owned.

For good measure, Lady Llanover expected her tenants and workers to abstain from drink. Once she saw the bicycle of one of her gardeners propped up outside the Waun y Clare pub, near Pontypool, and made a point of rebuking him when the opportunity arose. His silent and witty response was to leave his bicycle one night beneath her bedroom window.

Other areas had something of a surfeit of licensed premises. Edward Davies wrote of Chepstow:

> The inns will furnish ev'ry want and wish,
> For there you'll find good flesh, good fowl, good fish;
> And those who on crimp [firm] salmon wish to feast
> In great perfection there will find it dress'd.
> Here is good ale, good cider, and good wine,
> So that the sons of kings we here may dine.

In the 19th century there were 70 public houses in the town, which were reduced to a dozen by the 1990s. As late as 1901 there were 61 in Monmouth, one for every $83^{1}/_{2}$ inhabitants. The village of Gofilon once had 19, which are now down to two, the Lion and the Bridge. Of Grosmont's four, two (the Greyhound and the Duke of York) have gone and two (the Angel and, a mile away, Cupid's Inn) remain. Shirenewton's seven or eight are down to a modest four, the Tredegar Arms, the Tan House, the Carpenters Arms and the Huntsman Hotel (formerly called the Cross Hands).

Other places have now lost their only inn. The once famous Monmouth Cap at Llangua is now a farmhouse. By contrast, the Hostry Inn at Llantilio Crossenny has served customers since 1459, save for a gap of 50 years in the 19th century after a murder. The Star Inn at Llanfihangel Torymynydd also dates from the 15th century. Two stage coaches, Nimrod and Fusilier, changed horses there on their journey between Chepstow and Raglan. A ghostly coach seen nearby is one of many apparitions associated with public houses; others are described in chapter 3.

Many inns have their stories and traditions. A horseman is said to have won a wager at Pont-hir House Inn by riding his mount over the steeply-pitched roof. The Farmers Arms at Goldcliff, alternatively known as the Gluepot or the Dealers' Den, had an enclosure in front (now a carpark),

PLAY

round which farmers were said to run nine times after closing time to keep fit. The Horse and Jockey (see illustration on page 139) at Llanfihangel Pont y Moel formerly possessed a 13½ gallon jug and a five pint and one noggin tot. These were both previously kept at the Golden Lion in Abertillery, where at Christmas a sovereign was paid to anyone who could drink the tot's contents without a pause. The only recorded winner was a woman.

The Murenger, which claims to be Newport's oldest inn, preserves the name of the official who collected 'murages', taxes devoted to maintaining the town walls. The Skirrid Inn at Llanfihangel Crucorney calls itself the oldest in all Wales, claiming a Norman origin, though the present building is mediaeval. After being convicted in the court held there, sheepstealers were hanged from the oak staircase which still exists. The Five Alls at Chepstow has no pretension to antiquity but its sign is said to be a copy of one painted in the 18th century by William Hogarth for an establishment at Marlborough. Publicans sometimes added a sixth to the list (see chapter 9) on the sign: 'The devil: I take all'.

More than one place in Monmouthshire was called after its public house; for example, Tafarnau Bach (Small Taverns) and Croes y Ceiliog (Cock's Cross), Cross Keys and Six Bells. Other Welsh names for pubs still in existence include Tafarn y Werin (People's Tavern) near Ebbw Vale, Rhyd y Blew (Ford of the Hairs) at Sirhowy, whose sign shows two horses being washed in a stream, and Ffwrrwm Ishta (Bench for sitting—as opposed-to bench for working, *ffwrrwm waith*) at Machen. Some inns have bilingual signs, such as the Carpenters Arms / Tafarn y saer at Llanishen and near Trellech the Gockett Inn / Tafarn y Grugiar Ddu, which means black grouse.

It was formerly the custom to entice travellers by rhymes extolling public houses' hospitality and fare. At Croes y Ceiliog, which may take its name from the 'cock' or additional horse added to draw loads up a hill, rather than a cockerel, this is carved in stone:

> Dwma Dafarn Croes y Ceiliog
> Groesaw I Bob un am ei ceiniog
> Cwrw da I bawb trwy dalu
> Dewch I mewn chwi gewch ei brofi
> (Here is an inn the Cross of the Cock
> A welcome is yours for a penny
> Good beer waits you all for payment so small
> Come in taste our ale good as any).

The inn sign at Llantarnam's Y Ty Gwyrdd (Green House) which reads: Good beer / And cider for you / Come in / And taste it

The Gate at Llanfrechfa advertised itself with the couplet, 'The gate hangs high and hinders none / Refresh and pay and follow on'. At Monmouth the Robin Hood, which cherishes the tradition that Shakespeare stayed there, displayed until the 18th century this sign:

> Walk in, kind sirs, my ale is good,
> And take a pot with Robin Hood;
> If Robin Hood is not at home,
> Pray take a pot with Little John.

The Old Bonny Thatch at Tutshill did not display a verse, but was the subject of one. When John Kitchen was landlord between 1830 and 1846, a letter is said to have arrived from William Makepeace Thackeray in an envelope marked:

> Postman, my hearty,
> Use your utmost despatch
> In taking this letter
> To the Inn Bonny Thatch,
> John Kitchen the landlord,
> A fine English host,
> Good cheer was his motto,
> Good ale was his boast.
> On Tutshill, near Chepstow,
> On the banks of the Wye
> You will find it with ease,
> So. old fellow, good-bye.

A Caerleon man, a brazier called Williams, spent a good deal more time in drinking than he did at home. One evening he was at the Ship Inn, just over the Usk from Caerleon, in what the Romans called *Ultra Pontem* and is now known as the Old Village. The hours passed and his wife became increasingly incensed at his absence. Despite stormy weather she lit a lantern—this was in 1772—and marched off to find him. As she was crossing the wooden bridge over the Usk it collapsed under the pressure of floodwater and she was swept downstream clinging to the wreckage.

Her husband, having heard her screams, came to the inn door in time to see her disappearing, lantern still alight. 'What a good job I wasn't on the bridge', he is said to have remarked as he went back to his drink. Mrs Williams held on to the woodwork and managed to shoot one of the arches of Newport Bridge, over three miles downstream from Caerleon. She was rapidly heading for the estuary when she was spotted by a sailor on *The Hawk*, a Plymouth vessel which lay at anchor in the river. A boat put out to rescue her, and the captain hired a chaise in which she went home. When her husband turned up the following day his reception can be imagined.

Playing, Dancing, Singing
The musical tradition of Monmouthshire includes the classic choirs and brass bands which still flourish. Churches and chapels also made a vigorous contribution. In some villages there are records of the old singers and instrumentalists akin to those evoked by Thomas Hardy in *Under the*

Colliers 'stepping' to the harp during the strike of 1873

Greenwood Tree. At Grosmont there were galleries over the north and south transepts of the church occupied respectively by singers and musicians—a cellist, a clarinettist and a fiddler. When the fiddle player was absent the parish clerk, who happened to be the village blacksmith, would boom up in a deep bass voice to his daughter, who led the singing, and say: 'Now, Polly, pitch the kay [key]'.

There were once so many fiddlers that John Byng, visiting Newport in 1787, complained of 'an eternal fiddling, from the fondness of the Welsh for dancing.' He remarked on the absence of a harp, but the instrument was common enough for colliers to be dancing to its music when they were on strike in 1873. At the same period, harpers and *baledwyr* (ballad singers) were said to be a common sight in Ebbw Vale's public houses on a Saturday evening.

Lady Llanover's attempts to encourage Welsh music led her to employ a series of harp players. In her book, *River Diary*, published in 1950, Dorothy Eastwood describes meeting at Pant-y-Goitre a 95 year-old woman whose father had been the Llanofer harpist in the late 19th century. She herself had played the harp for Lady Llanover of whom she said:

> She was one of the first people to collect and preserve the old Welsh songs, although in those days it was thought a ridiculous thing to do. But she persevered, and later other people began collecting them, too, but it was late then, and many of them were lost.

As she left, Mrs Eastwood noticed that the strings of the woman's harp 'hung limp and frayed from its polished golden wood.' She later found out that the woman's husband died 'and her only son was killed, and so she broke the strings and never played again.'

The Welsh oral tradition of song was indeed in a parlous state by the 1840s, as we can judge from the celebrated compilation by Maria Jane Williams, *Ancient National Airs of Gwent and Morgannwg*. This includes only a handful of items from Monmouthshire, of which one is given on page 111, above. However, the repertoire can be partly deduced from printed ballad sheets which appeared in the area. Carols which circulated in this way are described in chapter 11.

Charles Heath (1761-1830), born near Kidderminster in Worcestershire, was apprenticed to a Nottingham printer. He announced through an advertisement in the *Hereford Journal* in June 1791 that he was setting up in business in Monnow Street, Monmouth.

> H E A T H,
> PRINTER, BOOKSELLER, STATIONER, and BOOKBINDER,
>
> REspectfully announces to the inhabitants of MONMOUTH, and the county at large, that, under the patronage and encouragement of several respectable families in the town and its vicinity, he is fitting up
> A PRINTING - OFFICE,
> With all possible dispatch, in *Monow Street*: Flatters himself he shall have it in his power to execute every article in the Printing business with such neatness, accuracy, and expedition, as will render him worthy of their favour.
> BOOKBINDING IN GENERAL.
> STATIONARY OF ALL KINDS.
> A CIRCULATING LIBRARY
> is preparing, and Catalogues of the same will be ready for delivery in a short time.
> All the Genuine PATENT MEDICINES.
> ☞ A great variety of FISHING TACKLE, and other articles.

In 1783 Heath moved to premises in the Market Place, and in 1817 to 23 Agincourt Square, where he remained until his death in 1830. A monument was eventually erected to his memory in St Mary's Churchyard, where it still stands.

He was twice mayor of Monmouth, and on their visit to the town in 1802 he welcomed Lord Nelson and Lady Hamilton to his shop. He published many books, including editions of the Bible and Hume's *History of England*. He also wrote a good deal himself, dispensing with a pen by setting directly into type accounts of Tintern Abbey, the Wye, Raglan Castle, Chepstow and Monmouth. Coxe quotes from his books; Bradney had copies of them in his library.

In addition to carols in the form of single sheets, priced one penny, Heath issued 100-page books entitled *The Grand Hall of Conviviality: being a Collection of Rational, Manly, Humorous, and Other Songs* and *The Jovial Farmer's Chest of Conviviality; or, Journal, of his Social Mirth: being a Collection of Rational, Manly, and Other Songs. Calculated to promote the Pleasures of the Festive Table; mingling, at the same time, Hilarity with Reason.* The latter, which was sold also by

Charles Heath
(Nelson Museum, Monmouth)

Roberts, Ross, Mrs Kirby, Chepstow, and Allen, Hereford, contains the words of 77 songs, sometimes with indications of tunes such as 'Come haste to the wedding', 'Gee ho, dobbin' or 'Here's to the maiden of bashful fifteen'. Some items are listed as having been sung at the Hall of Conviviality, Overmonnow; in Monmouth at the Beaufort Arms or at the Harmonic Club in the White Lion; and at the Sportsman's Hall on the Gadder Hill, Abergavenny.

There are one or two traditional songs, such as 'John Barleycorn' and 'The Barley Mow', but most are the professional compositions of Charles Dibdin, James Hook, William Shield, and the like. The national pool of songs—'The Golden Days of Good Queen Bess', 'The Roast Beef of Old England', 'The Post Captain', 'High-mettled Racer', 'How stands the glass around?'—is complemented by a few local pieces.

Of one writer, Heath has this to say:

> Parry ... was a tradesman in Ross, who afterwards engaged as a soldier, and went to America, where he lost his right arm at the famous battle of Bunker's Hill. He afterwards returned home, and, with the addition of his pension, supported himself by writing these local and descriptive songs.

One of three of Parry's songs included, 'The Prospect of Ross', begins:

> Since Poet's soft lays round fair Albion oft ring,
> Permit me, although but a shepherd, to sing,
> Not of dark solemn groves, nor yet beds of green moss,
> But my theme is the delicate Prospect of Ross.
>
> From whence, oh how grateful, appear to the eye,
> The serpentine form of the sweet river Wye,
> Whose surface unruffl'd displays such a gloss,
> As the stream smoothly glides by the Prospect of Ross.

'The Pleasures of Harvest', 'Set to Music and Sung by Mr John Watkins, Organist, Monmouth', has a similarly idyllic view of country life:

> Farewell, ye sweet virgins, ye beauties in bloom,
> The saffron looks gay now the Harvest draws on,
> Come men to your reaping, with sickles so keen,
> Come lads to your labours, come lasses to glean.

PLAY

>   Plough and sow,
>   Reap and mow,
>   Lambs to rears
>   And sheep to shear,
> Health and content is the countryman's fare. ...
>
> Honest Hodge, cross his shoulders, from the barn bears the flail,
> Nell, on her head, she supports a full pail,
> 'The cattle all fodder'd, to the kitchen let's haste,
> No other pains take, - good- brown ale crowns the feast.
>   Plough and Sow, &c.

A song 'never before printed' by Reverend Thomas Price of Trellech celebrates, to the tune of 'God save the King', the presentation of colours in 1799 to the Monmouth Volunteers, a sort of Home Guard of the time. Another, 'The Monmouth and Brecon Shire Lasses Delight', expresses joy at different soldiers' return after seven years' absence.

A further item 'never before printed' is a song written to the tune of 'Hearts of Oak' 'by a Lady, - in compliment to the Welch Nation, for their gallant conduct in defeating the French army, under General Tate, in Pembrokeshire' [in 1797]. It runs as follows:

> While St George and St Patrick are handed to fame,
> St David, for ever renown'd be thy name;
> If ever to heroes just glory belongs,
> May the honest, brave, Welchmen enliven our songs.
> Round the national leek shall the laurel be twin'd,
>   And the Welchmen's great merit,
>   And generous spirit,
> Be honor'd, while freedom is dear to mankind.
>   Round the national Leek, &c.
>
> For freedom how oft have the Cambrians bled,
> And untam'd to the mountain recesses have fled;
> Preferring the frown of the damp rocky caves,
> And dying as freemen, to living as slaves.
> Round the national leek shall the laurel be twin'd,
>   And may this old story,
>   Be told to their glory,
> And honor'd, while freedom is dear to mankind.

THE FOLKLORE OF MONMOUTHSHIRE

When Harry of Monmouth, in Azincourt's field,
Made the French our inveterate enemies, yield;
The Welchmen that day of their courage might boast,
Which many an enemy felt to his cost.
Round the national leek shall the laurel be twin'd,
    And may the French fear them,
    And ever revere them,
While honor and freedom are dear to mankind.

Other nations degenerate; but Welchmen so bold,
Are as brave and victorious as Welchmen of old;
As of late fourteen hundred false Frenchmen have found,
Who presum'd to set foot upon Cambrian ground.
Round the national leek shall the laurel be twin'd,
    And firm be they ever,
    Degenerate never,
While honor and freedom are dear to mankind.

The Frenchmen imagin'd they soon might prevail,
When they long'd to enjoy toasted cheese and Welch ale;
The Welchmen were rous'd, the French mice were entrapp'd,
And the ale and the cheese, thank St David, escap'd.
Round the national leek shall the laurel be twin'd,
    May their cheese still be toasted,
    Their enemies roasted,
And Welchmen for ever be dear to mankind.

Then honor the Welch, each heroical soul;
To the Welch, fill ye topers, the mellowing bowl;
Ye pious remember the Welch in your prayer;
Reward the brave Welchmen with smiles, O ye fair.
Round the national leek shall the laurel be twin'd,
    May their courage and glory,
    Be honor'd in story,
Remembered while freedom is dear to mankind.

James Hiley Morgan, a younger contemporary of Heath's, arrived from Brecon to set up his press at 3 High Street, Abergavenny, in about 1820. As well as being a printer he was a bookbinder, bookseller, stationer and dealer in patent medicines. For over a year in 1855-6 he published a weekly newspaper, the *Abergavenny Herald*. He died in 1868.

Sweet Caroline my Store.

As I walked down the Greenwich Road one evening in June,
I never saw so fine a sight as on that afternoon,
I'm sure there were 10'000 folks, and if I say ten more,
All waiting to receive our Queen, sweet Caroline my Store.

A finer sight you never saw, nor one I'm sure so good,
Than for to see our Royal Queen supported by a Wood,
That Wood shall never be cut down, but stand for ever more.
For he'll protect our innocent sweet Caroline my Store.

A Minister, I heard some say, a man of mighty fame,
A foe unto our loving Queen, I dare not say his name;
O may the heavens change his mind, aye him and many more,
That try to ruin our innocent sweet Caroline my Store.

The Judges on their seats alone will sit to try our Queen,
I hope to God in them there will no malice then be seen.
The lords are summon'd to attend, and if as many more,
May God above inspire their minds, for Caroline my Store.

You said you lov'd her G---g-y, ah! why did she believe,
She never thought an Englise heart was made for to deceive,
The mighty power you have on earth, nay heaven can grant no more,
May cease when you assay to wrong sweet Caroline my Store.

I've heard some say I am too bold, and that I may offend,
For fear I should I'll take my leave, and so I make an end,
So farewell ovr Royal Queen until your trial's o'er,
And may you conquer all your foes, sweet Caroline my Store.

THE LADS OF Thorney-moor Woods.

IN Thorney-moor Woods in Nottinghamshire,
Three keeper's houses stood three squares,
And about a mile from each other were,
Their orders were to look after the deer.

I with my dogs went out one night,
The moon shone clear, and the stars gave light,
O'er hedges, ditches, gates, and rails,
With my two dogs close at my heels,
To catch a fat buck in Thorney-moor fields.

The very first night we had bad luck,
One of my very best dogs got stuck,
He came to me both bloody and lame,
And sorry was I to see the same,
For he was not able to follow the game.

I search'd his wounds and found them slight,
Some keeper has done this out of spite,
But I'll take my pike-staff in my hand,
I will range the woods till I find the man,
I will ta s hide right well if I can.

I ranged the woods and groves all night,
I ranged the woods till it proved daylight,
The very first thing that here I found,
Was a good fat buck laying dead on the ground
I know my dogs gave him his death wound.

My dogs they know me by my call,
I out with my knife and cut the bucks throat,
And you would have laugh'd to see limping Jack
Strutting about with the buck on his back,
He carried it like some Yorkshireman's pack.

I hired a butcher to skin the game,
Likewise another to sell the same,
The very first buck he offered for sale,
Was to an old whore who sold bad ale,
And she sent us three poor lads to gaol.

But the Quarter Sessions were drawing nigh,
At which we were all to be tried,
The Gentlemen laugh'd them all to scorn,
That such an old whore should be forsworn;
She all to pieces ought to be torn.

The sessions ere over and we are all clear,
The sessions are over and we all sit here;
The very best game I ever did see,
Was a buck or a deer, but a hare for me,
And Thorney-moor fields this night I'll see.

Morgan, Abergavenny.

Morgan ballad sheet (Abergavenny Museum)

James Hiley Morgan and his former premises at Abergavenny

Morgan issued only one sheet of carols (see chapter 11) and a number of other single sheets with ballads which seem to have been pirated from elsewhere. These include 'Lancashire Dick', 'The Bristol Tragedy', 'The Lads of Thorney-Moor Woods', a rather curious piece on the death of Lord Dudley Ward, dedicated to 'the Colliers of Miners of Dudley and its Vicinity', and several dealing with Queen Caroline, George IV's unhappy wife, who died in 1821.

Morgan's ballad sheets, some still pinned to the racks where they had been hung for the ink to dry, only came to light in 1961, when a new owner of the premises broke into the loft at 3 High Street, Abergavenny.

CHAPTER 11

Calendar Customs

During the 19th century Welsh calendar and other customs took a battering through the combined impact of militant teetotalism, religious revival and industrial revolution. By depopulating the countryside the last of these, as Trefor M. Owen has pointed out, 'effectively removed the main upholders of traditional customs.' In addition, 'In their new terraced houses in the industrial valleys of Glamorgan and Monmouthshire, the harsh industrial regime which directed their labour left little time, and probably less energy, for the seasonal customs of the countryside they had left, which, in any case, had less meaning for them in the new milieu.'

New forms of organised sport and mass entertainment came in to fill the vacuum. The trend continued in the 20th century, when seasonal observances became confined to a few, heavily commercialised, national occasions, of which the foremost is Christmas.

In Wales St David's Day (1 March) is still very much a spontaneous celebration, with ordinary people choosing to wear or display the leek or daffodil. The spirit is akin to that shown in the past when people felt a deeply rooted compulsion to participate in certain seasonal rituals, and derived a profound sense of satisfaction from doing so.

New Year
Church bells were muffled at Caldicot to ring the old year out, then pealed to ring in the new. From Redwick comes the curious story of ringers one year whiling away the time until midnight by playing cards. The door of the ringing chamber flew open once, twice, then a third time even though one of the ringers had bolted it. The men were so frightened that they dared not ring the bells that night, nor play cards in the church again.

THE FOLKLORE OF MONMOUTHSHIRE

Until the First World War at Newport ships sounded their sirens from the docks at midnight to welcome the New Year, whilst watch-night services were held (as they still are) in churches and chapels, and cheering crowds sang 'Auld Lang Syne' in the streets. Until at least the 1950s it was the custom in Monmouthshire to leave open both back and front doors of a house 'to assist', wrote the Opies in *The Lore and Language of Schoolchildren*, 'the Old Year's departure and the arrival of the New.' Coins, 'especially silver money', had to be left outside the door.

In the early hours of New Year's Day farmers went round. their fields 'burning the bush' to drive out any evil influence and to ensure good fortune for the coming twelve months. One of the bundles of twigs used was carefully preserved on the farm until the following year's ceremony. Copious libations of cider were drunk in the festivities, and animals were wassailed— sung to. With regard to Monmouthshire, H.C. Ellis wrote in 1904:

> I once saw a flat cake with a hole in the middle put on the horn of the leading cow of the herd, and the family servants standing around, singing:
>> Here's a health to thee, Brownie, and to thy white horn,
>> God send thy master a good crop of corn.
>> Thee eat thy cake and I'll drink my beer,
>> God send thy master a happy New Year.
>
> But the cow did not eat the cake; she tossed it by throwing up her head, as she objected to the weight of it on her horn, and it depended on where the cake fell—in front or behind her—whether the year would be good or bad for her master.

Wassailers went round at Monmouth both on 1 January and Twelfth Night with songs such as this:

> Good master and good mistress and all your house so fine,
> Rise from your beds this morning while yet the stars do shine.
> Open your door and greet us with good cheer:
> May the good Lord God grant you a happy New Year.
>
> We come here designing to taste of your good ales
> So tap us a new barrel, we'll want none of the stale.
> Surely you'll not leave us in frost and snow out here,
> May the good Lord God grant you a happy New Year.

[Musical notation with lyrics:]

Good master and good mistress and all your house so fine, Rise from your beds this morning while yet the stars do shine O-pen your door and greet us with good cheer. May the good Lord God grant you a hap-py New Year.

> So here's to you, Brownie, and to your white horn,
> May God send your master a good crop of corn.
> You eat your oats and we will drink our beer:
> May the good Lord God grant you a happy New Year.
>
> So here's to your cider and here's to your cake,
> And here's to a score, lads, must go before daybreak;
> For our time it is precious, we can no more stay here:
> May the good Lord God grant you a happy New Year.

Husbands and wives at Llanishen raced each other on New Year's Day from the church to a well in the field off Vicarage Lane. The first to reach the goal would be acknowledged by his or her partner as top dog for the ensuing year. The well itself was dressed with sprigs of box or yew as a thank-offering for never running dry.

Starting at midnight, or later, depending on the locality, people, and especially children, went round to collect gifts. Even though Christmas was past they sang:

> The snow lay on the ground,
> The stars shone bright
> When Christ our Lord was born
> On Christmas Night.
>
> 'Twas Mary,
> Daughter of holy Ann,
> That brought him to this word,
> Our Lord made man.

THE FOLKLORE OF MONMOUTHSHIRE

> She laid him on the straw
> At Bethlehem;
> The ass and oxen shared
> The room with them.

Calennig, New Year's gift in Welsh, was the word used to describe both the food and money collected and also of the object carried from door to door. Arthur Machen (born in 1863) wrote:

> When I was a boy ... , there was a very queer celebration on New Year's Day in the little Monmouthshire town where I was borne, Caerleon-on-Usk. The town children—village children would be nearer the mark, since the population of the place amounted to a thousand souls or thereabouts—got the biggest and bravest and gayest apple they could find in the loft, deep in the dry bracken. They put bits of gold leaf upon it. They stuck raisins into it. They inserted into the apple little sprigs of box, and then they delicately slit the ends of hazel nuts, and so worked that the nuts appeared to grow from the ends of the box leaves, to be the disproportionate fruit of those small trees. At last, three bits of stick were fixed into the base of the apple, tripod-wise, and so it was borne round from house to house; and the children got cakes and sweets, and—those were wild days, remember—small cups of ale. And nobody knew what it was all about.

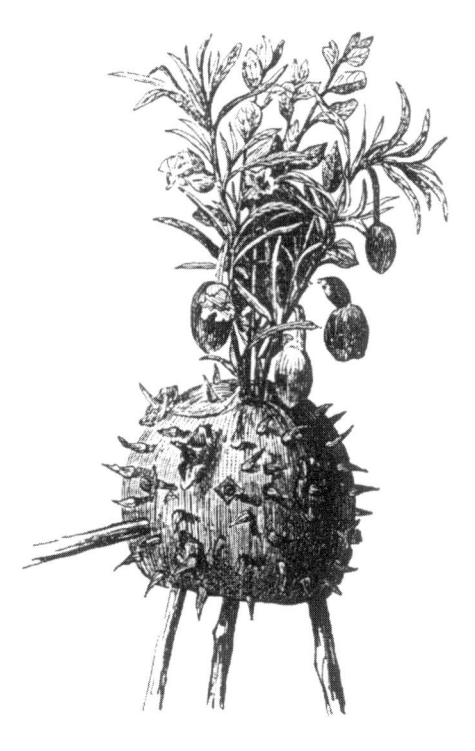

The Calennig, or New Year's Apple (from Coxe's Historical Tour Through Monmouthshire*)*

Machen's attempt to trace the custom back to Roman times is undoubtedly fanciful though the giving of New Year's gifts is certainly ancient. In the calennig the three components of fruit, nuts and wood were supposed to represent the Three Wise Men's presents of sweetness, wealth and immortality.

At Chepstow, where the calennig was called a 'monty' (allegedly from 'Good morn to ye') an orange was often used instead of an apple, and holly instead of box. Between 6 a.m. and noon boys and girls went from house to house, chanting:

> Monty, Monty, happy New Year,
> A pocket full of money and a cellar full of beer.

The custom had died out by 1914 in Chepstow, but continued elsewhere. Fred Hando was given a personal calennig early in the Second World War by a lady brought up in Chepstow who told him not to remove the orange 'until it was quite withered whereupon I should see a happy year.' He complied; the prediction came true. At the same period he saw a calennig on the mantelpiece of the Masons Arms at Devauden which boys had taken there 'to see the New Year in' and been rewarded with threepence apiece. A Mrs Rose of Tintern remembered that twice that amount was given by her husband, a builder, each year to the two sons of one of his employees who called every New Year's Day with a monty for him, which he kept for luck until it rotted or withered away. As late as 1987 Edmund J. Mason wrote:

> An old Welsh custom still kept up at Devauden is that of the calennig. An apple is chosen for its red skin, and a sprig of holly is pushed in at the top, from which hang raisins and small fruit. Hazel twigs, covered with silver paper are pushed into the base of the apple, and small pieces of silver paper decorate the skin. The apple stands for a fruitful life and when rotted is thrown away, but as long as it is kept it is said to bring good luck to the household.

Twelfth Night

When the calendar was reformed in 1752 some people who obstinately refused to accept the change did not celebrate Christmas until Twelfth Night, which they termed Old Christmas Day. Once common in rural

Monmouthshire, this was confined by the 1880s to Shirenewton, where carol singers went round on Old Christmas Day. For good measure, though, they would already have been out on Christmas Day proper, and also on New Year's Day.

The Feast of the Epiphany on 6 January marks the traditional anniversary of the Three Wise Men's visit to the infant Jesus. Since it comes at the end of the Twelve Days of Christmas it is also known as Twelfth Day, and its eve as Twelfth Night. Until the 1920s in some of the industrial areas to the west of Monmouthshire 'Christmas loaves'—dough cakes with yeast and spice, otherwise known as 'barm bracks'—were made for all the family to eat on Twelfth Night.

At midnight on Twelfth Night, it is believed, bloom scions of the Glastonbury thorn, said originally to have grown from a staff planted in the ground there by Joseph of Arimathea. One specimen stood near the White House at the bottom of the hill just before Grosmont on the road from Skenfrith. 'My gardener's boy heard of the legend', wrote Canon Barron in 1916, 'and determined to test it, so he and another boy started off [from Skenfrith] at 10 pm on January 5th and witnessed the blossoming at 12.' Another tree, in Monmouth's Priory Street, was remembered as late as 1935. Like the holy thorn, rosemary is still believed in the Wye Valley to blossom at midnight on Twelfth Night.

In the Llanvapley area until the 1860s and 70s, 13 bundles of straw, 12 of a certain size and one bigger, called Epiphany Lights, were lit in high places during the first minutes of Twelfth Day. The ceremony seems to have been a relic of apple tree wassailing, when 13 fires were lit and one, known as the Judas Fire, subsequently put out.

Movable Feasts

Easter Sunday falls between 22 March and 25 April, and in turn dictates other points in the religious calendar. Lent is the period of 40 days (not counting Sundays) from Ash Wednesday to Easter Saturday. Mothering Sunday is the fourth Sunday in Lent.

In 1784 a correspondent wrote to the *Gentleman's Magazine* that the previous year, in Chepstow, he had heard for the first time of Mothering Sunday:

> My enquiries into the origin and meaning of it were fruitless; but the practice hereabouts was, for all servants and apprentices, on

CALENDAR CUSTOMS

Midlent Sunday, to visit their parents, and make them a present of money, a trinket, or some nice eatable; and they are all anxious not to fail in this custom.

A century later Wirt Sikes commented that the custom was 'nowhere popular in Wales at present'; yet iced buns sprinkled with hundreds and thousands continued to be associated with the day until the 1970s. Now, Mothering Sunday is almost completely forgotten, having been eclipsed by the commercial Mother's Day (the second Sunday in May) imported from America. Oddly enough, though, the new event has fostered the sort of family gatherings favoured by the old custom.

In another act of family piety, on Palm Sunday, a week before Easter, people put on their best clothes and went to lay flowers on their relatives' graves (see also chapter 7). At Trellech on Good Friday small loaves were baked to be kept for good luck for a year, save for some that were ground up to be taken for various illnesses. The custom at Risca was for children to take their hot cross buns into the fields for a picnic. These buns are now available in shops for many weeks before Easter, so the special thrill has been weakened. Young people from Newport traditionally walked up Twm Barlwm for their picnic but this custom has fallen into disuse since the 1970s. Good Friday is now a working day for many, and for those who are free, more sophisticated entertainment is readily available.

Until the 1950s on Easter Sunday at Goytre, Blaenafon and no doubt elsewhere, children went hunting in the garden, first thing in the morning, for hard-boiled, hand-painted eggs. At Pontypool children rolled them down a grassy slope, where the last to break was declared the winner. The ceremony of walking the wheat (see chapter 9) took place on the same day.

Whit Sunday is the seventh after Easter; Trinity Sunday, the eighth. On Whit Sunday and Monday, Whitsun Ale (see chapter 10) was given to all those taking part in sports. During Whitsun Week at Bedwellty, Mynyddislwyn and elsewhere, Lamb Ale competitions were held in which women with hands tied behind their backs attempted to catch a fat lamb in their teeth, no doubt with some assistance from the weight of their bodies. The first winner acquired the title of Lady of the Lamb for the ensuing year and presided over a feast at the Church Inn where her health was drunk in Lamb Ale.

Whitsuntide was the season for processions with banners and bands of the benefit clubs which provided some kind of insurance against unem-

Whitsun turnout at Tredegar in the 1950s

ployment and sickness, and also death grants, before the days of the welfare state. At Blaenafon the Old Benefit Club was based at the Old Crown public house, Dic Shon Ffyrnig's Club (*ffyrnig* means fierce) at the Bridgend (its members wore hats with a red ribbon tied in a true lover's knot to signify fidelity), and the Phoenix Club, whose people favoured yellow ribbons, at the New Inn. Each procession concluded with the club's annual feast.

The rather more sedate chapel walks, which took place mainly on Whit Monday, are still fondly remembered by many people. For D.L. Driscoll, this was one of the great childhood treats at Machen:

> Whitsun Monday was our Parade Day when we did a lap of the village, each Sunday School behind its own banner, the Silver Band in front playing, as we sang our school songs, 'Hold the Fort', 'Marching to Zion', though I confess that we were not so anxious in getting to Zion as we were in getting back to our chapel for the tea. And what a tea it was. The tables were loaded with all kinds of dainties while our mothers in starched white aprons bustled to and fro, carrying huge pots of tea and refilling the

quickly emptied plates. We did full justice to our Whitsun tea; it's a wonder that we had enough energy for the sports which took place afterwards, but we did, and were ready too for the left-overs brought to the field after in baskets.

Adults, too, enjoyed such events. A woman from Fleur-de-Lis recalled:

The Whitsun March was a grand event with banners flying and much competition amongst all denominations for the loudest singing, which only ceased as chapel passed chapel in close proximity as the procession turned either at Pengam post office (now closed) or 'Flower Square'. After the tea and 'tramline' cake (plain cake sandwiched with jam and cream—only seen on Whit Monday) everyone joined in the fun on the Ynys field. ... 'Kiss-in-the-ring' was especially popular. Many a couple met their destiny on the Ynys field—in spite of the clouds of coaldust—by the end of the evening.

Sunday School procession in Broad Street, Blaenafon, in 1908 (Village Publishing)

The dust came from two local collieries, Britannia and Pengam, which are now no more.

Until the 1920s on Whit Tuesday brass band and choral contests attended by large crowds were held at Chepstow Castle. The pleasure fair at Risca near St Mary's Church on the Tuesday was very tame, compared with the 'wild pleasures', as one writer put it, of Stow Fair at Newport a little later (see chapter 10).

Many events once held at Whitsuntide are now discontinued. Others have transferred to the May Bank Holiday, the first Monday after 1 May.

May and Midsummer

On *Calan Mai* (1 May) by ancient tradition chieftains moved from winter to summer quarters (*hendre* to *hafod*), as summer began six months of domination over its perennial enemy, winter. A distant echo of that strife might be discerned in the May battles, called 'muntlings', at Monmouth, in which the young men of 'Cappers' Town' (Overmonnow), or Cat-a-thumpings, met the Up-town boys on the Monnow Bridge for a free-for-all. Both sides belaboured each other with besoms ('muntles') reinforced with stones, and a return fixture took place on 29 May, until the whole thing was banned in 1858.

Monnow Bridge and Gate, scene of the 'muntlings'

CALENDAR CUSTOMS

The maypole in Wales was called a *bedwen* since a *bedw* (birch tree) was used. It would often be decorated for luck with plates, pots, pails and silver dishes as well as flowers. In 1781 John Byng noticed Chepstow's maypole in Beaufort Square 'well hung round with garlands'. T.D. Fosbroke noted in his book, *The Wye Tour* (1818):

> A little below White-brook, appears on the left side [of the river] a considerable eminence, called Pen-y-van Hill, the summit of which usually exhibits a May-pole, around which the Peasantry now or recently celebrated the Roman Floralia, called by us May-games, with dances and feasting.

The pole, no doubt renewed from time to time, stayed on the hill until 1951, when it was brought down to stand by Llandogo School. Other villages, too, had maypoles, which they were obliged jealously to guard against raiding parties from rival places.

Windows, doors and porches were festooned with green sprays and flowers. The hawthorn, birch and mountain ash used had the additional virtue of keeping away witches. Some twigs, fashioned into small crosses, were kept over the doors of houses and stables, a practice which continued in some areas—Chepstow, for example—until at least the 1920s.

Some girls drank dew at sunrise on May Day in the belief that so doing would speedily bring them a husband, and perhaps make them beautiful, too:

> The young lass who on the first of May
> Rises at dawn and goes her way,
> And washed with the dew of the hawthorn tree
> Will ever after handsome be.

Other girls carried beribboned hoops of primroses and harebells as they competed to be chosen as May Queen. Boys, too, went out in 'Maying' parties, collecting money. As late as 1890 girls styling themselves May Queens went round doing the same in Chepstow. About 60 years earlier a correspondent related in Hone's *Every-Day Book* (1827) what he had seen in the town on May Day. His letter deserves to be quoted in full:

> After I had sailed up the river Wye, and arrived at Chepstow-castle, my attention was arrested by one of the prettiest processions I

remember to have enjoyed. It consisted of milkmaids dancing and serenading round an old man, whose few gray hairs were crowned by a wreath of wild flowers; he held a blossomy hawthorn in his right hand, and bore a staff, with cowslips and bluebells, in his left. A cow's horn hung across his shoulders, which he blew on arriving at a house. The youths and lasses were more than thirty in number. Their arms, and heads, and necks, were surrounded by clusters of lilies of the valley and wild roses. Then came an apple-cheeked dame with a low-crowned, broad-brim hat; she wore spectacles, mittens were drawn up to her elbows, her waist trim, a woollen apron round it, her petticoat short, blue worsted stockings, a high-heeled pair of shoes with silver buckles, and a broad tongue reposing on each instep. In one hand she held a brass kettle, newly-scoured, it was full of cream; in the other, a basket of wood strawberries. To whoever came up to her with a saucer or basin, she gave a portion of her cream and fruit, with the trimmest curtsey I ever saw made by a dainty milkwoman betwixt earth and sky. She was 'Aunt Nelly', and her 'Bough Bearer', called 'Uncle Ambrose', was known for singing a song, ''Twas on one moonshiny night' which with his defective pronunciation lisped 'meann sheeiney'. Ambrose strummed an instrument in his turn, partly harp, and partly hirdy-girdy. Six goats, harnessed in flowers, carried utensils in milking and butter making; and the farmer of the party rode on a bull, also tastily dressed with the produce of the fields and hedges. A cheese and a hatchet were suspended behind him, and he looked proudly as he guided the docile animal to the public-house, into which the milkmaids and their sweethearts went, quickened in their motions by the cat-gut, which made stirring sounds up stairs. The flowery flag, was thrust upwardly into the street, facing the iron bridge; and, getting again into the fisherman's boats I sailed and loitered down the banks of the river, charmed by what I had seen, felt, and understood. Of the milkmaids, Miss Thomas of Landcote [Lancaut] was the darkest, the neatest, and the tallest—she stood *only* five feet, ten inches high.

Other May events such as a procession of decorated vehicles at Newport continued until well within living memory. The hiring fairs (see chapter 9) had disappeared by the First World War, though the side-shows and roundabouts which had accompanied them lingered in some places.

A May Day spectacular is currently organised each year by the Chepstow Round Table at Caldicot. This and the May Day fete at Magor

CALENDAR CUSTOMS

Pride of Wye Lodge, Manchester Unity of Oddfellows, at Tintern (Chepstow Museum)

and Undy are the successors of the earlier and rather more spontaneous celebrations of the arrival of summer.

Oak Apple Day (29 May) marked Charles II's escape from capture by hiding in the famous oak tree at Boscobel; some of its customs may simply have transferred from the first day of the month. In various places, including Caerleon, boys fought each other with branches of oak or ash, and united to chase with stinging nettles anyone omitting to sport oak leaves or an oak apple.

For some, this was Club Feast Day (see above). Until the First World War members of the Heart of Oak Lodge and their families paraded to the church at Llanishen with banners and the Catbrook Silver Band to the fore. Then they enjoyed a meal at the Carpenters Arms, followed by foot races for adults and children. Further amusements consisted of hoop-la, swing boats and a horsepowered roundabout. The band played on until midnight.

On Midsummer's Eve (23 June) the fairies revelled on Dancing Hill at Undy, and also elsewhere (see chapter 3). At Cwmcarfan, near Monmouth, slips of the flower known as midsummer men were stuck into a piece of clay and left overnight to show what the future held in terms both of sickness and death, courtship and marriage (see chapters 6 and 7). Until comparatively recently some farmers at Grosmont paid an annual rent to the lord of the manor on Midsummer Day of a single red rose only, in honour of the tradition that Henry of Lancaster took his emblem from the roses of Grosmont.

A number of churches held their patronal festival (*gwyl mabsant*) in June or July, a convenient time in terms of the farming year because it could fall between haymaking and harvest. In these months come the days of St Paul (7 June), St Bartholomew and St John the Baptist (both 24 June), Saints Julius and Aaron (1 July), St Odoceus (2 July); but even churches whose saints' days fell in the winter months might choose to celebrate them in the summertime.

Much to the consternation of Edmund Jones, Aberystruth's June *mabsant* was characterised not by 'devotion of any kind', but by 'abundance of sin committed'; in fact 'nothing else but sin is the work of the day, and the measure of sinning very great.' Mynyddislwyn's celebration, once the most popular of its kind in the whole of Monmouthshire, drew in merrymakers, and often troublemakers, from all the surrounding parishes. Local rivalries led to fights, both individual and collective. From Cardiff, Newport, Gloucester and even Bristol, came gingerbread sellers, pedlars of all kinds, jugglers prize-fighters and dice-swindlers. Classic rural amusements included competitions to win a hat by grinning and contorting the face, a flannel shift by running, and various prizes by gulping down hot hasty pudding (resembling a thick batter).

Souls and Doles

The year began in the old Celtic calendar on *calan gaeaf* (1 November), the first day of winter. Old Year's Night (31 October) was a time for witches, when a hobgoblin could be seen on every stile: *pwca or bob camfa*. George Greeves of Abertyswg tells how miners who spoke appreciatively of festivals such as Valentine's Day, Shrove Tuesday and Mabon's Day (18 November), felt distinctly apprehensive at Hallowe'en—despite the name, meaning All Souls' Eve, which the church had bestowed on the day in an attempt to allay such fears.

Precautions taken against witches included placing open Bibles near doors and windows, or under chair cushions before certain women came

Ducking for apples on Hallowe'en

in and sat down. Strong smelling herbs were spread round the house, and brooms (made of birch) fixed over doorways. Dishes of animal blood were put in grates and drawings of witches hung in windows or pinned to front doors.

Such expedients gradually fell into disuse, and Hallowe'en became a children's festival sometimes called Snap-apple Night, after the game of apple-bobbing. At Rhymney Thomas Jones ducked for apples in the wooden wash-tub. Shops in Caerleon formerly had tubs where anyone who so wished could go and try to bite an apple out of the water. At Cwmbrân until the 1950s a small apple or nut was placed on a mound of flour in a dish on the table. Each person present in turn scooped away some of the flour with a knife, trying not to dislodge the fruit. The one who eventually did disturb it had to pick it up in his mouth: 'If the apple is right in the flour you got your face covered with flour.'

At Griffithstown they took a swede, cut it in half, and hollowed out the inside. Incisions were made to represent eyes, nose and mouth, then the resulting face, with candle to light it from behind, was threaded on strings and fastened to a pole. These Jack o' Lanterns, as they were called, were used to startle the unwary: 'You go out into the street and if anyone comes along pop out from around a corner and frighten them.' At Pontypool they were positioned on gateposts to ward off evil spirits.

Children in the same town had their own variant of 'Snap Apple' or 'Apple on the Line':

> First of all some sort of hook or nail must be available over a doorway. An apple is cored and the end of a length of string about a yard long is tied through the centre of the apple. The other end of the string is tied to the hook or nail. The string is twisted and the apple is sent spinning ..., and people in turn try to catch the apple with their mouths and eat as big a mouthful as they can. This goes on until all the apple is eaten.

This description was given by a 12 year-old girl to the Opies in the 1950s. At the same period children at Garndiffaith sang 'Apple on the line/On which we dine' as a prelude to the game.

A rather more elaborate song was noted by Sikes:

> On the Welsh Border there prevails a Hallowe'en custom among the children of going about to the houses singing the rhymes which follow:
>
> > Wissel wassel, bread and possel,
> > Cwrw da, plas yma; [Good ale, this house]
> > An apple a pear, a plum or a cherry,
> > Or any good thing to make us merry.
> >
> > So[u]l cakes, So[u]l cakes,
> > Pray you, good missus, a So[u]l cake;
> > One for Peter, and two for Paul,
> > And three for the good man that made us all.
> >
> > The roads are very dirty,
> > My shoes are very thin,
> > I've got a little pocket
> > To put a penny in.
> > Up with the kettle and down with the pan,
> > Give us an answer and we'll be gan.

CALENDAR CUSTOMS

(A loud rap at the door).
Spoken. Please to give us a 'apenny.

The reference here to soul cakes shows that the song must originally have been sung on All Souls' Day (2 November), when, as Archdeacon Coxe noted in 1801, 'in many parts of the country, the poor of every persuasion still retain the custom of begging bread *for the souls of the departed* ... ; the bread then given is called Bara r[h]an, or Dole bread.'

Three days later came the celebration which is still with us. On Bonfire Night at Abergavenny there was a procession with an effigy of Guy Fawkes to a great fire fed with barrels of pitch in the middle of Cross Street. At Chepstow the occasion was even more lively, thanks to the plentiful supply of cordage, barrels and tar when the town was a port. Blazing barrels of tar were rolled down the steep streets, amidst riotous scenes. Policemen who intervened risked being stoned. 'Year after year', wrote Ivor Waters, 'the magistrates tried to punish the trouble-makers but were defeated by mass perjury and the shortage of policemen. Mobs threw mud and stones, kicked one constable's door in and soaked another in paraffin and tried to burn him.' From the 1890s more sedate torchlight processions and firework displays began to replace the rumbustious behaviour at the old Bonfire Nights.

Cross Street, Abergavenny

As the grip of winter tightened the poor were licensed by tradition to ask for help on St Thomas's Day (21 December). Records such as this at Llanarth Court near Raglan, recall the custom: 'Two sacks of wheat to be given away yearly to the poor and widows of Llanarth, hamlet of Clydach and Bryngwyn for ever in the lower passage of the house.' Fred Hando visited the Court in the 1950s and was shown a Llanarth Dole entry of '19 loaves of bread to be given to the poor of the Catholic congregation at the door of the Chapel after the Mass for the Faithful departed.' Thus the living poor benefited in the name of the faithful dead.

A widow called Kitty Meredith, who died in 1893 at the age of over 90, told the historian, Bradney, how she remembered the Lorymers of Perthir House, Rockfield, who gave a dole of bread to local children. It would be accepted to the accompaniment of this chant:

> Bara rhan, bara rhan,
> One for God and one for man.

As recently as the 1990s an 87 year-old gypsy called Ned informed Maria and Andrew Hubert: 'The women went out on St Thomas's Day. If they went round the farms they got a measure of corn in some areas, and breadcakes in others.'

Christmas
When school broke up at Blaenafon children in their excitement went round knocking on doors and running away. They also stuffed lighted pieces of paper up drainpipes and called the game 'Devil up the Drainpipe'. On Christmas Eve at Usk, says a newspaper report of 1866, pranks included 'unhinging gates, pulling down shutters, [and] wheeling barrows into the river.'

Well into the 20th century, on Christmas Eve, one farming family in north-east Monmouthshire gave each worker meat, oranges and sweets, together with a gold sovereign. A 'kissing bunch' made of two wooden hoops at right-angles to each other and covered in ivy and tinsel was hung from the ceiling. There was also a holly bunch from which red apples dangled on strings.

The same family received separate visits on Christmas Eve from carol singers and guisers. The latter, otherwise called mummers or Christmas Boys, went round and performed a play in large houses and inns. Two parties, 'followed by crowds of adoring youngsters', were reported from Pontypool in 1868 and again the following year. One of them, consisting of five lads from Abersychan, first recited, then acted out the ballad of 'Robin Hood and the Shepherd'. They finished with a traditional song, 'We'll hunt the buffalo' (a somewhat incongruous choice), took up a collection, and moved on to do the same again elsewhere.

Their choice of play was unorthodox. Normally, the characters included King (or Saint) George, who fought a boastful opponent, Turkish Knight (or Turkey Snipe). The villain inevitably died, to be restored to life, amid a certain amount of horseplay, by a quack doctor. Performances of this kind took place in Chepstow from the 1860s (and possibly earlier) until 1913.

In an article on amateur drama in Monmouthshire Sybil Hollingdrake wrote that her grandfather as a young man had taken part in performances of the play in Risca, though by 1963 he could remember only a few lines:

Party of mummers at Tenby, which may or may not have resembled those of Monmouthshire

THE FOLKLORE OF MONMOUTHSHIRE

> Here comes I, old Niddy Noddy,
> Got no head nor yet no body;
> No fingers, no toes, no eyes and no nose.
> Give me a penny and off I goes.

A further fragment was recalled in 1973 by Mr Gordon Owen of Dursley in Gloucestershire, who had learned it as a boy in Abercarn from his maternal grandfather, a Mr Hicks:

> In steps me, Old Father Christmas,
> Father Christmas is me name.
> Welcome here or welcome not,
> Old Father Christmas'll never be forgot.

Another version of the play was performed at Monmouth at least until the 1880s in the Punchbowl Inn and no doubt elsewhere. An incomplete text was turned up in a local bookshop by the Huberts:

Enter Father Christmas

> Here comes I, old Father Christmas, welcome or welcome not.
> I hope old Father Christmas will never be forgot,
> But old Father Christmas he has but a short time to stay.
> I be come to show you pleasure to while the time away.
>
> I travel far, I travel near,
> I come now for a jar o' your Christmas beer,
> If it be your best
> Then in heaven I pray your soul to rest;
> If your ale it be small
> We show you no cheer at all.
>
> Walk in, Room, again I say,
> And pray, good people, clear the way.
> Walk in, Room.

Enter Room

> God bless you all, ladies and gentlemen.
> It's Christmas time and I come again.

CALENDAR CUSTOMS

My name is Room, one sincere and true.
A merry Christmas I wish to you.
A king of Egypt is for to display,
A noble champion without delay.
A noble doctor, too, I declare,
And his bag of tricks to bring up the rear.
And let the Egyptian king straightway appear!

Enter Egyptian king

Here comes I, the Egyptian king,
Whose mighty deeds round the globe doth ring.
No other champion but me excels
Except my son-in-law, St George.
Indeed that wondrous knight whom I so dearly love,
Whose mortal deeds the world so well approve,
The hero whom no dragon could affright.
Come, valiant champion bold, your warlike ardour to display,
And show good England's enemies dismay.

Enter St George

Here comes I, St George,
That valiant champion bold,
And with my sword and spear
I've won three crowns of gold.
I slew the dragon 'He',
And brought him to the slaughter,
By which I gained fair Sabra,
The King of Egypt's daughter. ...

Enter the Turkish knight

Here comes I, the Turkish knight,
Come from the Turkish land to fight.
I'll fight St George, that man of valour bold,
And if your blood is hot
I soon will make it cold.

St George draws his sword

Large words, my worthy friend.
I am the man for thee,
Therefore prepare yourself to fight with me,
or else I'll slay thee instantly!

They fight. The Turkish knight falls, then rises on one knee

Oh pardon me, St George,
Oh pardon me, I crave;
Oh give me but my life,
And I will be thy slave.

St George

Is there no doctor to be found
To cure a deep and deadly wound?

Enter Doctor

I can cure lovesick maidens, jealous husbands, squalling wives and brandywine-doused dames with one touch of my triple liquid or a touch of Jerusalem balm.
And here is a pill called Pompomlouf,
Guaranteed to bring a man back to life.

Unfortunately, the text breaks off at this point. The doctor would have restored the knight, after which with a song and an appeal for money the play would have ended.

Plays, like doles, provided a welcome source of help for the poor. Carol singing was also useful. Ivor Edmonds (born 1906) of Llanishen devoted the money collected to buying new clothes. When D.L. Driscoll of Machen took home her collection in an old cocoa tin with a slit in the lid, her mother gave her a halfpenny to spend and kept the rest towards Christmas presents.

In the second half of the 19th century, to judge from the few carols that are named, the repertoire consisted of traditional items, often in local variants, such as 'While shepherds watched', 'The Joys of Mary', 'I saw three ships' and 'The Holly and the Ivy.' Some of these may well have stemmed from sheets issued for sale earlier in Abergavenny and Monmouth. Penny broadsides with up to four carols were printed by James Hiley Morgan of

The celebrated CAROL, called,
Dives and Lazarus.

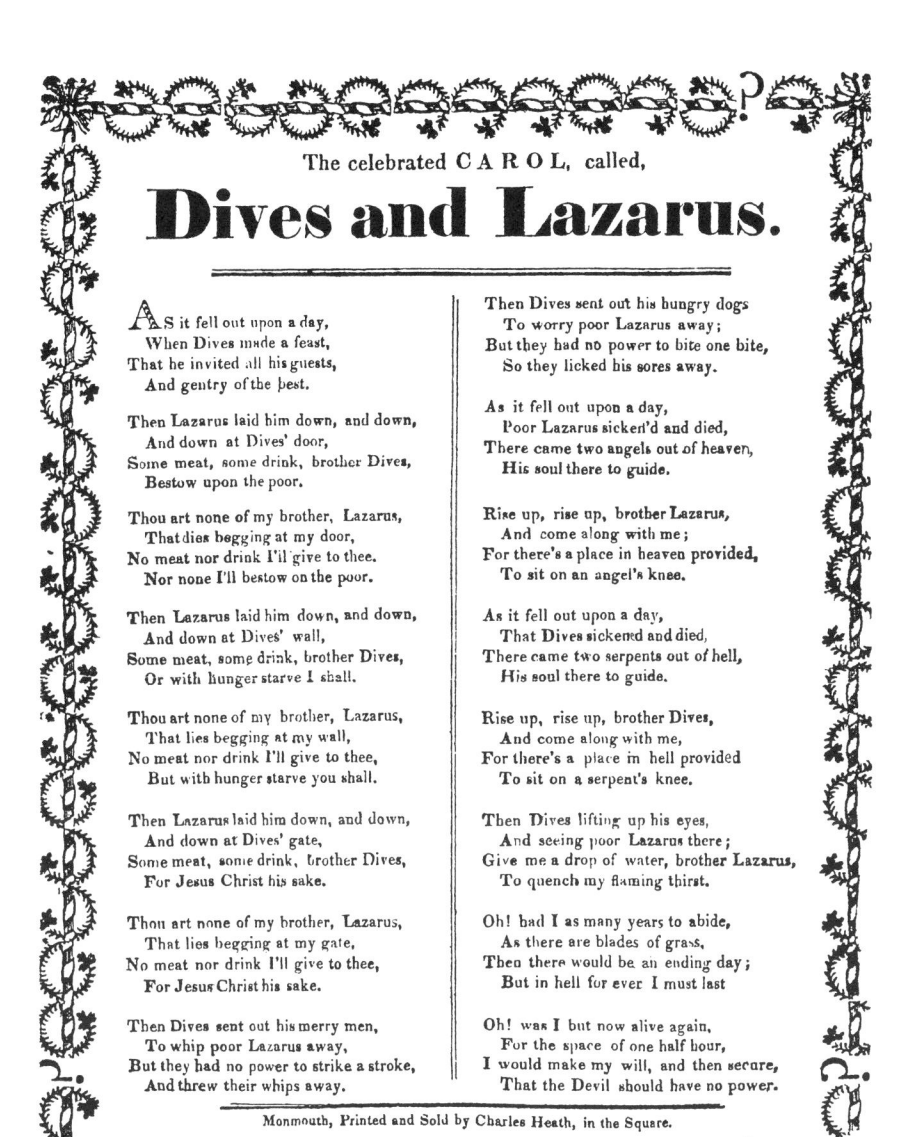

As it fell out upon a day,
When Dives made a feast,
That he invited all his guests,
And gentry of the best.

Then Lazarus laid him down, and down,
And down at Dives' door,
Some meat, some drink, brother Dives,
Bestow upon the poor.

Thou art none of my brother, Lazarus,
That dies begging at my door,
No meat nor drink I'll give to thee,
Nor none I'll bestow on the poor.

Then Lazarus laid him down, and down,
And down at Dives' wall,
Some meat, some drink, brother Dives,
Or with hunger starve I shall.

Thou art none of my brother, Lazarus,
That lies begging at my wall,
No meat nor drink I'll give to thee,
But with hunger starve you shall.

Then Lazarus laid him down, and down,
And down at Dives' gate,
Some meat, some drink, brother Dives,
For Jesus Christ his sake.

Thou art none of my brother, Lazarus,
That lies begging at my gate,
No meat nor drink I'll give to thee,
For Jesus Christ his sake.

Then Dives sent out his merry men,
To whip poor Lazarus away,
But they had no power to strike a stroke,
And threw their whips away.

Then Dives sent out his hungry dogs
To worry poor Lazarus away;
But they had no power to bite one bite,
So they licked his sores away.

As it fell out upon a day,
Poor Lazarus sicken'd and died,
There came two angels out of heaven,
His soul there to guide.

Rise up, rise up, brother Lazarus,
And come along with me;
For there's a place in heaven provided,
To sit on an angel's knee.

As it fell out upon a day,
That Dives sickened and died,
There came two serpents out of hell,
His soul there to guide.

Rise up, rise up, brother Dives,
And come along with me,
For there's a place in hell provided
To sit on a serpent's knee.

Then Dives lifting up his eyes,
And seeing poor Lazarus there;
Give me a drop of water, brother Lazarus,
To quench my flaming thirst.

Oh! had I as many years to abide,
As there are blades of grass,
Then there would be an ending day;
But in hell for ever I must last

Oh! was I but now alive again,
For the space of one half hour,
I would make my will, and then secure,
That the Devil should have no power.

Monmouth, Printed and Sold by Charles Heath, in the Square.

Carol sheet printed and sold by Charles Heath
(Abergavenny Museum)

High Street, Abergavenny, Charles Heath of Monmouth (for both of whom, see also previous chapter), and Pritchard of Monmouth. Surviving sheets from these printers consist of one by Morgan, 'Four New Carols' (including 'Dives and Lazarus', 'Rejoice and be merry, set sorrow aside', 'A virgin most pure' and 'Christmas now is drawing near at hand', two by Pritchard, 'The Carnal and the Crane' and 'Whilst shepherds watch'd' / 'Rejoice now, all good Christians', and 17 by Heath, containing 27 items:

>Away, dark Thoughts
>The Black Decree
>Christmas now is drawing near at hand
>Christ's Birth
>Come, Shepherds, listen
>Come, sound his praise abroad
>The Creation of the World; Or, The Wonderful Works of God
>Dives and Lazarus
>Divine Mirth: God rest you merry gentlemen
>The first good joy that Mary had
>The Fountain of Christ's Blood
>Good Christian People
>Hark, Hark, what News
>Hark, the herald angels
>In Slumbering Sleep
>Lift up your Heads
>Oh, for a thousand I
>Our Saviour's Love
>Rejoice and be merry
>Rejoice now all good Christians
>The Rising of the Dead
>Shepherds rejoice
>The Sinner's Redemption; Or, Let all that are to mirth inclined
>When Pilate rul'd
>While Shepherds watch'd
>A Virgin most pure
>The Virgin Unspotted

Of these, 'The first good joy' dates from the 14th century, 'Dives and Lazarus' and 'The Creation' from the 16th, 'The Sinner's Redemption' and 'The Virgin Unspotted' from the 17th. Nahum Tate's 'While Shepherds' first appeared in 1700; Charles Wesley (1707-88) wrote 'Oh, for a thousand tongues' and also 'Hark, the herald', though Mendelssohn's now-familiar tune for the latter was united with the words only in the 1850s.

The printed sheets carried only texts, some with decorative borders and illustrative woodcuts. Singers would have learned some tunes in church or chapel, but many of these carols were not sung in religious services. For example, 'The Carnal [crow] and the Crane', which deals with the miraculous restoration to life of a roasted cockerel, may have been excluded because it draws on the apocrypha; and 'Dives and Lazarus', though it stems from an authentic gospel, is unrelenting in consigning the rich man to hell, and ignores the redemptory message of Christmas.

Many of the carols were sung with tunes passed on through oral tradition. Unfortunately, none appear to have been noted or recorded from Monmouthshire singers, though many have turned up in neighbouring Herefordshire and Gloucestershire. As recently as 1977, five of the items on Heath's list were recorded by Bob Patten and Andrew Taylor from a native of Brockweir, Charlie Williams (1909-83), who learned them from his father, a native of the same village, which is separated from Monmouthshire only by the width of the Wye. The solitary verse of 'The Black Decree' which Williams remembered is given here, followed by a selection from the remaining 21 in Heath's text of what he called this 'celebrated and popular carol':

The black decree spread all the country round, To kill all young children in their turn. They took poor children from their mother's breast, Thinking to find Christ among the rest.

> The black decree spread all the country round,
> To kill all young children in their turn.
> They took poor children from their mother's breast,
> Thinking to find Christ among the rest.

But God above, who knew what would be done,
Had sent to Egypt his beloved son,
Where with his earthly parents he was fed,
Until the bloody tyrant he was dead.

What dangers and what hazards he [Christ] did run,
Both day and night, lest we should be undone,
What pains, what labour, did he not endure,
To save our souls, and happiness secure.

Was always doing good, to let us see,
By his example, what we ought to be,
He made the blind to see, the lame to go,
And rais'd the dead, which none but God could do.

Carols in Welsh, sometimes newly-written to well-known tunes, were sung very early on Christmas morning during *plygain* services (from the Latin, *pulli cantus*, cock-crow) at churches and chapels. The services, of which a feature was lavishly-decorated candles, once took place throughout Wales, but declined as the use of the Welsh language diminished. In Ebbw Vale the last recorded *plygain* was held at Penuel Chapel in 1859. There were others until the 1870s at Mynyddislwyn and until ten years later at Abercarn.

Probably the last in Monmouthshire took place at Llanofer. With the *plygain* due to start there at six on Christmas morning, everyone went to bed early on Christmas Eve, though before they did so there was a curious local ritual: the inspection of potatoes

Portrait of Augusta Waddington Hall, Lady Llanover, 1862, by C.A. Mornewicke

stored in cellars. Another custom was that young people met to eat *cyflaith* (treacle toffee) before the service. After it, all the estate's 200 tenants and workers met in the great hall of Llanofer Court, decked for the occasion with holly, mistletoe, and mottoes in Welsh. They sat down to a lunch of mutton, beef, goose, giblet pies, plum puddings, mince pies, rice puddings, apple tarts, currant and seed cakes, oranges, gingerbread, apples and nuts. Those too old or ill to attend were sent food, firing and clothes.

After lunch a harpist played for singing. Then prizes were presented to those who had won competitions for such things as Welsh sheep, vegetables, flowers, and even white-washing houses and outbuildings. In the evening, from six until midnight, there was dancing, with intervals for songs. Welsh country dances, jigs and reels, including the celebrated Llanofer eight-handed reel, were all in demand.

Liquid refreshments were restricted to gingerbeer, sherbert, lemonade and water from Ffynnon Ofer, thanks to the teetotal views of Lord and Lady Llanover which led to a local ryme:

> Grand house but small cheer;
> Large cellar but no beer;
> Lord Llanover lives here.

The formidable Augusta, Lady Llanover, was passionately devoted to Welsh music, customs and language, though she also found time to write a classic book, *The First Principles of Good Cookery*, published in 1867. 'There was no woman in Gwent, nor in the rest of Wales', wrote Mair Elvet Thomas, 'more enthusiastic than she for the Welsh language, although she was neither able to speak it at all well nor write it unaided.' Others, less charitable, said she 'spoke Welsh pretty well for a foreigner.' With her husband, a member of the Crawshay family, she ran at Llanofer an outpost of Welsh culture, as defined, revived, and sometimes even invented, by herself. When her husband died in 1867 she carried on alone until her own death at the age of 94 in 1896.

Mari Lwyd

A kind of mock horse with various costumed attendants once made appearances throughout Wales during the Christmas season, with local variations in timing. As the party approached a house, doors were barred.

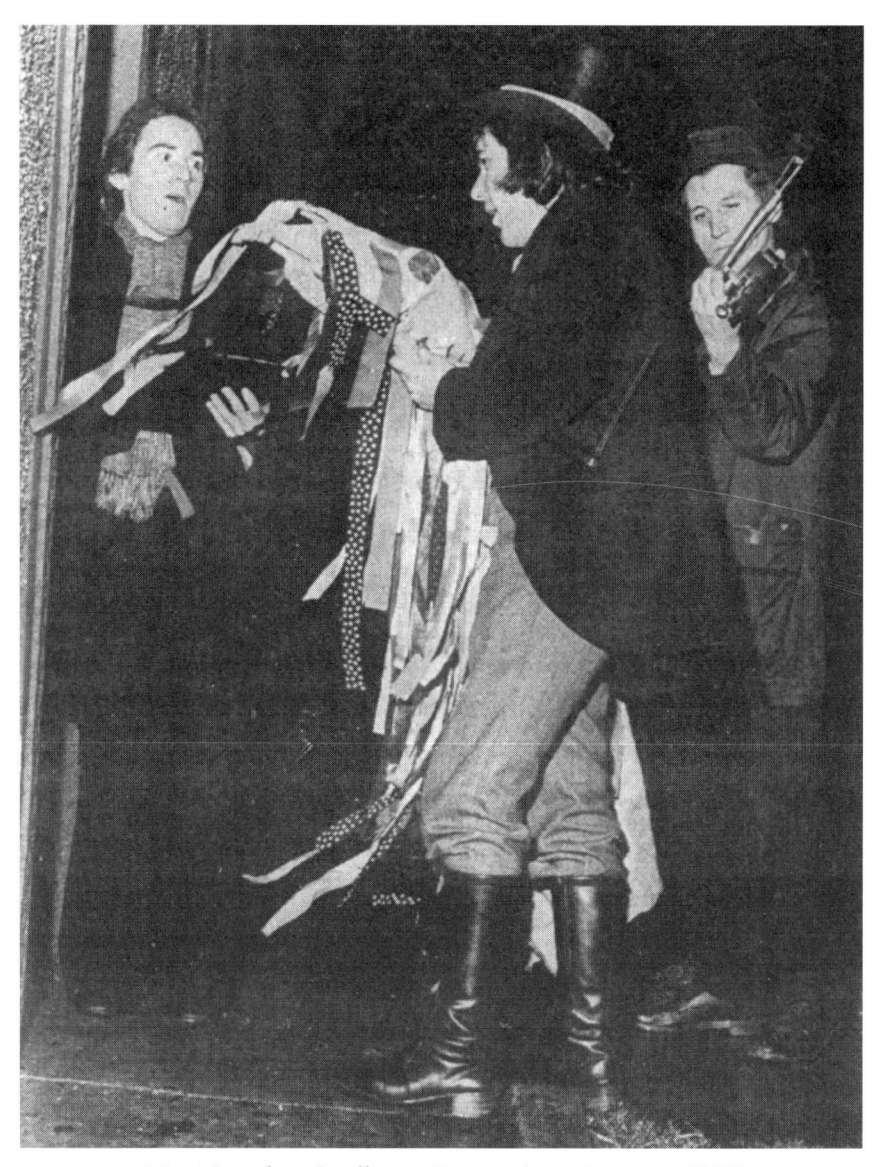

Mari Lwyd at Coelbren, Breconshire, January 1976

There followed an exchange between those inside and those outside of song verses, partly extemporised, after which the luck-bringing visitors were admitted for refreshments and rewards of money.

In Wales as a whole the ceremony was first recorded in 1800, though 35 years later in Monmouthshire as a result of an accident in which a child died and 10 men were injured. Fire broke out when they were preparing to decorate 'a *merry lwyd*, which, at Christmas, is carried from door to door, the bearers of it singing a Welsh song', said a local newspaper.

Three years later a correspondent wrote approvingly of the custom to the *Monmouthshire Merlin*:

> I am happy to say it continues to delight young and old every winter, in the parts of Gwent about Pontypool, Govilon, Abergavenny, and the mountainous district generally. The parties going about with the horse's head are denominated *Merry Lhwyd*, who sing Welsh songs and dance, the great amusement consisting in the spectre horse's antics, he being well skilled in frightening the maidens, who, peeping through the half-opened door are put to flight by his gambols.

Others were less appreciative. William Roberts, a Baptist minister at Blaenau, writing in 1852, expressed the anxious wish that people should withdraw their support from such 'old Pagan and Popish ceremonies which have come down to use from the darkest ages in learning behaviour and religion.' Specifically of the Mari Lwyd he commented: 'I wish of this folly, and all similar follies, that they find no place anywhere apart from the museum of the historian and the antiquary.'

Within about 30 years Roberts's hopes were fulfilled, at least so far as Tredegar was concerned. Evan Powell wrote in 1884: 'The custom of carrying "Mari Lwyd" on Christmastide, was of a corrupt nature, and existed until recent years, but as present is extinct, having "died a natural death" through want of patronage.' Powell had little sympathy for the tradition, and talked with heavy sarcasm of the 'witty and intelligent masqueraders', with their 'rigmaroles' of verses.

Despite being greatly influenced as a poet by Powell, William Williams (1849-1900) wrote much more sympathetically of the custom. Williams, born at Tredegar, was still a child when his father died in an accident at Bryn Bach Colliery. He learned the trade of blacksmith at Sirhowy ironworks, where several fellow-workers also wrote poetry. As Myfyr Wyn, Williams wrote poems for eisteddfodau and also published two volumes of popular verse. He contributed many articles in Gwentian

THE FOLKLORE OF MONMOUTHSHIRE

Welsh to local newspapers, a selection of which was published posthumously as *Cân, Llên a Gwerin* (Song, Lore and People). These were his thoughts (translated by Frank Olding) on Mari Lwyd,

> Or, as the old timers used to call her *Fari Lwyd*. It used to be very popular years ago at Christmas Time, but you don't hear a lot about it nowadays ... The ones I saw were pieces of wood carved into the shape of the head of a horse or mare (if there's any difference in them) and dressed in ribbons of different colours, and its mouth made in such a way that the man who was working it could move it up and down from a cord as if it were alive. The fellow that was performing inside was hidden under a big white sheet that covered him entirely, with another lad leading him by a bridle with a red or blue ribbon, like leading a horse.
>
> A company went with the 'Feri' round about through the town or villages and before they'd begin acting, one part of the company would go into the house and shut the door against the other part. Then the part that was outside would begin a *pwnc* through the keyhole, with those inside *pwnco* (chanting) against them. One or two were very funny at this, and if there was somebody clever inside, he would keep the 'Fari' out until the boys were almost frozen stiff. The *pwnco* went something like this:
>
> | Agorwch y drysa, | Open the doors, |
> | Gadewch i ni wara, | Let us play, |
> | Mae'n or yn yr eira | It's cold in the snow |
> | Y Gwilia. | At Christmas. |
> | | |
> | Cer odd na'r hen fwnci, | Get away you old monkey, |
> | Ma d'anadl di'n drewi, | Your breath stinks, |
> | A phaid a baldorddi | Stop trumpeting off |
> | Y Gwilia. | At Christmas |
> | | |
> | Ma'r gaseg o'r perta, | The mare's of the prettiest, |
> | Gadewch i ni wara, | Let us play, |
> | Mae 'phen yn llawn cnota | Her head is full of knots |
> | Y Gwilia. | At Christmas. |
> | | |
> | Yn lle bo chi'n sythu, | Instead of you freezing, |
> | Wel, ledwch y 'Feri' | Well, lead the 'Meri' |
> | I fiwn i'n difyru'r | Inside to entertain us |
> | Nos heno. | Tonight. |

Then they would march in singing some old nonsense like this:

> T dy lodl lidl,
> Tym tidl odl idl,
> Tym, tym, tym.

If there was a young girl there somewhere, the 'Meri' would bolt in a wink, with her mouth open and the girl screaming as only girls can scream—louder than the Dowlais hooter. After performing like that for a while, they'd put a cap or hat in the 'Meri's' mouth to go round and collect for the cause, and they often made a pretty penny before the end of 'Y Gwilia'—the Twelve Days of Christmas.

There, I've given you a fairly close account of how the Meri Lwyd used to carry on; but education and enlightenment have driven her from the land by now and she is very little mentioned, and that's no loss at all for all I know. Still, we like to recall the old customs and ways, and that's the reason for my saying so much about this old custom ...

Like the *plygain*, this custom declined in parallel with the Welsh language, though unlike the *plygain*, it was actively opposed by the chapels, by whose intervention, according to W. Scandrett, a recent historian of Tredegar, 'The Mari Lwyd was banned and traditional folk dances and songs were lost.' Nevertheless, it was reported as taking place at Llandegfeth in 1886 and '87, Caerleon in 1908 and Monmouth in 1913. George Greeves (born 1910) of Abertyswg pointed out that when he was a child old miners still talked of the Mari Lwyd, and he and his playmates 'trotted round after Christmas on a stick with a horse's head handle which we painted white.'

Men whom Fred Hando interviewed in 1950 at Caerleon took part in performances only 20 years previously. Gus Sergeant (born 1886) made the startling comment that they 'sang in Welsh but didn't understand the words.' They toured from Newbridge to Goldcliff, and were invited into houses to be given home-made cakes, beer and money. Sam Tripp (born 1885) remarked: 'I wouldn't say [we were] exactly welcome. We were kind of accepted as part of the Christmas duties.' He remembered how some English incomers at Glenusk, having heard the Mari (pronounced *Merri* in Caerleon) was about to arrive, loosed their bulldog. To the high glee of the Mari men, the animal took to its heels as soon as the horse's champing jaws seemed to threaten it. The performers' pride was hurt, though, and they decamped to the Bell Inn at Caerleon, where normally after a night of touring they shared their takings at eight in the morning.

Many commentators have tried to explain the Mari Lwyd, but even the name remains obscure. 'Holy Mary' has been suggested as its meaning, but *lwyd* in the sense of holy is part of the usage of bardic convention only. Its everyday meaning is 'grey', so Mari Lwyd may simply be 'Grey Mare'.

William Roberts preferred 'Holy Mary' because it helped to sustain his thesis of papist origins. He also saw pagan influence, suggesting that the custom was linked with enchantment, 'in connection with a warlike princess, reputed to have flourished in Gwent and Morgannwg in the early ages, and who is to be seen to this day [1852], mounted on her steed, on a rock in Rhymney Dingle.'

Even the highly-respected Iorwerth Peate nodded homerically in 1943 when he stated, 'No one, as far as I am aware, doubts the fact that the *Mari Lwyd* is a pre-Christian horse-ceremony which may be associated with similar customs spread over many parts of the world.' If it did date from such early times it would indeed be strange to find no reference to it in the whole of Welsh history and literature prior to 1800. On the other hand, it does resemble customs from elsewhere in which

The Mari Lwyd at Llanofer Post Office as sketched by Fred Hando in 1950

the effigy of an old horse is taken round at the turn of the year to bring good luck to the visited and good cheer to the visitors.

The Mari Lwyd always performed at Llanofer during the lifetime of the august Augusta, lady of the house. When Llanofer Court was sold in 1934, lot 52 in the catalogue was 'two carved wood, horses' heads, as used in the old Welsh Christmas Custom, known as Mari Lwyd.' Lot 53 was 'a quantity of old iron.' Another sad relic is still to be seen, a painting over the door of Llanofer post office which, until Lady Llanover closed it down, was an inn called the Penceiffel (Nag's Head). It shows the Mari Lwyd arriving by moonlight at Llanofer Court, and was painted some 150 years ago.

The Mari Lwyd was very successfully revived during the 1970s in parts of Breconshire and Glamorgan. One day this might be done in Monmouthshire too. The old words would ring out once more, and the old magic return.

> Dymunwn ich lawenydd
> I gynnal blwyddyn newydd;
> Tra par o'r gwr i dincian cloch
> Wel wel y boch chwi beunydd.
> (We wish you joy
> To provide for a new year;
> As long as the man tinkles his bell
> May you improve daily.)

THE FOLKLORE OF MONMOUTHSHIRE

Sources

Anon. *The Chartists in Newport* (Newport, 1995)
    Folklore of Blaenau Gwent (Abertillery, 1995)
    The Gwent Village Book (Newbury and Usk, 1994)
    'Peculiar Marriage-custom in Wales', *Chambers's Edinburgh Journal*, n.s. 5 (Jan-Jun 1846). 175-6
Arnot, Robin Page *South Wales Miners* (1967)
D.A.B. Letter in *Gentleman's Magazine*, 44, Pt 1 (1784), 343
Bailey, Stanley James 'Village Life in Llanvihangel Crucorney', *Gwent Local History*, no. 48 (Spring 1980), 14-17
Baker-Gabb, Richard *Hills and Vales of the Black Mountain District* (Hereford, 1913)
Bagnall-Oakley, M.E. and W. *An Account of the some of the Rude Stone Monuments and Ancient Burial Mounds in Monmouthshire* (Monmouth, 1889)
'Baledi a Cherddi', vol. 17, National Library of Wales
Barber, Chris *Arthurian Caerleon in Literature and Legend* (Abergavenny, 1996)
    Mysterious Wales (1983)
Baring-Gould, S. *A Book of South Wales* (1905)
Baring-Gould, S. and John Fisher *The Lives of the British Saints* (1907)
Barnett, Cefni Part of letter to Dr Iorwerth Peate, dated 10.7.1959, MS 4.946, Museum of Welsh Life, St Fagans
Biekski, Alison *Flower Legends of the Wye Valley* (Chepstow, 1974)
Bloomfield, Robert *The Banks of Wye* (1811)
Bord, Janet and Colin *The Secret Country* (1976)
Borrow, George *Wild Wales* (1862)
Bradley, A.G. *Shropshire, Herefordshire and Monmouth* (1908)
Bradney, Joseph *A History of Monmouthshire*, 4 vols (1907-33)
    A Memorandum, being an attempt to give a Chronology of the Decay of the Welsh Language in the Eastern Part of the County of Monmouth (Abergavenny, 1926)
Brett-James, Norman G. *Walking in the Welsh Borders* (1942)
Briggs, Katherine *A Dictionary of Fairies* (Harmondsworth, 1977)
Brooks, J.A. *Ghosts and Legends of Wales* (Norwich, 1987)

Browning, Lewis *Blaenavon, Monmouthshire. A Brief Historical Sketch* (Abergavenny, 1906; repr. Cowbridge and Bridgend, nd).
Bruning, Ted *Guide to Real Cider* (St Albans, 1996)
Byng, John *The Torrington Diaries*, ed. C. Bruyn Andrews (1954)
Calennig (Mick Tems and Pat Smith) *Songs and Tunes from Wales* (LP record, Greenwich Village, GVR 214) (1980)
Centerwall, Brandon S. 'The Name of the Green Man', *Folklore*, 108 (1997), 25-33
Children, George and Nash, George *A Guide to Prehistoric Sites in Monmouthshire* (Logaston, 1996)
Clark, Arthur *The Story of Monmouthshire*, vol. 1 (Llandybie, 1962)
Clark, J.H. *Reminiscences of Monmouthshire* (1908)
Clark, Leonard *Grateful Caliban* (1967)
Clarke, Stephen *Ghosts and Legends of Monmouth and Hereford* (Monmouth, 1977)
Condry, William *Exploring Wales* (1970)
Conran, Tony *Frontiers in Anglo-Welsh Poetry* (Cardiff, 1997)
Coxe, William *A Historical Tour through Monmouthshire* (1801)
Davies, Dewi *Welsh Place-names and their Meanings* (Brecon, nd)
Davies, D.S. 'Some old inn signs of South Wales', *Wales and Monmouthshire*, no. 4 (Feb. 1939), 19-24
Davies, Edward *Chepstow: A Poem* (1786)
Davies, Elwyn *A Gazetteer of Welsh Place-Names* (Cardiff, 1957)
Davies, E.T. *Bradney's 'History of Monmouthshire'. An Assessment* (Abergavenny, 1986)
   A History of the Parish of Mathern (Chepstow, 1950)
   The Place Names of Gwent (Risca and Newport, 1982)
Davies, Gwilym and Palmer, Roy (eds) *Let us be merry. Traditional Christmas Carols and Songs from Gloucestershire* (Lechlade, 1996)
Davies, Idris *The Angry Summer. A Poem of 1926*, with an intro. by Tony Conran (Cardiff, 1993)
   The Complete Poems of Idris Davies, ed. Dafydd Johnson (Cardiff, 1994)
Davies, L. Twiston *Men of Monmouthshire* (Cardiff, 1933)
Davies, Lynn 'Aspects of Mining Folklore in Wales', *Folk Life*, 9 (1971), 79-107
Davies, Owen 'Healing Charms in Use in England and Wales, 1700-1950', *Folklore*, 107 (1996), 19-32
Davies, Paul R. *Historic Inns and Taverns of Wales and the Marches* (Stroud, 1993)
Davies, T.A. 'Folklore of Gwent. Monmouthshire Legends and Traditions', *Folklore*, 48 (1937), 41-59
Davies, R.R. *The Revolt of Owain Glyn Dwr* (Oxford, 1995)
Davies, Thomas, Jones, William, and Davies, J.D. Griffith, 'Parish Names in Monmouthshire', *The Monmouthshire Review*, 2, no.1 (1934), 51-77

SOURCES

Davies, Walter Haydn *The Right Place - The Right Time. Memories of Boyhood Days in a Welsh Mining Community* (Llandybie, 1972)
   Ups and Downs (Swansea, 1975)
Davies, Wendy *The Llandaff Charters* (Aberystwyth, 1979)
Davies, W.H. *Collected Poems* (1942)
Defoe, Daniel *A Tour through the Whole Island of Great Britain* (Harmondsworth, 1971; orig. 1724-6)
Donovan, E. *Descriptive Excursions through S. Wales and Monmouthshire, in the Year 1804*, 2 vols (1805)
Driscoll, D.L. *Candle-light. Old Machen* (np, nd)
Duckham, Helen and Baron *Great Pit Disasters* (Newton Abbot, 1973)
Dunnill, E.J. 'Welsh Folklore Items: Monmouthshire', *Folklore*, 24 (1913), 107-110
Durant, Horatia *Raglan Castle* (Pontypool, 1966)
Eastwood, Dorothea *River Diary* (1950)
Edwards, Ness *History of the South Wales' Miners Federation* (1938)
Edmonds, Joyce *Tales of the Llanishen Parishes* (Chepstow, 1992)
Ekwall, Eilert *The Concise Oxford Dictionary of English Place-names* (Oxford, 1991: repr. of 4th ed. of 1960)
Ellis, H.C. 'Monmouthshire Notes', *Folklore*, 15 (1904), 221
Evans, C.J.O. *Glamorgan and Monmouthshire* (1963)
Evans, J. (ed.) *The Text of the Book of Llan Dav reproduced from the Gwynsaney Manuscript* (Oxford, 1893)
Eyre, L.M. 'Folklore Notes from St Briavel's', *Folklore*, 13 (1902), 170-77
Eyre, Margaret 'Folk-lore of the Wye Valley', *Folklore*, 16 (1905), 162-179
Fisher, J. 'Welsh Church Dedications', *Transactions of the Honourable Society of Cymmrodorion*, session 1906-7 (1908), 76-108
Fletcher, H.L.V. *The Coasts of Wales* (1969)
Foord, Edward *Hereford and Tintern* (1925)
Fosbroke, T.D. *The Wye Tour* (Ross, 3rd ed., 1826; orig. 1818)
Fox, Cyril *Illustrated Regional Guides to Ancient Monuments. Vol.IV, South Wales and Monmouthshire* (1950)
Fox, Cyril and Lord Raglan *Monmouthshire Houses* (Cardiff, 1951)
Fraser, Maxwell 'Christmas at Llanover', *Presenting Monmouthshire*, no. 14 (Autumn 1962), 25-9
   West of Offa's Dyke. South Wales (1958)
Frere, Sheppard *Britannia. A History of Roman Britain* (1978; orig. 1967)
Friar, Stephen *A Companion to the English Parish Church* (Stroud, 1998)
Frost, John *The Horrors of Convict Life* (1856)
Gascoigne, Russell *The Haunting of Glamorgan and Gwent* (Llanrwst, 1993)
Geoffrey of Monmouth *The History of the Kings of Britain*, trans. Lewis Thorpe (1969)
Gerald of Wales *The Journey through Wales*, trans. Lewis Thorpe (Harmondsworth, 1978)

Gibbings, Robert *Coming down the Wye* (1942)
Gilbert, H.A. *The Tale of a Wye Fisherman* (2nd ed., 1953; orig. 1928)
Gilpin, William *Observations on the River Wye* (Oxford, 1991; orig. 1782)
Greene, W.H. *Greene's Gossip about Monmouth* (Pontypool, 1870)
    Jack o' Kent and the Devil. Stories of a Welsh Border Hero told in Verse (Chepstow, nd)
Greeves, G[eorge] 'Interesting Information Collected from Old Retired Monmouthshire Miners, with Old Customs, Practices, Treatments and Superstitions', typescript (1970), Misc. MSS 1001 in Gwent Record Office
Grieve, M. *A Modern Herbal* (Harmondsworth, 1980; orig. 1931)
Grigson, Geoffrey *The Englishman's Flora* (St Albans, 1975)
Grinsell, Leslie V. *Folklore of Prehistoric Sites in Britain* (Newton Abbot, 1976)
Gruffydd, Eirlys 'Ysbrydion a Cheolion Gwent', *Llafar Gwlad*, no. 21 (1988), 9-10
Gruffydd, W.J. *South Wales and the Marches* (1951)
'Gwent' Articles in the *South Wales Argus*, 27 Jul. 1935; 10, 18, 29 Aug., 2, 22, 30 Sep., 19, 27 Oct., 27 Nov., 23 Dec. 1936; 4 Jan., 11. 17 Mar. 1937
Gwyndaf, Robin 'A Classic of Welsh Folklore Reissued', *Folklore*, 92, pt ii (1981), 190-5
    'Storïau Gwerin Gwent', *Llafar Gwlad*, no. 21 (1988), 6-7
Hall, S.C. *The Book of South Wales, the Wye, and the Coast. Part I. The Tourist's Companion from Gloucester to Ross and Monmouth* (1861)
Hando, Fred *Journeys in Gwent* (Newport, 1951)
    Out and About in Monmouthshire (Newport, 1958)
    The Pleasant Land of Gwent (Newport, 1944)
Harper, Charles G. *The Marches of Wales* (1894)
Hearth-Arthur, R.R.A. *Cromwell and Folklore in Gwent* (Monmouth, 1975)
Heath, Charles *Descriptive Account of Tintern Abbey* (Monmouth, 1793)
    The Excursion down the Wye from Ross to Monmouth (Monmouth, 1799)
    Monmouth (Monmouth, 1804)
Henken, Elissa R. *National Redeemer. Owain Glyndwr in Welsh Tradition* (Cardiff, 1996)
Hodges, Geoffrey *Owain Glyn Dwr* (Logaston, 1995)
Hollingdrake, Sybil 'Amateur Drama in Monmouthshire', *Presenting Monmouthshire*, no. 16 (Autumn 1963), 11-15
Howell, Raymond *Fedw Villages. A Lower Wye Valley History* (Old Cwmbrân, 1985)
Howells, W. *Cambrian Superstitions* (1831; repr. Felinfach, 1991)
Hubert, Maria and Andrew *A Monmouthshire Christmas* (Stroud, 1995)

SOURCES

Hutton, Ronald *The Pagan Religions of the Ancient British Isles* (Oxford, 1991)
    The Stations of the Sun. A History of the Ritual Year in Britain (Oxford, 1996)
Jackson, M. N[ewton] *Bygone Days in the March Wall of Wales* (1926)
James, Grantley *So Who Really Haunts the Anchor Inn?* (Tintern, 1996)
Johns, W.N. *Historical Traditions and Facts* (Newport, 1881 and 1897)
Jones, Edmund *A Geographical, Historical, and Religious Account of the Parish of Aberystruth* (Trevecka, 1779)
    A Relation of the Apparitions of Spirits in the County of Monmouth and the Principality of Wales (Newport, 1813; orig. 1767)
Jones, Francis *The Holy Wells of Wales* (Cardiff, 1954, repr. 1998)
Jones, Ifano *A History of Printing and Printers in Wales and Monmouthshire* (Cardiff, 1925)
Jones, John *Welsh Place Names* (Cardiff, 1979)
Jones, John B. *Offa's Dyke Path* (1976)
Jones, P. Thoresby *Welsh Border Country* (1938)
Jones, T. Gwynn *Welsh Folklore and Folk-Custom* (1930)
Jones, Thomas *Rhymney Memories* (Aberystwyth, 1990; orig. Newtown, 1938)
Jones, Thomas (trans. and ed.) *Brut y Tywysogyon or The Chronicle of the Princes* (Cardiff, 1952 and 1955)
Kilvert, Francis *Kilvert's Diary*, ed. William Plomer (1964)
Kissack, Keith *The Lordship, Parish and Borough of Monmouth* (Hereford, 1996)
Lias, Anthony *A Guide to Welsh Place-Names* (Llanrwst, 1994)
Lord, Peter *Words with Pictures. Welsh Images and Images of Wales in the Popular Press, 1640-1860* (Aberystwyth, 1995)
Lulham, Maurice A. *The Wye Valley Otter Hounds* (Gloucester, 1936)
Machen, Arthur (Arthur Jones) *Dog and Duck* (1924)
    Far Off Things (1922)
    Things Far and Near (1923)
Mais, S.P.B. *Highways and Byways in the Welsh Marches* (1939)
Mason, Edmund J. *Portrait of the Brecon Beacons* (1975)
    The Wye Valley from River Mouth to Hereford (1987)
Massingham, H.J. *The Southern Marches* (1952)
Matthews, John Hobson 'Monmouthshire Folklore', *Folklore*, 15 (1904), 348-9
Mee, Arthur *Monmouthshire* (1951)
Meyrick, Samuel Rush 'Cambrian Eccentricities Containing a Brief Sketck [sic] of the Antient Customs, Legends and Superstitions of the Welch, together with an account of their weddings and Burials', MS in the Pilley Collection, Hereford City Library
Mitchell, Elizabeth Harcourt *The Crosses of Monmouthshire* (Newport, 1893)
Prys Morgan 'A Welsh Snakestone, its Tradition and Folklore', *Folklore*, 94, Pt ii (1983), 184-191

Morris, John (trans. and ed.) *Nennius. British History and the Welsh Annals* (London and Chichester, 1980)
Myrddin ap Dafydd *Welsh Pub Names* (Capel Garmon, 1991; orig. in Welsh, 1988)
Neill, Dennis O. and Meazey, Peter (eds) *Broadsides. Topical Songs of Wales* (Cardiff, 1973)
Olding, Frank 'Fairy Lore in 18th-century Monmouthshire', *Third Stone* forthcoming
    'Gwent and the Arthurian Legend'. *Gwent Local History*, no. 66 (Autumn 1987), 23-9
Opie, Iona and Peter *The Lore and Language of Schoolchildren* (Oxford, 1959)
Opie, Iona and Moira Tatem (eds) *A Dictionary of Superstitions* (Oxford, 1989)
Osborne, G.O. and G.J. Hobbs *The Place-names of Western Gwent* (Rogerstone, 1992)
Owen, Elias *Welsh Folk-Lore. A Collection of the Folk-tales and Legends of North Wales* (Felinfach, 1996; orig. Oswestry and Wrexham, 1896)
Owen, Trefor M. *Welsh Folk Customs* (Cardiff, 1959)
    What Happened to Welsh Folk Customs? (1985)
Palmer, Roy *Britain's Living Folklore* (Felinfach, 1995; orig. Newton Abbot, 1991)
    The Folklore of Gloucestershire (Tiverton, 1994)
    The Folklore of Hereford and Worcester (Logaston, 1992)
    'Welsh Ballads and Broadsides', *Poetry Wales*, 26, no. 4 (Apr. 1991), 6-8
Palmer, William T. *The Verge of Wales* (1942)
Parry, Charles ' The Past and Present History of Ebbw Vale', TS copy of MS (1869), Gwent Record Office
Parry-Jones, D. *Welsh Country Characters* (1952)
    Welsh Country Upbringing (1948)
    Welsh Legends and Fairy Lore (1953)
Peate, I.C. 'Jackie Kent', *Folklore*, 48 (1937), 218-9
    Tradition and Folk Life, a Welsh View (1972)
Peate, Iorwerth C., 'Mari Lwyd. A Suggested Explanation', *Man*, 43 (1943), 53-8
Phillips, Edgar (Trefin) *Edmund Jones, 'The Old Prophet'* (1959)
Phillips, Olive *Monmouthshire* (1951)
Pickavance, Sue (ed.) *A Living in Torfaen. Memories of Life in Pontypool, Cwmbran and Blaenafon* (Pontypool, 1993)
Piggott, H.E. *Songs that Made History* (1937)
Porter, Gerald '"Who talks of my nation?" Resisting Voices in the Broadside Ballad', in *Visions and Identities. Papers from the 24th International Ballad Conference in the Faeroe Islands*, ed. Eythun Andreasson (Torshavn, Faeroe Islands, 1994)
Powell, Evan *History of Tredegar* (Cardiff, 1885)

SOURCES

Powell, Walter *The Diary of Walter Powell of Llantilio Crossenny (1603-1654)*, transcribed and ed. Joseph Bradney (Bristol, 1907)
Price, V.G.H. 'Trellech', *Journal of the Anthropological Institute*, 9 (1880), 51-3
Raglan, Lady 'The "Green Man" in Church Architecture', *Folklore*, 50 (1939), 45-57
Rainsbury, Anne (comp.) *Chepstow and the River Wye in Old Photographs* (Stroud, 1989)
Raven, Michael *A Guide to Herefordshire* (Market Drayton, 1996)
    Song of the Fox. Poems, Songs and Ballads (Market Drayton, 1996)
Rees, W.J. (ed.) *Liber Landavensis* (Llandovery, 1840)
    Lives of the Cambro-British Saints (1853)
Rhys, John *Celtic Folklore, Welsh and Manx*, 2 vols (London, 1980; orig. Oxford, 1901)
Richardson, John *The Local Historian's Encyclopedia* (New Barnet, 1974)
Roderick, Alan *The Folklore of Gwent* (Cwmbran, 1983)
    (ed.) *A Gwent Anthology* (Sketty, 1988)
    The Gwent Christmas Book (Newport, 1995)
    Haunted Gwent (Newport, 1995)
    'A History of the Welsh Language in Gwent', pt I. *Gwent Local History*, no. 50 (Spring 1981), 13-39; pt II, *Gwent Local History*, no. 51 (Autumn 1981). 2-32
    The Music of Fair Tongues. The story of the Welsh Language in Gwent (Newport, 1987)
Saer, D. Roy (ed.) *Caneuon Llafar Gwlad* (Cardiff, 1974)
Salway, Peter *The Oxford Illustrated History of Roman Britain* (Oxford, 1993)
Sayce, A.H. *Reminiscences* (1923)
Scandrett, W. *Old Tredegar*, vol.I (Tredegar, 1990)
Searle, Elsa J. *The Rivers of Monmouthshire* (Swansea and Llandybie, 1970)
Senior, Michael *Portrait of S. Wales* (1974)
The Shell Guide to Wales, introd. by Wynford Vaughan-Thomas; gazetteer by Alun Llewellyn (1973)
Simpson, Jacqueline *The Folklore of the Welsh Border* (1976)
Snell, F.J. *The Celtic Borderland* (nd)
Sikes, Wirt *British Goblins* (1880)
Slater, Montagu *Stay Down Miner* (1936)
Somerville, Christopher *Philip's Welsh Borders* (1991)
Spink, A.G. *The History of the Holy Trinity Church, Christchurch, Newport, Gwent* (Christchurch, 1965)
Stephens, Meic *The Oxford Companion to the Literature of Wales* (Oxford, 1986)
Stephen, D. Rhys *Pwka'r Trwyn* (London and Newport, 1851)
Stevens, Catrin 'The Funeral Wake in Wales', *Folk Life*, 14 (1976), 27-45

Summers, John 'Salmon-stoppers of the Wye', *The Countryman*, 89, no.2 (Summer 1984), 130-4
Taylor, G.S. 'Aust, the Place of Meeting', *Transactions of the Bristol and Gloucestershire Archaeological Society*, 24 (1901), 159-171
Taylor, Robert *The Stranger's Guide to the Banks of the Wye* (Chepstow, nd)
Thomas, Edward *Beautiful Wales* (1905)
Thomas, Mair Elvet *The Welsh Spirit in Gwent* (Cardiff, 1988)
Thomas, W.H. *Tinterne* (1839)
Thompson, Dorothy *The Chartists* (1984)
Trevelyan, Marie *Folk Lore and Folk Stories of Wales* (1909)
Tucker, Anna *Abergavenny in Old Photographs* (Abergavenny, 1983)
Vaughan, Herbert M. 'Augusta, Lady Llanover (1802-1896)', *The Monmouthshire Review*, 2, no.1 (1934), 10-17
Wade, G.W. and J.H. *Monmouthshire* (1909)
Walton, Isaak *The Compleat Angler*, ed. John Hawkins and W. Oldys (1760)
Waters, Brian *Severn Tide* (1947)
Waters, Ivor *Customs and Folklore of the Lower Wye Valley* (Chepstow, 1969)
   Folklore and Dialect of the Lower Wye Valley (Chepstow, 1973)
   Inns and Taverns of Chepstow, 5 parts (Chepstow,1975-6)
   The Parish Doctor (Chepstow, 1955)
   The Port of Chepstow (Chepstow, 1977)
   There was a young lady from Gwent (Chepstow, 1976)
Waugh, Julian (arr.) '"Hark Forward". Hunting Song', MS D 396.422, Gwent Record Office
Westwood, Jennifer *Albion. A Guide to Legendary Britain* (1985)
Wherry, Beatrix A. 'Miscellaneous Notes from Monmouthshire', *Folklore*, 16 (1905), 63-7
   'Wizardry on the Welsh Border', *Folklore*, 15 (1904), 75-86
Willett, M. *The Stranger's Guide to the Banks of the Wye* (Bristol, 4th ed., 1845)
W[illiams], C[harles] H[enry] *Legends of Gwent* (Newport, 1857)
Williams, Idris *Trefil, a Monmouthshire Quarry Village. An Essay* (np, nd ? 1947 or 8)
Williams-Davies, John *Cider Making in Wales* (St Fagans, 1982)
Williams, Maria Jane (coll. and arr.) *Ancient National Airs of Gwent and Morganwg* (Llandovery and London, 1844)
Williams, Raymond *Border Country* (1960)
Williams, William (Myfyr Wyn) *Cân, Llên a Gwerin* (1908)
Wood, Eric S. *Historical Britain* (1995)
Wood, Juliette 'Perceptions of the Past in Welsh Folklore Studies', *Folklore*, 108 (1997), 93-102
Wright, Arthur *The Church Bells of Monmouthshire* (Cardiff, 1942)
Wright, Sid *Shop Talks* (Hereford, 1941)

Index

Place names are given in the version commonly used, with correct Welsh forms added where appropriate in square brackets. Variant spellings may be found in passages quoted in the text, where authors' preferences have been respected. Numbers in italics refer to illustrations.

Aberbeeg [Aber-big] 86, 183
Abercarn 209, 272, 278
Aberffraw [Aberffro], Anglesey 5
Abergavenny [Y Fenny] 5, 132, 164, *164*, 236, 248, 250, *252*, 269, *269*, 274, 276, 281
Abergavenny Castle 32, 33
Abersychan 159, 271
Abertillery [Abertyleri] 128, 155, 209, 243
Abertyswg 283
Aberystruth 53, 65, 150, 155, 239, 266
Adam of Usk 37
adultery 153
Afon Lwyd 26, 182
All Hallows' Eve 58
All Souls' Day 269
All Saints' Day x
Alteryn [Allteuryn] 185, *186*
Ancient Druid Inn, Argoed 180
angels 9
annwn 11, 155
'Ap Siencyn' 88
aphrodisiac 130
apple-bobbing 267, *267*
Argoed 77, 180
Arthur, King 9, 20, 26-31, *27*
ash tree 135
Aubrey, John 148
Aust 16

Baker-Gabb 157, 159
Bailey, Crawshay 198, 199-203
  Joseph 198
  Richard 198

ball games 65, 68, 239-40
ballads 46, 49-52, 138, *138*, 168-71, *208*, 209, *210*, 213, *251*, 271
Bannavem Taburniae 4
Baptists 19
Bardsey Island (Ynys Enlli) 9
bare-knuckle fighting 235
Barry Island 14
Basaleg 57, 66, 98
Bath 9
Beachley 16
  Point 124
Beauchamp, Richard, Earl of Warwick 34
Beaufort [Cendl] 75, 185, 198
Beaufort Arms, Tintern 115
Bedivere, Sir 12
Bedwas 14, 98, 108
Bedwellty [Bedwellte] 108, 157, 259
beer 241-5
Bell Inn, Llanbadoc 113
Bell Inn, Skenfrith 76, *76*
bells 7, 11, 143-4, 153, 154, 158
'Bells of Rhymney, The' 206-7
benefit clubs 259-60, 265
Bettws Newydd 31
Bevan, Aneurin 204
  Monument 103, *103*
Bible 149, 266
bidding 150
Bielski, Alison 128
Bigsweir 85
birch 82, 263
births 152-3
Bishton [Trefesgob] x, 15, 185
'Black Decree, The' 277-8

black magic 69
Black Mountain [Mynydd Du] 2, 81
Black Rock Hotel 45
Blackwood [Coed-duon] 47, 52, 200
Blaenafon 69, 128, 140, 149, 153, 190, *197*, 209, 235, 259, 260, *261*, 270
Blaenau 26, 47, 77, 149, 281
Blaenau Gwent x
blood sports 231-6
Bloomfield, Robert 115
Blorenge, The [Blorens] 40, 103
Boat Inn, Argoed 78, *78*
Boch Rhiw Carn 12
bonesetters 145-6
Bonfire Night 269
Boxing Day 232
Boyce, Max 240
Brace, William 214
Bradney, Joseph 42, 110, 270
Braose, Eva de 164
   William de 32
   William (the last) 164
Bridstow 19
Bristol 15
Bristol Channel 4
Brittany 7
Brockweir 277
Browning, Lewis 84, 190, 209, 235
Brychan 11, 12
Bryngwyn 31, 108, 162, 223
Brynithel 110
Bryn-mawr x
Buckholt Camp 46
'Bugeilo'r Gwenith Gwyn' 88
burning the bush 254
Byng, John 115, 177, 263

Cadair Arthur 31
Cadwaladr 138, 185
Caerleon [Caerllion] x, 1, 85, 137, 183, 244, 283, 284
Caerleon Fair 70
Caerwent x, 4, 5, 174

Caldicot x, 31, 253, 264
calendar customs 253-85
calennig 256-7, *256*
Capel Newydd 57, 153
Capel-y-ffin 91, *92*, 174, 187
Caractacus 10, 25
Caradog, King 4, 31
Carlyle, Thomas 41
carols 274-8
Carpenters Arms, Llanishen 160
   Shirenewton 87
Carreg y Derwydd 99
Cas Troggy [Trogi] 182, *183*
Castell Arnallt 32, 182
   Bryn Buga 182
   Bwch 182
Cath Palug 25
Cefn 47
   Hills 85
Cefntilla Court 44, 84
Celtic mythology 155
Ceridwen 130
Chain Bridge 232, *232*
changeling 60
chapel walks 260
Charles I, King 40, 42, 43, 44, 45
Chartist movement 25, 46-52, 186, 197, 206
Chartists' Cave, Dukestown 52
Chepstow [Cas-gwent] x, 121, 128, 131, 149-50, 184, 191, 224, *225*, 231, 237, 242, 243, 257, 258-9, 269
Chepstow Castle 28, 95, 262
Christchurch (Eglwys y Drindod] 11, 133
Christmas 232, 270-9
   Boys 270
   loaves 258
church ales 241
church founding 4, 5, 6, 54-5
churchyard and wayside crosses 101, 159-60
cider 226-30, *227*, *228*

INDEX

Civil War 40-6
Clare, Richard de 187
Clarendon, Lord 43
Clark, J.H. 193
Clarke, Arthur 4
Claudius, Emperor 25
Cleddon Brook 129, *129*
Clevedon 125
club moss 130
Clwyd y Sarn 26
Clydach 40, 61
Clynnog Fawr 6
Clytha [Cleidda] 31, 182
   Arms 229
Coach and Horses, Blackwood 52
Cobbett, William 46
Cock and Feather, Grosmont 140
cockfighting 231
Coed Dial 187
Colmer Stone 133-4, *133*, *134*
Coity Mountain 69, 88
conjuror 57, 127, 156
coracle 20, *116*, 117
Cordell, Alexander 49
corn cockle 222
corn dollies 222
corpse bed (deryn corff) 156
corpse candle (canwll corff) 155
Corpus Christi Day 133
Cowbridge School 201
Coxe, William 59, 71, 105, 110, 119
Craig-y-Dorth 34
Crawley, Richard 222-3, *223*
cricket 135, 239
Croes Penmaen 90, 200
Croes-y-ceiliog 180, 231, 243
Croft-y-Bwlla 85
Cromwell, Oliver 40, 44-6, 87
Cross Keys 185
Cross Keys Inn, Pontypool 140
Cross Keys, Usk
Cross Oaks Inn, Penmaen 87
Crumlin [Crymlyn] 48, 75, 184

curses 79
Cwm 80, 86
Cwm afon 153
'Cwm Rhondda' 216
Cwm Pwca 61
Cwmbrân 88, 180, 267
Cwmcarfan 72, 156, 265
Cwmfelinfach 216
Cwmtillery [Cwmtyleri] 59, 69, 77, 159
Cwmynyscoy 89, 180
Cwmyoy [Cwm-iou] 148, 173, *173*
Cwrt-y-bella 161
cwrw da (good beer) 241-5
cyhyraeth 154
Cyndrwyn, King 17

'Dafydd y Garreg Wen' 88
dairy maids 58
dancing 56, 57, 58, 60, 67
Darby Brothers 201
Davies, E.T. 30
   Idris ix, 206, 214
   James 221
   L. Twiston 201
   R.R. 39
   Rev. T.A. 71, 135, *135*, 155, 157, 162, 218
   W.H. 185, 203
   Walter Haydn 214
death 147-78
   omens 153-6
demons 11
'Deryn Pur, Y' 88
Devauden 82, 85, 142, 144, *145*, 151, 221, 257
Devil's Lappit 72
Devil's Pulpit 70
Devil, the 65-75, 162, 203
'Devil up the Drainpipe' 270
devil's brew 65
Devil's Quoit 100
Dibdin, Charles ix, 248

Dingestow [Llanddingad] 32, 184
   Court 147
Dixton 9, 46, 175
Dog Days 129
   Star 130
dole bread 269
Donovan, E. 133, 134
Dowlais Top 145
Drayton, Michael 1, 113
Driscoll, D.L. 220, 238, 260, 274
Druids 25, 130
Druidstone 99
Dukestown 52, 185

Easter 161, 222, 259
Eastwood, Dorothy 246
Ebbw Vale [Glynebwy] 47, 88, 212, 246, 278
Edward IV, King 45
elder 82, 129
Elgar, Edward 26
Elizabeth I, Queen 15
Ellis, H.C. 254
elvering 119
elves 63
English Stones 44
Epiphany Lights 258
epitaphs 41, 168-78
Erging 9
Ernisius 2-3
evil eye 145
Ewias, Vale of 2, 81
exorcism 92
Eyre, Margaret 58, 91

Fairfax, General 44
fairs 236-8
fairies 53, 56-61, 110, 155, 188, 265
fairy ring 57, *57*, 59, 60
Fairy Well of Llwydu 110
farm workers 220-30
Farmers Arms, Goldcliff 242
fertility rites 166

Ffynnon Efa 93
   Gwaed 110
   Issui 17, 108, *109*
   Oer 109
   Wen 110
   y Cleifon 110
   y Garreg 110
   y Rhiw Newydd 110
   Wenog 110
Ffynnonau Oerion 110
   Ofor 111
Fiddler, Will the 88
fieldnames 185-90
fishing 114, 117, *118*, 125
Five Alls Inn, Chepstow 224, *225*, 243
Flat Holm (Ynys Echni) 14
Fleur-de-lis 194, 261
floods 126
Flowering Sunday 161, 259
flowers 58, 121, 128-9, 130-1
foot races 235-6
football 240
Fordd Rhufeinig, Y 26
fortune telling 144-5, 148
Fosbroke, T.D. 263
foxhunting 232-5
Frontinus, Julius 10
Frost, John 46-52, *47*
funerals 156-61
   processions 158

Gam, Dafydd 36, 192
Garn Clochdy 11
Garn Llwyd, Y 102, *102*
Garndyfaith 268
Garway Church 75
Garway Hill 72
Gate, The, Llanfrechfa 244
Geoffrey of Monmouth 1, 28-30, *29*, *30*
Gerald of Wales 32
ghosts 53, 82-94, 183

298

INDEX

giants 28, 32, 85, 96, 182-3
Gildas 22
Gilfach Fargoed 219
Gilpin, William 115
Gilwern x
Gilwern Hill 40
Glastonbury Thorn 258
Glenusk 283
Glyn 85
Glyn Dwr, Owain 15, 34-40, *38*
Glywys 11
Glywysing 11
Godwin, Francis 15
Gockett Inn, nr. Trellech 86, *87*, 243
Gofilon 77, 108, 242, 281
Goldcliff x, 93, *94*, 125, *125*, *126*, 184, 242, 283
Goldcliff Priory 125
Goose & Cuckoo, Llanofer 242
gorgon 164
Goytre [Goetre Fawr] 259
Gray Hill 100, 101, 104
Great Castle House, Monmouth 46
green man 165-7
Greeves, George 131, 144, 218, 283
'Grey Lady' 84
Griffithstown 185, 267
Grigson, Geoffrey 129
Grosmont [Y Grysmwnt] x, 71, *71*, *74*, 140, 237, 242, 246, 266
 Castle 31
 Fair 74
Gruffydd ap Llewelyn 31
Guinevere, Queen 9
guisers 270
Gutto Nyth Brân 236
Gwent x, 4, 182, 230, 279
 Rural Life Museum 220
Gwent, Dr John 74
Gwernesey [Gwernesni] 142
Gwladys 11-13
Gwydden Valley 62
Gwynllwg x, 11
Gwynllyw 5, 11-13

Hafodyrynys 63, 89
Hafodafel 56
hallowe'en 80, 266-9, *267*
Hanbury Arms, Caerleon 26
Hando, Fred 81, 132, 222, 257, 283
hares 81
'Hark Forward' 233-5
Harold, King 31
Harold's Stones 102, *102*
Harper, Charles 112
harvest home 221
 mare 221
Hatterel Hill 153
hawthorn 263
Hay-on-Wye [Y Gelli] 33
hazel 59
healing powers 77, 109-13
Heath, Charles 120, 246-8, *247*, *275*, *276*
Helen of the Legions 21
Helena, mother of Constantine the Great 21
'Hen Gelynen, Yr' (The Old Enemy) 88
Hen Gwrt 36
Henllys 61, 93, 147
Henry I, King 2
Henry V, King 34, 250
Henry VIII, King x
Hentland 9
Herbert family 10
Herbert, William 43
Heston Brake 26
hiring fairs 224-5
Hogarth, William 243
'Hold the Fort' 216
Hollingdrake, Sybil 271
Hollybush 185
Holy Island [Ynysgybi] 22
Holy Mountain (*see Skirrid*)
Holyhead [Caergybi] 22
Hooke, James 248
Horse and Jockey, Llanfihangel Pont-y-Moel *139*, 140, 243

house leek 129, *130*
Howells, William 90
Hubert, Maria 85, 270
Hugh, Charles 139
hymns 157
Hywel Dda 15
Hywel, Lord 62

Iddon, King 5
Industrial Revolution 185, 195
Iorwerth of Caerleon 32
infusions 131
Islwyn x
Ithel, King 22
Itton [Llanddinol] 151, 185
   Court 232

Jack o' Lantern 268, *268*
Jack (John) of Kent 37, 71-75
James, James & Evan 180
Jeffreys, Judge 87
Jenkyns (a healer) 69, 140-3
John, King 33
Johns, W.H. 238
Johnson, Nicholas (a charmer) 142-3
Jones, Edmund 53-6, *54*, 75, 139, 154, 183, 239
   Francis 109
   Thomas 132, 146, 152
   P. Thoresby 17
   William 22-4
   William (Chartist) 46

Kay, Sir 12
Kemeys [Cemais] 125, 190, *190*
Kemp, John 74
Kent, John 74
   Dr John 75
Kentchurch 74
   Court 37, *37*
Kilgwrrwg [Cilgwrrwg] 13
Kilvert, Francis 55
Kings Head, Monmouth 22

Kings Head, Newport 46
kissing bunch 270
knobblers 240
Kymin, The *188*, 189

Lacy, Hugh de 2
   William de 2
Lady's Well 13
Land Girls 85
Landor, Walter Savage 3
Langstone 99, 188
Lasgarn Hill 83
Leather, Mrs E.M. 67, 91
leeks 2
leprosy (cure) 110
Lewis, William T. 214
Lewis family (of St Pierre) 44, 84
Lhuyd, Edward 111
life 147-78
'Lili Lon' 198
Livox 86
Llanarth 6, 270
   Dole 270
Llanbadoc [Llanbadog Fawr] 113, 142
Llancarfan 13, 14
Llandafal 80
Llandaff Cathedral 9
Llanddewi Fach 106, 147
Llanddewi Rhydderch 2
   Skirrid [Ysgyryd] 2
Llanddingad (Dingestow) 20
Llandegfedd 17, 90, 163
Llandenny [Llandenni] 44, 80
Llandevaud 96, 192
Llandogo 22, 119, 263
Llanelen 21, 40
Llanfaches 5, 65
Llanfair Discoed 65, 100, 189, *239*
Llanfapley 17
Llanfihangel Court 83, *84*
   Crucorney [Crucornau] 39, 83, 87, 162, 176, 182, 243

INDEX

Gobion *175*, 176, 182
Llantarnam 36, 90, 96, 182, 244
Pont-y-moel *139*, 140, 182, 243
Rogiet 65, 100, 182
Torymynydd 182, 229, 242
Troddi (Mitcheltroy) 182
y Fedw (Michaelstone) 99, 182
y Traethau 182
ystern Llewern [Ystum Llywern] 5, 182
Llanfoist [Llan-ffwyst] 184, 200
Llanfrechfa 20, 89, 189, 244
Llangattock [Llangatwg] 54
   Lingoed 42, 174, 181, 239
   Vibon Avel [Feibion Afel] 110, 177, *181*, 181
Llangeview [Llangyfiw] 142, 184
Llangofen 17
Llangybi 22, 40, 96, 108, 167, 168
   Hunt 232
Llangwm 19, 165, 166, 171, *172*
Llanhiledd 17, 56, 96, 163
   Mountain 82
Llanigon 159
Llanishen [Llanisien] 40, *135*, *143*, 160, 255, 265
Llanmelin Camps 26
Llanofer 21, 60, 153, 154, 278-9, *284*, 285
Llanofer Uchaf 57
Llanover, Lady 21, 60, 241-2, 246, *278*, 279
Llanover, Lord ix, 279
Llanrwst 49
Llansoy [Llan-soe] 172
Llanthony [Llanddewi Nant Hodni] 1-4, *3*, *4*, 81, 148
Llantilio Crosseny [Llandeilo Gresynni] 6, 7, 36, 98, 165, *165*, 188, 226, 242
   Pertholey [Bertholau] 6
Llantrisant 19, 61, 113, 186
Llanvetherine [Llanwytherin] 21, 61, 163, 239

Llanveyno [Llanfenno] 5, 105
Llanwenarth 19, 183
Llanwern x, 134
Llewelyn ap Iorwerth 11
Llowes 33
Locke, Mary Ann 144
Locrinus 122
Longtown 2, 91
love potion 130
Lydney 156

Mabinogion 30, 152
mabsant 88, 266
MacColl, Ewan 216
Machen x, 5, 96, 164, 220, 238, 260
Machen, Arthur xi, 97, 106, 113, 229, 256
Maches 5
Maesglas x
Magnus Maximus 21
Magor [Magwyr] x, 96, 165, 264
Mais, S.P.B. 28
Mamhilad [Mamheilad] 14, 110
Mari Lwyd 279-85, *280*
Markham 185
marriage guidance 147-9
Marten, Henry 40-2, *41*, 42
martyrs 1, 10-7, 14, 15
Mason, Edmund J. 83, 194
Mason's Arms, Devauden 144, *145*, *146*, 257
Massingham, H.J. 106
Mathern [Matharn] x, 15, 176
Maud, Queen 2
Maud de St Valerie 33
May Bank Holiday 262-5
maypole 263
Meibion Glyn Dwr 39
Meilyr 137
Merlin 66
metalworkers 197-203
Methodists 157
Michaelmas Eve 105
Midsummer's Day 266

301

Eve 156, 188 265
midsummer men 148, 265
Midwinter's Day 102
miners 127, 156, 203-220, 266
miracles 5
miscarriages 130
mistletoe 128
Mitchel Troy [Llanfihangel Troddi] 72, 86, *173*, 182
'Mochyn Du, Y' 198
Monkswood Forest 35
Monmouth [Trefynwy] ix, x, xi 87, 91, 94, 114, *114*, 153, *177*, 247, 248, 254, 158, 262, *262*, 272, 274, 276, 283
  Castle 46
  Priory *29*
Monnington-on-Wye 37
'monty' 257
Mordred 29
Morgan, James Hiley 250, 252, 274, 276
  William 15, 179
Morgannwg, Iolo 88
Morris, Lewis 189
Mothering Sunday 258-9
Mothers' Day 259
Mountain Air Inn, Llanfrechfa 89
mountain ash 82, 135, 263
Mounton 234
  Brook 131
mummers 270-4, *271*
'muntlings, the' 262
Murenger, The, Newport 243
music 56, 88-9, 97, 216, 245-52, 274-8
Mynydd Carn y Cefn 65
  Gadair Fawr 153
  Maen 96
  Mulfraen 99
Mynyddislwyn 98, 155, 184, 259, 266, 278
Mynde, The 26

N.U.M. 198
Nant Mair 17
Nant-y-glo 149, 198, *198*, 200
Narth, the 79, 218
Nash 125, 154, *154*, 188
Nedern Brook 5, 183
Nennius 108
New Passage Ferry 44
New Year 253-7
Newbridge-on-Usk 13, 98, 128, 148, 283
Newcastle [Y Castellnewydd] 39, 59, 99, 184
  Oak 39, *58*, 59, *59*
Newchurch [Yr Eglwys Newydd ar y Cefn] 144, 144, 160, 172
Newland 22
Newport [Casnewydd-ar-Wysg] 10, 46, 47-8, 85, 93, 125, 132, 148, 151, 160, 161, 174, *193*, 207, 237, 240, 241, 243, 154, 159
nicknames 191-4, 217
Nodens 155
Nowy 20

oak 39, 59
Oak Apple Day 265
Oakdale 161

Offa's Dyke 96
Old Bonny Thatch, The, Tutshill 244
Old Christmas Day 257
Old Passage *122*, *124*
'Old Woman of the Mountains' 82-3, *83*
Old Year's Night 266
Oldcastle, Sir John 75
Olding, Frank 282
Ormond, John 204
Opie, Iona 128, 268
Orpine 148, *148*
Ostrich, The, Newland 23
Owen, Trefor M. 253

INDEX

Packing Stone, the 73
pagan ceremonies 66
Palm Sunday 52, 161, 259
Pandy 81
Panteg [Pant-teg] 91, 241
paranormal 53
Parry-Jones, D. 53
pastai 149
Patricio [Patrisio] *16*, 17, 108, *109*, 110, 147, 167, *167*, 175
patronal festival 266
Paynter, William 197, 198
Peate, Iorwerth 284
Pecked Stone, the 72
Peibio, King 9
Penallt 58, 72, 77, 79, *150*, 151, 160
Penarth, Caernarfonshire 6
Pencoed Castle 95
Pendragon, Uther 28
Pengam 55
Penhow [Pen-hw] 192
Penmaen 54, 87
Penrhiwellech 80
Penrhos x, 10, 110, 156
Pentwynmawr 87
Peterstone-Wentloog [Llanbedr Gwynllwg] 11
phantom carriages 85
   dogs 155
   funerals 155
Phillips, Olive 96, 184, 240
Phillips, Thomas 47
Pickavance, Sue 204
Piercefield 84
pirates 13, 16
place names 1, 180-5
plant lore *(see also flowers and individual plants)* 128-32
plygain 278
pneumonia 132
Pont-hir 26, 180, 242
Pont y Saeson 14, 81
Pnt yr Escob 187
Pontllanfraith 66, 180, 241

Pontnewnynydd 54, 128
Pontrilas 39
Pontrhydyrun 180
Pontypool [Pont-y-pwl] 57, 140, 152, 180, 191, 192, 200, *205*, 240, 259, 268, 281
Portishead 125
Portskewett [Porth Sgiwed] 4, 44
Powell, Rev. David *162*, 163
   Mary 163, *163*
Price, William 186
Pritchard, Miss 67, 75, *161*, 162
prize fighting 186-7, 235
prophecy 42-3, 53
Prosser, Ted 197, 198
public houses *(see also by name)* 86-88, 241-5
Puck 61
Punchbowl Inn, Monmouth 272
pwca 61-4, *61*
Pwll Melyn 35
Pwll Meyric [Pwllmeurig] 15
   Meurig 108
   Trachwant 104

quarrymen 195-7
Queens Head Inn, Monmouth 40, 87

rabies (cure) 131
Raglan [Rhaglan] 229
   Castle 42-4, *43*, *44*, 84, 95
   Lady 165-6
Raven, Michael 39
Redbrook 79
Redwick 253
Reformation 158
remedies *(see also plants, individual plants and illnesses)* 219, 226
Rhisiart Cap Du 139
Rhyd Gwrthebau 13
Rhyd-y-Meirch 154
Rhymney [Rhymni] ix, x, 149, 152, 205, 206-7, 211, 212, 215, 217
Rhys, Sir John xi, 27, 63

Risca [Rhisga] 192, *208*, 209, 214, 259, 271
Rising Sun, Monmouth 87
River Ebbw [Ebwy] 13, 113
  Ebbw [Ebwy] Fach 66
  Ebbw [Ebwy] Fawr 91
  Ebwy 155
  Honddu 1
  Monnow 71, *71*, 106, 114
  Rheidol 121-2
  Rhymney [Rhymni] x, 11, 99, 113
  Severn [Hafren] 16, 44, 108, 122
  Sirhowy [Sirhywi] 70, 180
  Usk [Wysg] 11, 113
  Wye [Gwy] 9, 114-21
Riverside Hotel, Monmouth 87
Roberts, P. 158
Robin Hood Inn, Monmouth 236, 244
'Robin Hood and the Shepherd' 271
Rockfield 12, 108, 185, 270
Roderick, Alan 94
Rogationtide 100
Rogerstone [Ty-du] 184
Romans 10, 25-6
roping 151
rosemary 161
Royal Oak, Blaenau 47
  Newport 46
rue 152
Rumney [Tredelerch] 113
Ruperra [Rhiw'rperrai] Castle 45, 96

sabbath 85
saints (*see also under individual names*) 1-24, 107-8
  days 266, 270
Salway, Peter 26
Sarn Hir, Y 26
Satan 11
Saxons 6
St Aaron 10
St Alban 10
St Albans 10

St Amphibalus 10
St Anne's Well, Trellech 111, *112*
St Arfan 20
St Arvans [Saint Arfan] 20, *20*, 151, 189
St Athan 5
St Augustine 16
St Barrog 14, 108
St Bernard 166
St Beuno 4-6
St Brechfa 20
St Brides-Wentloog [Llansanffraid Gwynllwg] 11
St Bridget 17-19, *18*
St Cadfan 16
St Cadwg 10
St Cenedlon 12
St Cybi 7, 21, 108
St David 1-4, *2*, 24
St David's Church 2
St David's Day 2, 253
St Davids 9
St Dingat 20
St Dyfrig 1, 6-9, *8*, 21
St Freide's Well 19
St George 9
St Gofor 21
St Govan 17
St Gwennarth 19
St Gwyndaf 21
St Gwynllyw 11-3, *11*
St Gwytherin 21, *21*
St Hiledd 17
St Illtyd 17
St Illtyd's Church 96
St Issui 17
St Julian's (house) 10
St Julius 10
St Mabli 17
St Mary 19, 21
St Maughan 108, 109
St Melon 21
St Mellons [Llaneirwg] 21, 154

INDEX

St Meurig 14
St Michael 9
St Michael's Chapel 105
St Michael's Church 181-2
St Mofor 21
St Noe 108
St Odoceus 22
St Padarn 8, 21
St Patrick 1-4, 108
St Peter 108
St Pierre 188
 Pill 30
St Sannan 108
St Tathan 4-6
St Tecla's Island 16, *120*, 124
St Tedeoc 9
St Tegfedd 17
St Teilo 6-9, *6*, 188
St Tewdrig's Well 15
St Thomas's Day 270
St Tysoi 20
St Woolos Cathedral *12*, 13, 48, 161, 174
St Wyndaf 21
Scandrett, W. 283
Scapula, Ostorius 25
Scotch Cattle 88 200
scrofula (cure) 110
Seeger, Pete 206
Seisyll ap Dyfnwal 32
self-heal 129
Seven Whistlers, the 156, 218
Severn Sea 121-6
Shakespeare 25, 38, 244
Shield, William 248
Ship Inn, Pontypool 57
 Raglan 229
Shirenewton [Drenewydd Gelli-farch] 15, 87, 185, 242, 258
shooting star 152
Sikes, Wirt 62, 65, 82, 259
Silures 10, 26
Siôn Cent 37, 71-5

sin-eating 158
Sirhowy Valley ix
Six Bells 185
Skenfrith [Ynysgynwraidd] x, *18*, 19, 67, 108, *108*, 162, 167, 181, 188, 189, 236-7, 239, 241
 Castle 31, 67
Skirrid [Ysgyryd] Inn 39, 65, *65*, 87, 105, *105*,b 243
 Fawr 9, 105-6, *106*, 153, 225

sleeping warriors 27
Sloop Inn, Llandogo 119
Snakestone 135-6, *136*
Snap-apple night 267
soldiers 25-52
Sons of Glyndwr 39-40
Southey, Robert 3
sphagnum moss 129
spirits 53-94
springs 6, 15, 77, 107-113
spurge *(see flowers)*
standing stones 73, 99-103
stoolball 240
Stow Fair 237-8
 Hill 12
strikes 199, *211*, 212-7
stye stone *(maen magl)* 135
Sudbrook 160
 Camp 26
Sugar Loaf [Moel Fannau] 31, 103, *103*, 153
suicides 101
Sul y Blodau 161
supernatural powers 37-8
superstitions 127
Swift, Rev. William 43

Talgarth 11
Taylor, Bishop Jeremy 40
Tegiwg 5
Tangwyn 5
Tennyson, Alfred, Lord 26

Thackeray, William Makepeace 244
The Bryn 93
Thomas, Edward 107
  Mair Elvet 279
  William (Islwyn) ix
  W.H. 86, 240
Thorpe, Lewis 29
Three Castles, the 31
Three Cranes, Chepstow 231
Three Horseshoes, Pentwynmawr 87
Tintern [Tyndryn] x, 15, 86, 189, 227, *265*
  Abbey 14, 240
  furnace 195, *196*
tolaeth 154
Torfaen x, 113, 182
Tostig 31
Townsend, J. 236
trade unions 199, 212-7
Tranch, the 54
treacle pits 192
treasure 67
Tredegar 149, 151, *260*
  House 42
  Park 13
Tredunnock [Tredynog] 13, 163
Trefethin 10, 57, 110, 209
  Oak 60
Trefil 181, 186, 197
Tregare [Tr'r-gaer] 42, 140, 140, 156
Trellech [Tryleg] x, 40, 58, 72, 79, 86, 95, 99, 100, *100*, 102, 111, 112, 151, 259
  Beacon 73
  Grange 14, 222
  Moor 81
Trevella 95
Trevelyan, Marie 81
Trinity Thursday 133
Trosnant 89
Trostrey [Trostre] 44
  Court 232
trows *114*, 119-20, *119*

Tudor, Jasper 46
tumuli 97-9
tunnels 95-6
Tutshill 244
Twelfth Night 254, 257-8
Twm Barlwm [Twyn Barllwm] 96-7, *97*, 259
Twrch Trwyth 30
Twyn y Calch 98
Ty Dial 187
Ty Gwyrdd 244
Ty pwca 61
Ty Trist 62
  Colliery 204, *204*
Tylery [Tyleri] Valley 65

Undy [Gwndy] 21, 188, 265
Usk [Brynbuga] x, 86, 185, 191
  Castle *34*, 35
  Priory 85

Valerian 156
vervain 130
Vincent, Henry 47
Virgin Mary 13
Virtuous Wells, the 58, 111, *112*

wake (*gwylnos*) 157, 236-7, 239
Wales ix, x, 1, 10, 17, 19, 25, 29, 30, 31, 32, 34, 46, 50, 53, 55, 114, 121, 138, 139, 156, 168, 179, 181, 222, 240, 241, 253, 279
walking the wheat 222
warts (cure) 132
wassailing 254, 258
water 107-26
  lily 130
Waters, Ivor 70, 181
Wattsville 185
Waunafon 59
Waun-y-Clare Inn, Nr. Pontypool 242
Waun-y-Pound 103
wayside crosses 101, 159

INDEX

weather lore 226
Webb, Beatrice 79, 214
   Sidney 214
weddings 148, 149-52
Wellington Inn, Newcastle 59, *59*
wells 107-13, 255
Welsh (language) 15, 179-80
'Welsh Fortune Teller, The' 138, *138*
Wentwood Forest 27, 135
Westgate Hotel, Newport 47, *48*
Westwood, Jennifer 143
Wheeler, Mortimer 26
Wherry, Beatrix 60, 135, 142
Whistle Inn, Blaenafon 235
White Castle x, 31
White Hart, Llangybi 40, 96, 232
White Lady 83, 84
Whitebrook 79, 263
whitethorn 82
Whitson 93, 188, 189
   Court 125
Whitsuntide 161, 259, 260-2
whooping cough 135

wife-beating 153
William II, King 31
Williams, Idris 181, 196
   Jane 111
   Maria Jane 246
   William 281
   Zephaniah 46
wise men 16, 127
witches 75-81, 266
witchfinder 82
witch-mark 82
wizards 97, 138, *138*
Wolvesnewton [Llanwynell] 90, 185
Wonastow [Llanwarw] 184
Wood, Eric 166
Wroth, William 65
Wye Valley Otter Hunt 231-2, *233*
Wylie 185

Ynyr 5, 182
Ynys-ddu ix, 55
Ystruth brook 66

Also from Logaston Press

Vol. II, Monuments in the Landscape Series: Castles & Moated Sites of Herefordshire

by Ron Shoesmith. 256pp with some 65 photographs, plans and maps. £9.95   ISBN 1 873827 59 8

Herefordshire is a county of castles and moated sites, reflecting its position as a well populated agricultural county bordering disputed territory. The history of defence within the county is explained, as is that of castle building, their use and, finally, demise. There is a comprehensive gazetteer of all the sites set out parish by parish with much recent information.

Vol. IV, Monuments in the Landscape Series: Prehistoric Sites of Monmouthshire

by George Children and George Nash. 144pp with 40 photographs, plans and maps. £7.95   ISBN 1 873827 49 0

This details the early settlement of Monmouthshire, an area which has interesting Stone Age finds along the shores of the Severn Estuary, in addition to Bronze Age complexes, standing stones and later Iron Age hillforts.

The Rivers Wye and Lugg Navigation, A Documentary History 1555-1951

by Victor Stockinger. 564pp with 57 illustrations, Hardback. £25
ISBN 1 873827 89 X

A collation of much of the documentary evidence assembled for the Public Enquiry into the navigation rights on the Wye. Documents include Acts of Parliament, surveys, terriers, leases, public notices, personal letters and other writings, including from the case of the Free Fishery in Archenfield. All brought together with an introduction comparing the development and current situation of the Wye with other waterways.